Vaqueros
in
Blue & Gray

Sgt. José Lino Hinojosa and an unnamed Union sergeant, probably Luis Gonzales, his brother-in-law. Both *Tejanos* were in the Second Texas Cavalry (Union). *Courtesy Eva Hinojosa and the Hidalgo County Historical Museum.*

VAQUEROS
IN
BLUE & GRAY

BY
JERRY D. THOMPSON

foreword by
FÉLIX D. ALMARÁZ, JR.

illustrations by
LEO GARZA JR.

NEW EDITION

STATE HOUSE PRESS
Austin, Texas
2000

Copyright © 1977 Presidial Press
Copyright © 2000 Jerry D. Thompson
All Rights Reserved

Library of Congress Cataloging-in-Publication Data

Thompson, Jerry D.
Vaqueros in blue & gray / by Jerry D. Thompson ;
foreword by Felix D. Almaraz ; illustrations by
Leo Garza, Jr.–New ed.
p. cm.
Includes bibliographical references and index.
ISBN 1-880510-71-5 (alk. paper)
ISBN 1-880510-72-3 (pbk. alk. paper).
1. United States—History—Civil War, 1861-1865—
Participation, Mexican American.
2. Texas—History—Civil War, 1861-1865—
Participation, Mexican American.
3. Mexican American soldiers—Texas—History—19th century.
4. Mexican American soldiers—Texas—Genealogy.
5. United States—History—Civil War, 1861-1865—Registers.
6. Texas—History—Civil War, 1861-1865—Registers.
I. Title: Vaqueros in blue and gray.
II. Title

E540.M54 T47 2000
973.7'0896892073—dc21   99-46351

Printed in the United States of America

cover design by David Timmons
cover photograph: Captain Joseph De La Garza
courtesy of Helen Yturri

STATE HOUSE PRESS
P. O. BOX 818
Buffalo Gap, TX 79508

Contents

Foreword vii
Introduction ix
Preface 1
Acknowledgements 3
I. Prologue 5
II. The Rio Grande Frontier 15
III. Tejanos for the Confederacy 25
IV. War Along the River 41
V. Vidal 71
VI. Union Tejanos 81
VII. The Rio Grande Expedition 97
Appendix A: Confederates 127
Appendix B: Federals 193
Footnotes 223
Bibliography 233
Index 241

Illustrations

Colonel Santos Benavides, and his wife
    Agustina Villarreal de Benavides............32
General Edmund J. Davis....................33
General Juan N. Cortina, 1866 34
Laredo Confederates: Refugio Benavides,
    Atanacio Vidaurri, Cristobal Benavides and
    John Z. Leyendecker.....................35
Captain Manuel Yturri II 36
Brigadier General Hamilton P. Bee..............37
Captain Cristobal Benavides...................38
Colonel John L. Haynes and his wife
    Angelica Wells 39
Bivouac of Texas State troops on
    Las Moras Creek.......................62
Main Plaza, San Antonio, 1861.................63
Laredo, Texas around 1878...................64
Ringgold Barracks and Rio Grande City..........65
Fort Duncan, near eagle Pass 66
Roma, Texas 67
Confederate evacuation of Brownsville,
    November 2, 1863......................68
Union Soldiers on Elizabeth Street,
    Brownsville..........................69
Gravestone of Capt. José Rafael de la Garza......126

Foreword

In the four decades before the close of the twentieth century, Jerry Thompson, the pride of Pie Town, New Mexico, perfected his craft as a writer along the banks of the Río Grande at Laredo, Texas. Our initial encounter occurred in the mid-1960s at the University of New Mexico. As graduate students we enrolled in a Southwestern history seminar, conducted by Dr. Donald C. Cutter who ultimately became our mentor.

For a few years after New Mexico our career paths diverged, occasioned by Thompson's residency at Carnegie-Mellon University in Pittsburg, Pennsylvania, and my return to Texas to accept a faculty appointment at St. Mary's University. Eventually, Jerry meandered down to Laredo where he established himself as a serious scholar of the Civil War and of its impact upon Texas and the Southwest. Our paths reconnected permanently in the programs of the Texas State Historical Association to which we contributed (and continue to participate) in various capacities.

Shortly after Thompson's arrival in Laredo, the folklore enshrouding the life of Colonel Santos Benavides and his cadre of Confederates motivated the young scholar to explore the involvement of *Tejanos* in the Civil War, a topic that had been generally overlooked in the over-arching design of the state's military historiography. Under the auspices of a research grant to study the *Tejanos'* presence in the bitter conflict, Thompson devoted an entire summer in Austin, working in the facilities of the Texas State Library and Archives, critically examining the muster rolls of *Tejanos* who had served in the Union forces. Inspired by the abundance of information, Jerry requested additional muster rolls of Mexican

Texans in military service. As the clerk disappeared into an adjacent room to retrieve the documents, an elderly lady who had overheard the request, gently took Thompson aside. "Young man," she counseled, "you must remember that Texas was part of the Confederacy. No one from Texas served with the Yankees." Reflecting upon the incident afterward, the acculturated researcher from Laredo acknowledged that social conditions indeed had changed by the early 1970s, because the lady had not referred to the Union forces as "those damned Yankees."

Dr. Thompson's painstaking research on Civil War issues culminated in several publications, notably *Vaqueros in Blue & Gray* and *Mexican Texans in the Union Army*. Additionally he composed articles and other monographs reflecting on the life of such *Tejanos* as Colonel Santos Benavides, the leader who achieved distinction as the highest ranking Mexican Texan in the Confederate army.

In this expanded edition of *Vaqueros in Blue & Gray*, much to the approval of genealogists and other researchers, Thompson includes an extensive checklist of individuals who participated in both the Union and Confederate forces. Next to Marc Simmons, celebrated writer of New Mexico, Jerry Thompson is the most dedicated researcher I have had the privilege of calling a friend and colleague in the fraternity of history. For this latest contribution, Thompson extracted data on *Tejanos* and *Mexicanos* from the National Archives in Washington, D.C., and the Texas State Library and Archives in Austin. In the process of compiling the appendix of names he consulted a vast number of primary sources, including muster rolls (company, detachment, and regiment), discharge lists, medical and hospital documents, enlistment papers, prisoner-of-war accounts, and court-martial records.

This new edition of *Vaqueros in Blue & Gray* fills a conspicuous gap in the saga of Civil War Texas, earning for its author the respect and salute of his peers in the profession.

Félix D. Almaráz, Jr.
The University of Texas at San Antonio

Introduction

Arriving on the Texas-Mexico border fresh from the University of New Mexico in 1968, I was astounded to discover that, despite the obviously long and rich cultural heritage of South Texas, little had been written about the role of *Tejanos* in the Civil War. Scholarly studies of Mexican Americans either entirely omitted the subject or dismissed it in a few, brief sentences. Not admitting that *Tejanos* had fought and died, much less that they had done so for reasons other than the defense of the South's "peculiar institution," scholars had, in effect, ignored information and insight about how *Tejanos* figured in Civil War history.

My original hope in the 1970s was to write a comprehensive history of all Mexican Americans in the war, not just *Tejanos*. A grant from the National Endowment for the Humanities enabled me to complete research at the National Archives, as well as at the Library of Congress, the Texas State Archives, and the University of Texas at Austin's Center for the Study of American History. I also had the chance to spend several weeks in Santa Fe, exploring such places as the New Mexico State Records Center and the Museum of New Mexico.

That *Tejanos* were important to Civil War history was not surprising to me. Previously, I had learned that *Nuevo Mexicanos* had played a significant role on the upper Rio Grande, and even a cursory examination of the *Official Records of the War of the Rebellion* confirmed the same for *Tejanos* on the lower part of the river. In what was actually a continuation of the 1859-1860 Cortina War, *Tejanos* had rebelled against state authorities in Zapata County at the same time that Fort Sumter fell on April 14, 1861. Moreover, *Tejanos* were in the last land battle of the war at

Palmetto Hill on May 13, 1865—more than a month after General Robert E. Lee and his Army of Northern Virginia surrendered at Appomattox Court House. Indeed, during the intermediate four years, *Tejanos* had followed the Lone Star and the Stars and Bars across a hundred different battlefields stretching from the New Mexico Territory's snow-capped mountains to Louisiana's swamps and bayous to Virginia's pine forests. Just as significantly, almost a thousand *Tejanos* and *Mexicanos* marched under the Stars and Stripes. In light of such information, I was confounded at how a leading author could conclude in a best-selling book on Texas history that Mexican-Texans "took no part in Anglo-American politics, regarded the war as a gringo affair and opted out." Something had to be done.

At long last, my modest book, *Vaqueros in Blue & Gray*, was published in 1976 by Presidial Press in Austin. Although issued in a limited edition, the book enjoyed a generally popular reception. In the years that followed, I was gratified to receive letters, telephone calls and, more recently, e-mails from descendants of those men and women depicted in the book. In a similar spirit, several graduate and undergraduate students from various schools were inspired to pursue the subject, writing me for suggestions and comments.

Other responses to *Vaqueros in Blue & Gray* have been less predictable than those dealing with further research. In February 1993, I was only too happy to speak at the dedication of a Laredo elementary school named in honor of Colonel Santos Benavides. Benavides, as it happens, was the single most important person to emerge from the nineteenth-century history of the community and, naturally, I had written about him. Equally exciting has been the professional progress of Leo Garza, Jr. As an aspiring artist at Laredo Community College, Leo illustrated *Vaqueros in Blue & Gray*; with equal skill and dedication, he also illustrated my biography of Confederate General Henry Hopkins Sibley. While our friendship thus grew, Leo went on to a distinguished career as a popular cartoonist for the *Laredo Morning Times* and, later, the *San Antonio Express-News*. All the while, though, his sketch of Captain Refugio Benavides' attack on Mexican guerrillas near Camargo in

January 1863 has remained proudly displayed in my office. On a less personal note, it was good to see the John L. Haynes papers, which I found while researching *Vaqueros in Blue & Gray*, donated to what is now the Center for the Study of American History at the University of Texas at Austin.

Sometimes, the use and influence of *Vaqueros in Blue & Gray* have been less than accurate or professional. Historians of all kinds, of course, know this problem as seemingly inevitable but no less maddening. Photographs that were first reprinted in my book began to appear in major histories of the war, often without proper credit or permission from me or the owners. A particularly rare image of captains Refugio and Cristobal Benavides (along with their brother-in-law Captain John Z. Leyendecker and Lieutenant Atanacio Vidaurri) is a case in point. One popular photographic history of the war credited the image as belonging to San Antonio's Ursuline Academy when, in fact, Laredo's Ursuline Academy Archives owns the image. Just as annoyingly, a recent Texas Historical Commission publication cropped Captain Leyendecker from the photograph, an act that would have made the Benavides brothers none too pleased.

In contrast to its misuse, *Vaqueros in Blue and Gray* has generated a great deal of solid research. For instance, additional biographical information has surfaced on Cecilio Valerio. On the morning of March 13, 1864, Valerio, a Union *Tejano,* fought a bloody skirmish against Major Mat Nolan deep in the brush country of what is now Duval County. Valerio's small force was supplied with gold coin, munitions, and clothing by both the Union Army (at Brownsville) and Navy (lying off the coast of Padre Island). Allegedly, Valerio's son Juan was captured while visiting Corpus Christi in March 1864, and Major Nolan subsequently coerced Juan into leading Nolan's small army to the senior Valerio's encampment at Los Patricios, fifty miles southwest of Banquete. Various attempts to find the exact location of the bloody skirmish have proved unsuccessful, although it has been discovered that Valerio and his son, after acquiring land on Rosita Creek in Duval County, returned to Mier at the end of the war. Indeed, a *corrido* recalling the skirmish at Los Patricios was part of the oral tradition in South Texas as late as 1950. In a similar vein, a wonderful poem surfaced that recalls how Confederate Lieutenant Joseph R. Garza gallantly died at the Battle of Mansfield on April 8, 1864.

Vaqueros in Blue & Gray was written, I would like to think, with both empathy and objectivity. Despite my efforts to consider every document I could find relative to *Tejanos* in the Civil War (including official reports, letters, journals, diaries, memoirs, and newspapers), I inevitably overlooked some pertinent facts. Even with the discovery of additional documents since 1976, though, I still hold to my major thesis—namely, that *Tejanos*, largely seen by the Anglo Texan community as second-rate citizens, joined the conflict for reasons less to do states' rights or slavery and more with class and economics. Many *Tejanos* saw enlistment in the military, especially the Union Army, as a way out of the *patrón* system's grinding poverty long a part of the Rio Grande frontier. That many *Tejanos* performed so admirably during the war only reflects their ambition to succeed in the economic system north of the border.

Some new information found since the publication of *Vaqueros in Blue & Gray* has amplified the importance of my thesis. Most notably, it is now evident that *Tejanos* served in a far wider scope than I had originally known. Not only were they active in South Texas, but *Tejanos* marched off to New Mexico, first with Lieutenant Colonel John Robert Baylor and later with Brigadier General Sibley. Like other Texans, they endured the disastrous retreat from northern New Mexico into the Mesilla Valley, finally passing through El Paso on their 650-mile march to San Antonio in the summer of 1862. A few *Tejanos* also left for Virginia with Hood's Texas Brigade, fighting there in the more well-known eastern theater. Other *Tejanos*, both Blue and Gray, fought and died in the swamps and bayous of Louisiana. In fact, after carefully examining records in both Austin and at the National Archives, I place the total number of *Tejanos* who served the Confederacy very close to 2,500—very close to what I had originally estimated (see appendix A). Union records, which are far more complete than those of the Confederacy, indicate that

958 *Tejanos* and *Mexicanos* were recruited into the Union Army, a fact that was not well known prior to the publication of my book and the subsequent release of my monograph, *Mexican Texans in the Union Army* (published in 1986 and reprinted in 1992). In all probability, then, in 1863 and 1864 the Union Army recruited many of the very men against whom the frontier army had fought during the Cortina War.

Other new information has confirmed certain characterizations in *Vaqueros in Blue & Gray*. For example, I stand firm in my original assessment of General Edmund J. Davis and Colonel John L. Haynes as opportunistic visionaries. Davis, who later became the controversial Reconstruction governor, and Haynes, who commanded the Union's 2nd Texas Cavalry, had both lived on the border for almost a decade when the war broke out, and both men understood and sympathized with the South Texas *Tejano* community. However, there is little doubt that both also saw the recruitment of *Tejanos* and *Mexicanos* into the Union Army and the eventual success of the North's cause as integral to their own ultimate political goals.

Still other information has not only confirmed, but intensified, my earlier characterizations. At the center of the *Tejano* Confederate experience was Colonel Santos Benavides' Regiment, a border cavalry unit that had largely grown out of the 33rd Texas Cavalry and must rank as one of the few Confederate regiments never to suffer defeat. Benavides, commander of the regiment that bore his name and the highest ranking Mexican American to serve the Confederacy, remains in my estimate a notorious figure. That Benavides hanged cattle and horse thieves in Laredo's St. Augustine Plaza during the war, a fact undiscovered when I wrote *Vaqueros in Blue & Gray*, thus reinforces my earlier conclusion that he was a hard-nosed, uncompromising authoritarian commander. If anything, perhaps I understated the case; a letter by Benavides, written following his defeat of the Mexican adventurer and revolutionary Juan Nepomuceno Cortina at Carrizo (present day Zapata) in May 1861, indicates that he executed prisoners of war.

Of course, not all my estimates or characterizations in

Vaqueros in Blue & Gray have remained unchanged. For example, I underestimated how bloody was the incident between Captain Mat Nolan and the Zapata County insurrectionists at Rancho Clareño (located on the Rio Grande downriver from Carrizo). In fact, a number of the insurrectionists who died at Clareño were probably unarmed and shot down in cold blood as they attempted to flee across the river. In *Mexican Texans in the Union Army*, I had the chance to incorporate this possibility, along with other new data about the Clareño incident. Elsewhere, I overlooked the political alliance and personal friendship between Colonel Santos Benavides and the powerful *caudillo* of Nuevo León and Coahuila, Santiago Vidaurri. Indeed, I came to know (largely through a letter of Colonel John S. "Rip" Ford) that Vidaurri, after being expelled from Mexico in March 1864, was staying in Laredo with Santos Benavides. Evidently, during the war (especially after the Union occupation of the Lower Rio Grande Valley in November 1863) Colonel Benavides became to the South Texas frontier upriver from Brownsville what Vidaurri had been to Nuevo León and Coahuila. Benavides, in other words, was as independent of Richmond as Vidaurri had been of Mexico City.

For me, perhaps the most important result of *Vaqueros in Blue & Gray* has been my further investigation into the life and times of Captain Adrian J. Vidal, the young and impulsive stepson of the wealthy and influential Mifflin Kenedy. While researching a biography of Juan N. Cortina, I found that Vidal, despite the influences of his father-in-law, was operating in Cortina's shadow and that Vidal's bloody revolt against the Confederacy in October 1863 focused on sacking Brownsville prior to his flight into Mexico. As a model for Vidal, Contina, in fact, might have been in contact with Federal authorities in New Orleans, especially Colonel John L. Haynes, prior to the occupation of Brownsville, and Cortina's brazen raid on Brownsville four years earlier in September of 1859 must have impressed Vidal greatly.

Whatever may be Contina's influence, Vidal remains as fascinating today as when I first learned of him in the 1970s—a soldier who had served both the Blue and Gray, deserted both, joined the liberal army of Benito Juárez, and was executed by the French imperialists. It turns out that Vidal, who was in the services of Cortina at the time, was captured by the French while hiding on a steamboat at Camargo. Although Kenedy used "powerful means" to save his stepson, Vidal was executed by a firing squad on the morning of June 14, 1865. Kenedy vividly recorded his emotions at the time: "I write with a heavy hand, as my boy has been shot at Camargo. As bad as he is, I would have saved him if [I] could, but my efforts have failed. . . . He died at 20 years, one month and five days old, and to all appearances less concerned than any one present. He took the bandage from his eyes, and faced the guard, requesting them not to shoot him in the face, which was not complied with. He requested his body be sent to his mother. My brother being at Camargo at the time with the *Alamo*, has brought him down, and [he] is buried here in Matamoros." Several years later, Vidal's remains were moved to the Kenedy family plot in a dark corner of the old Brownsville Cemetery.

Finally, additional information about those *Tejanos* who served in the Union Army continues to surface. For example, in my recent examination of the 1890 national census (the eleventh of its kind), I found listed the names and service records of those surviving from the Army, Navy, and Marine Corps. At the time of the census, forty-eight *Tejanos* were identified as alive, and, undoubtedly, many more veterans of the Texas Union Army were reluctant to identify themselves as such due to their desertion record. Two veterans, Félix J. Moreno, of Marlin in Falls County, and Juan Gonzáles, of San Diego in Duval County, reported having served in the United States Navy, the former on the steamer *Ericsson* and the latter on the *Harriet Lane*. One Spanish-speaking veteran, Cristóbal Torres of Brownsville, could remember "nothing definite, only that he was a U.S. soldier." Elsewhere, the census enumerator in Hidalgo County, while visiting the residence of Severo Delgado, was amazed that the elderly man claimed to be a Union veteran and was careful to note that Delgado was "a Mexican." Delgado was indeed a Mexican, and, like almost a thousand other *Tejanos* and *Mexicanos*, he played a small but important role in the crisis that was the Civil War.

All this prefatory material said, I can only hope that this second edition of *Vaqueros in Blue & Gray* will be as useful and provocative as the first. Having played my small part, I welcome any subsequent effort to refine the genuine history of this great state we call Texas.

Jerry Thompson
Texas A&M International University

Preface

On the same day Fort Sumter fell to Confederate forces in the harbor of Charleston, South Carolina, a mutiny against the Lone Star State erupted deep in the heart of the South Texas brush country. In May, 1861, more than a month later, on the same day the citizens of Virginia voted in favor of secession, the Zapata County revolt exploded into a bloody battle with a thirty-seven-year-old Confederate captain from Laredo, Texas, perilously leading his Confederates to victory. In February, 1862, one day before Confederate President Jefferson Davis was inaugurated in pouring rain at Richmond, Virginia, Union and Confederate forces clashed on the Rio Grande River in far off New Mexico. In March, 1864, nine days after General Ulysses S. Grant was commissioned a lieutenant general and given command of the Armies of the United States, the Confederate commander from Laredo courageously defeated a Union force attempting to seize control of Laredo and cut the Texas cotton trade. In early May, 1865, one month after Abraham Lincoln fell to an assassin's bullet at Ford's Theatre in Washington, Union and Confederate forces clashed in the lower Rio Grande Valley. After a bloody battle the Confederates were victorious.

More than 40,000 books and pamphlets, enough to fill several libraries, have been written on the Civil War, making the struggle the most written about war in the history of mankind. These books vary in nature from the opinions and correspondence of Karl Marx and Frederick Engels to the lives of prostitutes who followed the Army of the Potomac during Grant's Virginia Campaign. Books have been written about the role of every minority group in the United States except the Mexican-Americans of the Southwest. Even books which cover in some detail the war between the blue and the gray in the Southwest have very little, if anything, to say about the role of these proud people.

Acknowledgments

While the author was researching and writing *Vaqueros in Blue and Gray*, many individuals gave assistance, for which he is deeply obligated. The National Endowment for the Humanities provided a research grant that enabled him to take a year's leave of absence for travel to Washington, D.C., to examine valuable materials in the National Archives and the Library of Congress and to spend one summer of research in Austin and San Antonio.

At the National Archives Mike Musick of the Old Military Records Branch must be thanked for his able assistance as well as George Chalou for his valuable advice. In Austin the able staff of John Kinney at the Archives Division of the Texas State Library helped in many ways as did Chester Kielman's assistants at the Barker Archives of the University of Texas. The ladies of the United Daughters of the Confederacy Museum in Austin, where the John S. Ford papers are housed, must also be thanked.

In San Antonio Anita Saxine and her staff at the St. Mary's University Library were most cooperative as was Catherine McDowell at the Daughters of the Republic of Texas Library at the Alamo. At the Institute of Texan Cultures, Sam Nesmith and James P. McGuire were helpful in the location of several old photographs. James M. McCaffrey of the Houston Civil War Round Table was kind enough to read the manuscript and suggest changes. In Brownsville

Arnulfo L. Oliveira was an inspiring force. In Laredo Maria del Refugio Benavides, Maria Benavides Saenz, and Genoveva Benavides Vela, all granddaughters of Captain Refugio Benavides, were most gracious and have since become very close friends of the author. Cristobal Sanchez, grandson of Captain Cristobal Benavides, a most delightful man who exemplifies the individualism and ruggedness of the Benavides Brothers, has also become a close friend as a result of the research on *Vaqueros in Blue and Gray*. Other Laredoans for whose help I am grateful are Manuel Blanco, who read the manuscript and provided the badly needed grammatical expertise; Alma Gomez, who patiently typed the manuscript; as well as Art Innis, Hector Farias, Sara Cabello, Alma Saucedo, Tricia Netardus, Sister Mary Gabriel Macel, Consuelo V. Salinas, Ramiro Sanchez, Mike Volpe, Virginia Goodwin, Luciano Guajardo, Billy Hall, Lucy Molina and Ercila Uribe, all of whom helped in many ways.

Helen Yturri, a most gracious lady now living in Castroville who displays the vivacious determination of her ancestors, must be thanked for providing information on her grandfather, Captain Manuel Yturri.

And last but not least, thanks to my good friend Jay A. Matthews, editor and publisher of the Presidial Press, for his interest and concern in the printing and publication of this book.

>Jerry Thompson
>Laredo, Texas
>May 30, 1976

1

Prologue

It is estimated that 9,900 Mexican-Americans served in the Civil War, with the Territory of New Mexico contributing one-half of this number. Texas also contributed a large number of Mexican-Americans to the Civil War, with sizeable numbers of Tejanos serving in both the Confederate and Federal ranks. The Rio Grande Valley, specifically that area from Laredo downriver to Brownsville, contributed large numbers of men to the two armies. The lower Nueces Valley, in particular Nueces, San Patricio and Refugio Counties, sent many Tejanos into the struggle as did the City of San Antonio. Native Californians saw action in the war with a battalion called the Native California Cavalry recruited at San Jose, Napa, San Juan Bautista, San Francisco, Marysville, Monterey, and Los Angeles. The state of Louisiana raised a militia unit from New Orleans known as the Spanish Legion or Fifth Regiment of the European Brigade. Late in the war the Territory of Arizona attempted to raise a regiment, known as the First Battalion of Arizona Infantry, from Tucson, Tubac, and the southern part of the territory.

Spanish surnamed soldiers served in such varied units as the Fifty-Fifth Alabama Infantry, Manigault's Battalion of South Carolina Artillery, the Louisiana Pointe Coupee Artillery, Sixth Missouri Infantry, the Chalmette Regiment of Louisiana Infantry, Ogden's Louisiana Cavalry, and Gray's Louisiana Infantry. Spanish surnamed soldiers even served in units from the state of Vermont. Others fired on Fort Sumter and served the blue and the gray in most of the major battles of the Civil War.

Generally speaking, the role of the Mexican-Americans in the civil war is complex and difficult to assess and they have been severely criticized and made easy scapegoats for defeats which in reality were not of their making. The desertion rate in units comprised primarily of Mexican-Americans often ran as high as one-hundred percent, especially in units of New Mexico Volunteers and Territorial Militia. Desertions from Texas-Mexican Union companies was also high and the Native California Volunteer Cavalry had its share of these problems as well.

Little effort has been made by historians to examine and explain the reasons behind the apparent poor performance of Mexican-Americans in the epic struggle. There seems little doubt that prejudice against natives in both the Union and Confederate armies was common and in some instances disgraceful. Mexican-Americans often went without food and clothing for months, even to a greater degree than soldiers of other nationalities. The weapons supplied, particularly those issued to the Spanish-Americans of New Mexico, were old and outdated. Only a small percentage of the recruits could speak English, almost all having been citizens of the United States for only thirteen years or less. The vast majority did not understand the reasons for the struggle, were thus apathetic and did not join the blue and the gray for the same reason as did other Americans. Many in the Territory of New Mexico joined to escape the ruthless peonage system. A few in New Mexico and Texas joined to fight Indians. Many in South Texas joined to protect the Rio Grande Frontier. Others joined simply because the economic and political leaders from their communities enlisted, and by paternalistic tradition they too were obligated to follow. In many ways the military makeup in Mexican-American units was an extension of the socio-economic-political composition of the Mexican-American community and the merciless patron system.

Illiteracy in Hispanic companies averaged about ninety-five percent in New Mexico, and was almost as high in Texas and California. In some units of the New Mexico Militia, the illiteracy rate was as high as one-hundred percent with officers sometimes unable to sign their names.

An examination of the ages of more than three thousand Mexican-Americans listed on the various muster rolls in companies of the Confederate or Union armies from Texas, California, and New Mexico shows an average of twenty-eight years, revealing that the average Mexican-American who fought in the war was somewhat older than Americans of other nationalities. A similar examination of numerous muster rolls of state or territorial militia units from the same areas shows its members to be an average of thirty-one years. Men in their forties, fifties and even sixties, however, were not uncommon in Mexican-American companies.

Many officers, who were generally passed over when promotions were considered and who did not understand English, had a most difficult time comprehending a rash of military orders. Frustrated by a system they did not understand, Mexican-Americans tended to desert in flocks. The neglect, prejudicial treatment, and frustration produced a reaction which is well illustrated by the case of Captain Adrian J. Vidal, perhaps one of the most unusual stories of the entire war. Vidal joined the Confederacy and commanded a Mexican-American company in the lower Rio Grande Valley. He mutinied and with his entire company fled into Mexico. In 1864, with the Union Army in control of the lower valley, he recrossed the river, enlisted in the federal army and was once again commissioned a captain. Frustrated again, Vidal attempted to resign and when unable to do so deserted, fleeing across the waters of the Rio Bravo only to be executed for treason by the Imperialists in 1865.

One blazing exception to this rather dismal record was compiled by Tejanos from South Texas. These natives led by Santos Benavides, undeniably one of the most gallant leaders to wear a Civil War uniform, compiled a brilliant record of border defense. Benavides, as well as his brothers, Refugio and Cristobal, were legends in their own time. Santos, daringly brave, overcame numerous problems to become a colonel in the Confederate Army, thus becoming the highest ranking Mexican-American to serve the Southland. It is thus by no coincidence that the saga of the Tejanos in the Civil War centers around this great leader.

Warfare was nothing new to the Mexican-Americans of Texas. Ever since the first soldiers and missionaries had crossed the vast expanses of the American Southwest to colonize what would become the Lone Star State, daily survival had been a constant struggle against hostiles. This was especially true of the Mexican-Americans of South Texas who in 1860 comprised the vast majority of the population of that portion of the state. From the time that Jose de Escandon established the "villas del norte" in the newly created province of Nuevo Santander, Spanish and Mexican frontiersmen had struggled against hostile Indians to create and sustain a way of life in the desert wilderness.

Beginning in 1810-1811 a series of revolutions ravaged the villages along the Rio Grande. A large percentage of the population comprising the area supported Father Miguel Hidalgo in his fight for Mexican independence. In 1836 General Antonio Lopez de Santa Anna crossed through northern reaches of the area on his way to the Alamo and subsequent defeat at San Jacinto during the Texas Revolution. A few years later the area had become the focus of forces attempting to establish an independent republic. Laredo, on the Rio Grande, temporarily became the capital of the abortive Republic of the Rio Grande.

During the Second Texas Mexican War of 1840-42, the same Rio Grande villagers watched Mexican armies strike northward into Texas and Texan armies invade Mexico. It was not until the Mexican War erupted in the lower valley in

1846 that the state of Texas was able to extend its control over the Rio Grande frontier. Following the war the United States Army established a chain of military posts along the river and continued to garrison the forts until Texas seceded from the Union in 1861.

By late 1860, as the secessionist movement gained strength in Texas, mass meetings were held in several of the towns and villages south of the Nueces River. On December 3, 1860, many of the leading citizens of Corpus Christi met at the Nueces County Courthouse in what was called "one of the largest meetings ever convened in the county."[1] The sentiment at the meeting was overwhelmingly for secession. Those attending the assemblage elected delegates to a state convention at Austin and voted to "fully endorse the action of South Carolina."[2] At the conclusion of the joyous gathering, guns were fired, one for each of the southern states, and the mere mention of the Lone Star Republic brought cheers from those assembled. Although Mexican-Texans were a majority in Nueces County, they were not among the leading participants. Most of the Tejanos in the county were shepherds, rancheros, and poor campesinos having little, if any, wealth and no political influence.

Nine days after the Corpus Christi meeting, the leading residents of Refugio met in a similar gathering. The participants cheered the Lone Star Flag and listened to a number of speakers urge resistance to Abraham Lincoln and the Federal Government. As was the case in Corpus Christi, although a large percentage of Refugio County were Tejanos, none were listed among the leading participants at the meeting.[3]

On December 6, citizens of Starr County met at Rio Grande City. Several speakers expressed considerable attachment to the Union while others encouraged a rebirth of the Lone Star Republic. In conclusion, the participants agreed to abide by whatever action the State of Texas might decide to follow. Although Starr County was overwhelmingly Mexican-American, A. M. Palacios was the only Tejano participant listed.[4]

Upriver in Zapata County, residents met at Carrizo on December 27, 1860. Ysidro Vela, Zapata County judge, served as president of the meeting while Fenis Mussett, the local customs collector, was elected vice-president and Domingo Vela, secretary. Judge Vela in a few opening remarks explained the purpose of the meeting and invited Mussett to address the gathering. Mussett spoke of "the felonious aggression of the Abolitionists of the North upon Southern institutions and elucidated the inconsistency of submission to Black Republic rule."[5]

Among those chosen to draft a set of resolutions at this meeting was Pedro Diaz. The Zapata County constituency did not call outright for secession but agreed to request Judge Vela to call an election for the selection of delegates to the Austin convention. The events of the coming months would prove that the meeting at Carrizo did not reflect the political desires of the majority of the population. Those assembled, like Judge Vela for example, were the large landholding patrons who were a distinct minority.

Political leaders in Brownsville and Laredo also expressed political sentiments similar to those indicated by the Corpus Christi, Carrizo, Refugio, and the Rio Grande City gatherings. An election was held in January, 1861, in which the residents of Corpus Christi, Laredo, and the other villages and towns comprising the legislative district chose P. N. Luckett and H. A. Maltby, both from Nueces County, to a state secessionist convention in Austin.[6]

The Texas Secession Convention met in Austin on January 28, 1861. Of the 176 delegates who attended the convention, not one was Mexican-American although several counties represented at the convention, such as Starr, Hidalgo, Bexar, Cameron, Bee, El Paso, and Nueces, as well as Webb, Zapata, Refugio, and San Patricio, were predominantly Tejano. Delegates at the convention voted overwhelmingly to take Texas out of the Federal Union, and when a secessionist ordinance was presented to the Texas citizenry, it was approved by a vote of 46,129 to 14,697.[7]

The ordinance was strongly supported in those areas of the state which were predominantly Tejano. In the counties of Webb, Zapata, Cameron, Starr, and Hidalgo, or those having the largest percentage of Mexican-Americans, the ordinance was approved by a vote of 1,124 to 41. In Webb and Zapata counties, not a single vote was cast against secession, while downriver in Starr County only two negative votes were registered. The overwhelming vote in favor of secession in South Texas can be misleading. Only a small percentage of the Mexican-Americans in the above mentioned counties voted, cared to vote, or were eligible to do so.

The vote in favor of secession by Tejanos was certainly not due to a fear of abolitionism. In the entire Lone Star State Tejanos owned only sixty slaves, most of whom were in the San Antonio area.[8] In those counties along the Rio Grande having the largest percentage of Tejanos almost no slaves were recorded, due mainly to the fact that Mexico in most instances was only a stones throw away, making escape by Blacks relatively easy. Besides, few Tejanos had enough money to even dream of purchasing a slave.

On February 18, 1861, General David E. Twiggs, commander of the Department of Texas, surrendered all U.S. Military posts in Texas to state authorities, and within days Federal troopers on the Rio Grande frontier furled their flags and marched for the Texas coast, many to be captured at Indianola a few weeks later. John Salmon "Rip" Ford, a resident of Brownsville and veteran frontier fighter, who had served as a delegate to the secession convention, was granted authority to raise a regiment of troops and take control of the Rio Grande frontier.[9] All across the Southern part of the state, as elsewhere in Texas, many men flocked to serve the Lone Star State. In April, 1861, Santos Benavides of Laredo wrote Governor Edward Clark that sixty-eight men had been recruited and officers elected.[10] Benavides had set up headquarters at Fort McIntosh just outside of Laredo. There is no evidence that Benavides or the leading citizens of Laredo had ever expressed any Unionist sentiment. In fact, Benavides, who by the time of the Civil War had become one of Laredo's leading merchants, had acted as a slave catcher, even crossing into Mexico in pursuit of escaped Blacks.[11]

Santos Benavides had been born on November 1, 1823, the son of Jose Jesus Benavides and Margarita Ramon. His influence in the community was partially due to his wealthy uncle, Basilio Benavides, who had represented Webb County in the state legislature. Santos, during his lifetime, was to live under five flags: that of the Republic of Mexico, Republic of the Rio Grande, Republic of Texas, the United States, and the Confederacy. As a young man, he had first tasted the sting of battle during the Federalist-Centralist wars which had ravaged the Rio Grande Valley from 1838 to 1840.

During the Somervell Expedition of 1842, a motley band of rowdy and drunk Texans sacked Benavides' small store, yet the Laredoan refused to take up arms against the State of Texas or the American forces which occupied Laredo during the Mexican War. In fact, Benavides openly cooperated with the Americans and in 1856 became mayor of Laredo. By the time of the Civil War Santos had become a leading political and financial figure in the area. Benavides, who stood five feet ten inches and weighed 175 pounds, was in many ways similar to his great-great-grandfather, Tomas Sanchez, who founded Laredo in 1755.[12]

Santos' brother, Refugio, who had served two terms as mayor of Laredo in 1857 and 1859, and his younger half brother, Cristobal, also aspired to the secessionist cause. John Ford would later write that "the Benavides family broke ground in favor of secession" and "did the Confederacy an immense favor by declaring for her."[13]

No sooner had Captain Benavides set up headquarters at Fort McIntosh than trouble developed in Zapata County. Most of the problems seemed to have been instigated by "Rip" Ford's old enemy, Juan Nepomuceno Cortina.[14] Cortina, who has been called the "Rogue of the Rio Grande" by some, but the "Robin Hood of South Texas" by others, had previously fought corrupt Gringo politicians, land barons and even the United States Army. The elusive Cortina presented an interesting contrast to Santos Benavides. While the latter represented the more aristocratic Tejanos, or those who had been able to retain much of their land and wealth in the years following the Treaty of Guadalupe-Hidalgo; "Cheno" Cortina had become a leader to the poor vaqueros, campesinos, and the generally illiterate persons of Mexican descent on both sides of the Rio Grande, who had never known anything but poverty, exploitation and suppression. Following his defeat by Texas Rangers and United States forces in 1859-1860 in what has been called the Cortina War, the Mexican leader took refuge in Mexico but managed to maintain contact with many Tejanos on the-north bank of the Rio Grande.

The history of the past year bears testimony, miscontrovertible to the fact that you have . . . rendered the state and country much efficient and important service in crushing out the Rebellion in Zapata County, in expelling the outlaw Cortina and his followers, and in giving ample security to the lives and properties of your fellow citizens. Not a single complaint has been preferred or raised against you . . . I have passed several weeks amidst your company and sobriety, good behavior, and excellent discipline characterize them at all times and in all places.

     Charles P. Lovenskiold to Santos Benavides,
        January 25, 1862

2

The Rio Grande Frontier

Opposition to the Confederacy arose in Zapata County when about forty armed Tejanos under the leadership of Antonio Ochoa seized control of Precinct Three in the southern part of the county. This armed band then marched on Carrizo, the county seat seeking to prevent any of the county officials from taking their oath of allegiance, but they were met by the County Judge Ysidro Vela, who used threats and innuendos to persuade the Tejanos to return to their homes. The dissidents retreated downriver but proceeded to issue a "pronunciamiento" against the Confederacy.[15] Henry Redmond, an English immigrant who had come to Carrizo from

Refugio, was in a state of panic. Redmond, who owned a large ranch complex consisting of a store, warehouse, and several residences, wrote Ford on April 12, 1861, that the men had given their "pronunciamiento" to Vela and demanded that it be "forwarded to the U.S.," which Redmond claimed the petitioners thought was a "few miles on the other side of Bexar." Redmond expected an invasion of Carrizo momentarily. "It is hard to say how far their ignorance will lead them," Redmond wrote Ford.[16]

Pleas from Carrizo also went to Captain Benavides and Captain Mat Nolan, both of whom were then at Fort McIntosh. Since the insurrection in Zapata County was said to be in favor of "Old Abe" and the participants in the movement wanted to communicate with Federal authorities, the movement could easily be interpreted as Unionist in nature. In reality, however, it was more anti-Texan and appears to have had economic undercurrents. The poorer vaqueros and campesinos of Precinct Three doubtlessly had ideas of overthrowing large, politically influential landowners and thus control the county. According to Captain Nolan, the "men were not only attempting to keep the county officers from taking the oath of office," but were "also threatening to forcibly take all public money."[17]

To insure peace in the county, Nolan left Laredo on April 13 with twenty-two men and reached Carrizo, some sixty miles downriver, on the afternoon of the following day. Judge Vela swore out warrants for the arrest of Antonio Ochoa and other leaders of the revolt whose numbers Nolan reported were in excess of eighty. Nolan, along with Vela and the Zapata County Sheriff, immediately took up the line of march for the Clareno Ranch twelve miles downriver from Carrizo, the headquarters of some of the participants in the Zapata County revolt.

Arriving at the Clareno Ranch at daylight on the 15th, Nolan deployed his men around the ranch, at which time the Zapata Sheriff ordered the Ochoa's followers to surrender. When the ultimatum was met with gunfire, Nolan ordered his men to attack the ranch. Greatly outnumbered and surrounded, the Zapata County insurgents were easily defeated. Nolan reported that "nine Black Republicans" were killed in the battle. The leader of the movement, Antonio

Ochoa, was absent from the ranch in Guerrero, Mexico, but two other leaders, Nepomuceno Vela and Santiago Vela, were not so lucky and were killed in the attack.[18]

Ford, alarmed at the Zapata County revolt, also heard rumors that the elusive Cortina, with a party of men led by Teodoro Zamora, was planning to cross the Rio Bravo between Rio Grande City and Brownsville to join forces with Ochoa. Ford wrote Governor Edward Clark of the Zapata uprising: "I think Captain Nolan acted promptly, boldly, and properly. It is the only appropriate way to treat traitors who are against the authorities of the state. I hope the affair will end in nothing more serious, yet if as some suppose Cortina is implicated in the matter there is no telling what may happen."[19] Ford's suspicions were correct.

By early summer the Rio Grande frontier had become particularly vulnerable to raids from Mexico, since Ford was compelled to deploy his scattered forces from below Laredo to Fort Brown for fear of a Federal invasion of the Texas coast. Hearing of another Cortina instigated uprising in Carrizo, Benavides left Laredo on May 11 with a small detachment of troops for the river village.

What further angered the Confederate authorities along the Rio Grande were rumors, many of them purportedly passed by Cortina himself, that those resisting Confederate authority had formed an alliance with Federal authorities in the North as well as with Unionists in Texas. With money furnished by the Unionists, Cortina was reported to be buying arms and horses. Much of Ford's information came from Juan Villarreal of Camargo and Trinidad Flores of Reynosa, two men whom Ford trusted and had no reason to doubt. In reference to Cortina's impending raid, Ford wrote, "the scoundrels who set the Zapata rebellion . . . have aided in organizing a foreign force to invade Texas . . . I can not tell where the storm may burst. I shall endeavor to meet the bandit and drive him across the Rio Grande."[20]

As the numerous rumors spread up and down the Rio Grande Valley, many ranchers and sheepmen, especially those living in close proximity to the border, fled their homes for the more secure environs of the larger towns. From Roma northward to Laredo, the only villages which remained occupied were Carrizo and the small settlement of San Ygnacio.

With Nolan ordered downriver to join Ford, Benavides with thirty men took up quarters at Redmond's Ranch at Carrizo. Benavides wrote Ford of his arrival: "In consequence of the various reports that Cortina was going to cross the Rio Grande in this neighborhood, I came down here and have 30 men protecting this place, and intend to remain here until I hear positively of his whereabouts, and the number of his force."[21] Within hours of his arrival at Carrizo, Ysidro Vela reported to Benavides that Cortina was in camp at Malabucco sixteen miles from Mier on the road to Agualeguas. According to Vela, Antonio Ochoa, who had led the Zapata revolt the previous month, had "collected all the thieves, murderers, and assassins of Guerrero, and gone to Cortina."[22] Vela felt Cortina's intentions were to attack Carrizo.

Noah Cox, a leading secessionist from Roma agreed with Vela, feeling that Ochoa and Cortina were organizing men in Mexico for the purpose of crossing into Zapata County "with the avowed intention of plundering and burning the small frontier towns."

Cox organized a home guard for the protection of Roma and Starr County. "We . . . will defend ourselves as long as we can. Cortina and Ochoa are together, and they have possibly over one hundred men by this time," Cox reported.[23] Cox's small company consisted of forty residents of Roma thirty-four of whom were Tejanos. The company was hastily organized, poorly armed, and helpless against Cortina's veteran raiders.

Fearing Cortina, H. Clay Davis at Rio Grande, was also on the verge of panic. "I have just received an express from Juan Villarreal of Camargo," Davis wrote, "who says there is no doubt that Cortina with a considerable force is marching up the country, with the intention of crossing the Rio Grande near Guerrero."[24]

Upriver at Carrizo, Henry Redmond wrote Ford pleading for help. Redmond, convinced that Cortina would cross into Zapata County, wanted Benavides to station more troops at Carrizo. According to Redmond, Cortina had also joined forces with Octaviano Zapata and a man named Serna, one of Guerrero's leading political figures. Cortina, according to Redmond, was telling his partisans he would kill every Gringo in Zapata County, especially Redmond and Mussett. Redmond blamed most of Zapata County's problems on the residents of Guerrero, who Redmond felt were all followers of Cortina.[25] A correspondent for the *Corpus Christi Ranchero* echoed feelings similar to those of Redmond: "I will tell you that hellhole of iniquity, Guerrero, has got to be wiped out before perfect security will be obtained for our Rio Grande settlements. It is the nucleus around which Mexican bandits... gather."[26]

Mexican authorities in Matamoros had previously assured Ford that they would do everything possible to stop Cortina, but Judge Vela was skeptical. "The authorities of Mexico may insinuate that they will zeaously [sic] endeavor to prevent him from organizing an armed force to invade our soil, but it is vice versa. They would more zeaously [sic] encourage the scheme than use prompt measures to prevent it," the judge wrote. According to Vela, "Actions speak louder than words."[27] The judge had been forced to abandon his home and seek refuge at Redmond's Ranch. A band of Cortina's men had gone to Vela's ranch where they shot his cattle, stole his horses, and destroyed the corn fields; thus forcing the judge to flee to Carrizo for fear of his life.

From Carrizo, Benavides sent scouts to locate, if possible, the whereabouts of the wily Cortina. With most of the residents of Zapata County in sympathy with Cortina, it was impossible for Benavides to make a move without Cortina's hearing of it. Others, especially the large landowners and the handful of small merchants in Carrizo, as well as the county officeholders, were in sympathy with Vela, Mussett, and Redmond, and were reporting Cortina's movements to Benavides. "There is no doubt that he is organizing a force and that he intends to cross the Rio Grande near this place. I am constantly on the alert, and verily believe that I can repel his attack," Benavides wrote Ford from Carrizo.[28]

On May 19, Cortina with his raiders splashed across the Rio Grande about four miles below Carrizo and went into camp. The following day ten of Cortina's advance guard ran into three of Benavides' pickets, and a brief skirmish ensued. The three Confederates reported to Benavides that Cortina with the bulk of his raiders were safely on the Texas side of the river and that his force was growing hourly, being augmented by residents of Guerrero as well as citizens from Zapata County. Many of the Zapata County Tejanos were doubtlessly hoping to revenge the death of the men killed at the Clareno Ranch the previous month.

By the morning of the 21st, Cortina, by stationing various squads around Carrizo, had Benavides and the Laredo force surrounded and shut up in Redmond's Ranch. The bandit king had also succeeded in capturing two dispatch riders on the road from Roma to Carrizo.

All sorts of rumors reached the besieged Confederates. Cortina was reported to have between 1,500 and 2,000 men. Roma and Rio Grande City were purported to have fallen. Two residents of Carrizo, Anselmo Flores and Pedro Reyna, attempted to persuade Benavides to leave and let the Gringos defend themselves. Benavides, however, was determined to stand and fight.[29]

Benavides had no doubt that Redmond's Ranch could easily be defended, especially the largest of the buildings which was made of stone and had been used before the war by the United States Army as a fort. Furthermore, enough water and food were available to last several weeks. Morale was also heightened by the possession of a six-pounder cannon along with plenty of ammunition.

Several of Cortina's pickets were able to get within a few hundred yards of the ranch and fire a volley of shots at the defenders. Other than alert Benavides' green troops, the shots did little damage. Several of Cortina's men were easily visible on the small cactus covered hills surrounding the ranch complex and the village of Carrizo. Cortina's men did little more than ride around on their horses, however, a tactic Benavides felt was being used to confuse the besieged Confederates.

In the evening just as the sun began to set on the western horizon across the muddy waters of the Rio Grande, Benavides, Mussett, Vela, and Redmond positioned themselves on the large porch of Redmond's Ranch and took turns gazing through a spy glass at Cortina's men. Late into the evening, with a full moon out, the men could be seen marching about and deploying before the ranch complex.

On May 21st as nerves began to wear thin, the Laredo captain attempted to push an express through to Laredo for help. Private Angel Jimenez volunteered and set out for Laredo but was overtaken and captured a few miles outside of town. Within an hour another rider, mounted on Benavides' horse, with pistol in hand set out for Laredo at a full gallop. After a terrifying ride through Cortina's lines, the private reached Laredo safely.[30]

As the young private raced upriver to Laredo, Cortina's partisans continued to fire intermittently into the ranch complex. No casualties were reported, yet the Confederates spent an uneasy night.

The next morning, just as daylight broke across the South Texas desert, a lone rider came racing up to the ranch and almost collapsed from exhaustion. He was Refugio Benavides, Santos' brother who had raced his horse down the Mexican side of the river and had managed to avoid Cortina's pickets at the river crossing near Carrizo. Refugio brought word that the remainder of the Laredo Confederates were on their way from Laredo.[31]

Less than three hours later, a force of thirty-six men arrived at Carrizo. The force was headed by Basilio Benavides, Santos' uncle, and Lieutenant Charles Callaghan. With no rest the Laredoans had made the sixty-five mile ride from Laredo in thirteen hours. The men as well as horses were completely fatigued. The Confederates had been stopped briefly by the villagers at San Ygnacio who told the Laredoans that Cortina had 1,500 men deployed around Redmond's Ranch, and any attempt to break through his lines would be senseless. Believing the residents of San Ygnacio to be in sympathy with Cortina, the men had continued downriver. Just outside of Carrizo, within sight of Redmond's Ranch, the Laredoans ran through a squad of Cortina's men who were stationed on the Laredo Road.[32]

At the very moment the Laredo force reached Carrizo, Cortina and his men had entered the village and were in the process of breaking into the customs house and the court house. Believing Benavides to have surrendered, many residents of Zapata County joined Cortina and his men in the pillage.

Although exhausted from the long ride downriver from Laredo, Benavides within five minutes asked for volunteers to join him in an all out attack against the bandit chief and his men. Benavides, with forty men, caught Cortina and seventy of his followers a short distance from Carrizo and a bitter fight ensued. The Laredoans charged Cortina on horse and were successful in completely overrunning the partisans. With several of Cortina's men killed in the initial charge, the remainder broke for the Rio Grande. With swords in hand, the Confederates pursued the bandits to the river bank. Seven of Cortina's men were killed, fifteen wounded, and eleven captured. It was later learned that two of the bandits drowned while attempting to swim the Rio Grande to safety in Mexico. None of the Confederates were injured in the fight, although Lieutenant Juan Garcia Soto and Private Dario Aresola lost their horses in the battle. Private Angel Jimenez, who had been captured by the bandits the previous day, was recaptured. The entire battle had lasted only a few minutes.[33]

In his report of the battle to Ford, Benavides wrote: "Before attacking Cortina, I particularly ordered my men not to arrest any of the bandits, but to kill all that fell into their hands. Consequently I have no prisoners."[34] In a preceding paragraph of the same report, Benavides stated plainly that eleven prisoners had been taken in the fray. What happened to the captives can only be pondered. It is assumed that they were either shot or hanged as such was the custom along the Rio Grande frontier.

On the morning following the battle, Cortina was reported to be a short distance from Guerrero with a handful of men and moving down the country in full retreat. Benavides, who remained at Carrizo for several days, reported Cortina's force to be composed of the citizens of Guerrero and Zapata County, many of whom had been involved in the April uprising.

In Orders No. 21, Ford wrote of the battle at Carrizo: "Thanks are due to Captain Benavides and his men for their gallantry in expelling a foe from our territory. Their conduct merits the highest praise. Thanks are also due to the Hon. Basilio Benavides, Refugio Benavides and the citizens of Webb County for their promptitude in going to the rescue of their fellow citizens of Zapata County, when threatened by imminent danger. They have shown themselves to be loyal to the government of the Confederate States under trying circumstances and deserve the commendation of every true friend of the South."[35] In a personal letter to Benavides, Ford wrote: "Your judgement, ability, and gallantry in the affair receive encouragement from every quarter. I sincerely congratulate you upon your success. You and the people of Webb County have furnished indisputable evidence to the world of your devotion to the cause of Constitutional liberty."[36]

Ford did not hesitate in reporting Cortina's defeat to Governor Clark in Austin. Clark, who appears to have had some doubt about Benavides' loyalty prior to the battle at Carrizo, wrote the Laredo captain: "Whenever our enemies have appeared on our soil, you and your brave men have been present and driven them back, with great honor to yourselves and the gratification of your state." Clark even went as far as to send an elegantly engraved pistol to Benavides along with a letter which read, "I am happy to believe in your hands it will always be used in the defense of your country and prove an instrument of terror and destruction to her enemies."[37] Wallace E. Oakes, a friend of the governor, took the pistol to Benavides personally, and, although detained in San Antonio for some time, arrived on the border in November, 1861.

To Ford and Governor Clark, Benavides' continued loyalty to the Southern cause was critical. It is safe to speculate that had Benavides refused to serve the Confederacy and remained neutral or joined with the Federals, the war on the Rio Grande would have taken a much different course. Benavides, especially in late 1863 and early 1864, was the Confederacy on the Rio Grande, and without the loyalty of that element of the Mexican-Texan population which the Laredo captain represented, the entire southwestern flank of the Confederacy might have been exposed, and the Stars and Stripes might have waved over Austin long before the summer of 1865.

The thanks of the Legislature are hereby tendered . . . to Capts. Santos Benavides and Refugio Benavides and the officers and men under their command for their vigilance, energy, and gallantry in pursuing and chastising the banditti infesting the Rio Grande frontier.

> Joint Resolution of the Legislature of the
> State of Texas, March 30, 1863

3

Tejanos for the Confederacy

With the defeat of Cortina at Carrizo, the ferocity of what some were calling the Second Cortina War slackened, and Confederate authorities began to focus their attention elsewhere. The opening of hostilities between the Union and Confederate Armies in northern Virginia and the increased threat of a Union occupation of the Texas coast, stimulated thousands of young men from every walk of life to join the Texas Confederate Army. Tejanos were no exception as hundreds enlisted.

Many Mexican-Texans who enlisted in the Confederate Army saw action far from home. A few who enlisted in

Hood's Texas Brigade marched off to Virginia to see action at the battles of Gaines' Mill, Second Bull Run, Antietam, Fredericksburg, Gettysburg, Chickamauga, the Wilderness and Appomattox.[38] Thirty Tejanos recruited from San Antonio, Eagle Pass, and the Fort Clark area joined Trevanion T. Teel's Artillery Company and thirty-one more joined Charles L. Pyron's Company from Bexar County, both units of John R. Baylor's Second Texas Mounted Rifles, which marched across the vast deserts of West Texas to fight in New Mexico. These men, as a part of the Confederate Army of New Mexico commanded by General Henry Hopkins Sibley, fought bravely at the battle of Valverde. Other Mexican-Texans from San Antonio served in the Sixth Texas Infantry. The regiment comprised part of General Hiram B. Granbury's Brigade of General Patrick R. Cleburne's Division in the Army of Tennessee and saw action in several of the eastern campaigns, including the battles of Chattanooga, Chickamauga, the Atlanta Campaign, and at Franklin and Nashville in Hood's ill-fated invasion of Tennessee. Antonio Bustillos and Eugenio Navarro were two of the acknowledged leaders of the regiment.[39]

Manuel Yturri II, a Kentucky educated scholar who was fluent in both Spanish and English, was a Tejano of distinguished Spanish Basque-Canary Island ancestry, who enlisted in the Third Texas Infantry at San Antonio and served in Richard Waterhouse's Brigade of John Forney's Division in Arkansas and Louisiana. Yturri rose to the rank of Captain. Lieutenant Martiriano Rodriguez, a close friend of Captain Yturri's also served in the same regiment. Lieutenant Joseph De La Garza, another San Antonian after serving in the Confederate Army for three years and returning home, re-enlisted in 1864 and joined those Texans who were rushed north to resist the Union attempt to invade Texas in the Red River Campaign. He met his death in the bloody battle of Mansfield which turned back the northern columns.

Webb, Refugio and Bexar Counties probably contributed the most Tejano soldiers to the Confederacy. More than three hundred from Refugio and Bexar joined the Eighth Texas Infantry. Companies commanded by Joseph M. Penaloza and Angel Navarro were almost entirely Tejano, while fifty-five served in Edwin E. Hobby's Company E. The twenty-eight-year-old Penaloza and the thirty-four-year-old Navarro were to compile outstanding records during the war. In Penaloza's company Juan Sauceda served as second lieutenant, while in Navarro's company Sexto E. Navarro rose to the rank of captain with Tomas A. Rodrigues and Erasmo J. Chavez serving as second lieutenants.[40]

Several Mexican-Texans from the Eighth Infantry participated in the repulse of a Union force in the Battle of Corpus Christi in August, 1862. When Major A. M. Hobby had refused to surrender the town, Union warships outside Corpus Christi Bay bombarded the town for several hours and later landed a small force attempting to seize the town by storm. Confederates were said to have driven the Union Marines back in "gallant style."[41] Eight months later the Eighth Infantry helped drive a Union force from St. Joseph's Island on the Texas Coast and served at Fort Esperanza on Matagorda Island before being transferred to the lower Rio Grande Valley.[42]

Other Tejanos enlisted in Philip Nolan Luckett's Regiment of Infantry, eighteen of whom were recruited at Corpus Christi by Captain James N. Morgan. The men were enlisted for the war and saw action in the lower valley with Rip Ford. Most of the men were in their early twenties. Several were from Mexico, listing their birth places as Jalapa, Zacatecas, Vera Cruz, Chihuahua, San Fernando, Monterrey, and the Rio Grande towns of Camargo, Mier, Reynosa, and Guerrero.[43] Another company in Luckett's Infantry Regiment, commanded by F. J. Parker, were all Tejano, except for three officers. Although Francisco Barrera served as second lieutenant, the company was typical in that most of the companies comprised of a majority of Tejanos tended to have Anglo officers. Of the sixty-two men in Parker's company, only three had been born in Texas. Many of the men had been born in the interior of Mexico at Guadalajara, San Luis Potosi, Tampico, Puebla, Ciudad Victoria, Zacatecas, Guanajuanto, and Jalapa, while a few had been born in the northern frontier towns of Monterrey, Linares, Reynosa and Matamoros. The men varied in age from eighteen to fifty and were listed on the company muster roll as very small in stature. Several were listed as five feet one and five feet two with no one taller than five feet eight.[44]

Clemente Bustillo, a resident of San Antonio, raised a company of ninety-three Tejanos in the Alamo City as early as March of 1861. The communication problem faced by all Mexican-Texans in the war was evidenced on the face of Bustillo's muster roll which stated: "Those desires to enter the Cervice of the State of Texas for the term of six months commencing from the time they are mustered into Cervice." Antonio Cuellar, Jesus Garza, and Pedro Flores served Bustillo as "Leutenants" while Fermin Martinez, Jesus Rodrigues, Ignacio Sandoval and Cristobal Arellano were listed as "Sargeants." Bustillo's muster roll was perhaps one of the more interesting of the war. Not only were the men's age and rank listed but the color of their skin, the thickness of their whiskers, the texture and color of their hair, and their occupation. Bustillo's men varied in age from sixteen to fifty; their hair was listed as either straight or curly; their whiskers as thick, scattered, or none; their complexion as white or dark; and their occupation as laborers, blacksmiths, bakers, or carpenters.[45]

Clemente Zapata raised a company of Tejanos at San Diego in Nueces County. As was the tradition early in the war, the men elected their officers. At a meeting held in March, 1862, at the house of E. N. Gray, a San Diego Lawyer, Zapata was chosen as captain. Zapata, however, proved to be disloyal and deserted to join the Federals at Brownsville serving in their ranks until the end of the war.[46]

In June, 1861, Governor Edward Clark, using the Militia Act of 1858, directed that a state militia be organized. Adjutant General William Byrd, in charge of the organization, ordered that groups of men numbering not less than thirty-two and no more than one hundred were to be formed into companies. The companies were then divided into two groups: First, active companies to be composed of men willing to march at the call of the governor, and secondly, reserve companies composed of men unable to leave their immediate neighborhoods but willing to organize for home protection. Active companies were to be formed into battalions, consisting of between two and not more than five companies, with two battalions constituting a regiment.[47]

In most towns, large and small, thousands of men enrolled in the various companies. Tejanos also joined by the hundreds. Enlistment in the militia was in fact quite popular among Mexican-Texans, mainly because by joining the militia, especially the reserve forces, the Tejanos had no fear of being marched out of the state. The militia also permitted more of a retention of the patron system than did the regular Confederate service which had a tendency to undermine and destroy the system. The militia was therefore popular among Tejano political leaders.

In Precinct Two of Refugio County, Captain Rafael Alderete formed a militia company consisting of thirty-six Tejanos. Alderete called his company the Jeff Davis Home Guards and listed Trinidad Alderete and Cusoforo Lozano as officers.[48] In October, 1861, also in Refugio County, Captain Edward P. Upton raised a militia company, mostly of Tejanos, called the Lamar Home Guard Volunteers.[49] In the same month, Theodore Hermann mustered in a militia company of Mexican-Texans on the Medina River twelve miles southwest of San Antonio. All of Hermann's men were listed as having horses, but only a very few possessed rifles.[50]

In June, 1862, Adolphus Glaneke raised a militia company in the lower Rio Grande Valley called the Cameron County Coast Guards. The men, almost all Tejano, were mostly from Rio Grande City, rather than Cameron County.[51] In September, 1861, Captain Serapio Garza, assisted by Lieutenants Leonard Farias and Jorge Trevino, raised a militia company of Mexican-Texans at Rio Grande City called the Minute Men. The men were stationed at Ringgold Barracks at Rio Grande City and were utilized as scouts along the river. Usually a squad of ten men would be formed and sent out for as long as five days. Captain Garza was paid five dollars a day for his services, while Farias and Trevino drew two dollars per day and the enlisted men one dollar and fifty cents per day.[52]

In Precincts Six and Nine of Bexar County, Silas L. Stanfields raised a company of militia largely of Mexican-Texans called the Medina Guards. Juan Mercado served as the only Tejano officer.[53] James W. Gray's company of militia from Bexar County, called the Gray Town Pioneers, listed Juan M. Rodriguez, Papinesino Rodriguez, and M. M. Rodriguez as officers. Captain A. M. Barrera's company from Precinct One in Bexar County was Tejano, as was Antonio Sierra's Company from Precinct Eleven.[54]

In March, 1862, Captain Francisco Jimenez raised a militia company in Wilson County with Jesus Alderete, Matias Cuellar, and Ramon Falcon as officers. Another militia company from Wilson County, headed by Manuel C. Herrera with Mariano Flores, Acencio Alderete and Nuncio de la Zada as lieutenants, appears to have been entirely Tejano.[55]

Numerous Texas counties raised militia companies which contained small numbers of Mexican-Texans. Such was the case with William P. Graves' Davis Guards, S. W. Hill's Victoria Aides, and companies raised by J. E. Furgeson, John H. Cross, and Otto Von Roeder, all from Victoria County. The Lamar Home Guards from Refugio County, Bexar Guards from Bexar County, John Hynes' Bee County Militia, Isaac W. Engledow's Company from Nueces County, Sam C. Skidmore's Company from San Patricio County, Captain Asa Mitchell's Company of Minute Men and Captain M. J. Brinson's Company from San Antonio also contained small numbers of Tejanos.[56]

A militia company called the Pedernales Cavalry, which was raised at Groom's Springs and Westbrook in Blanco County, listed a few Tejanos. The men from Blanco County joined to fight Indians and not Yankees, however, as was the case in many companies raised by the Texas Frontier. "The neighborhood of the company has been troubled by Indians for the last two years and the men joined the company for the protection of the settlements," wrote George Freeman, captain of the company.[57]

Mexican-Texan militia companies like that of Joseph A.

Durand in Atascosa County continued to be raised throughout the war. Most of Durand's men owned their own weapons with a few not only owning a rifle but a shot gun and a six shooter as well. A few, however, owned no weapons at all.[58]

Hector Farias

Santos Benavides and his wife
Agustina Villarreal de Benavides.

Texas State Library

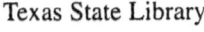

Gen. Edmund J. Davis.

General Juan N. Cortina, 1866

Ursaline Academy Library

Laredo Confederates: Left to right, Refugio Benavides, Atanacio Vidaurri, Cristobal Benavides and John Z. Leyendecker.

Courtesy Helen Yturri

Captain Manuel Yturri II

Brigadier General Hamilton P. Bee

Courtesy Cristobal Sanchez

Captain Cristobal Benavides

Col. John L. Haynes and his wife Angelica Wells.

I especially recommend Major Benavides for his untiring energy and patriotism, and would respectfully suggest that the general commanding recognize officially the distinguished services of Major Benavides, and the firm, unyielding support which the companies of Laredo, commanded by Captains Refugio and Cristobal Benavides, all Mexicans, have ever given to our cause.

> Hamilton P. Bee to Edmund P. Turner,
> September 11, 1863

4

War Along The River

The fighting between Tejanos and Cortina partisans did not end with the battle at Carrizo. On May 28, 1861, a skirmish broke out at the Clareno Ranch, near the site where Captain Nolan had previously defeated the Zapata County insurgents, when a group of Confederates went to the river for water and were fired on by Mexicans from the opposite bank. The Confederates returned the fire, and for the next two days the shooting across the Rio Grande continued. Several of Cortina's men were reported killed, although rumors that Antonio Ochoa had perished in the skirmish later proved to be false.

At Brownsville, Colonel Ford faced a dual problem of preventing further raids by Cortina and at the same time maintaining friendly relations with the Mexican government. To ease matters, General Guadalupe Garcia, Mexican commander at Matamoros, crossed the Rio Grande to confer with Ford at Fort Brown. General Garcia, having internal problems of his own, could ill afford a war with the Confederacy. Garcia had previously rejected a proposal presented to him by John Horsehead, a Seminole-Negro Chief, who upon his arrival in Matamoros attempted to persuade Garcia to allow him to raise three hundred Negroes to fight the Confederacy. Not until Garcia threatened to place the chief under arrest and put him to work in the public brick yard did Horsehead leave Matamoros. Garcia agreed in a signed treaty not only to allow Confederate authorities to cross the Rio Grande in pursuit of Cortina and his elusive raiders but to assume offensive operations against the bandit king himself. The Mexican general seemed to further agree with Ford that many of the Confederates' problems were with the citizens of Guerrero who openly cooperated with the raiders.

Garcia, at Ford's request, even journeyed upriver to Laredo to confer with Santos Benavides. In a meeting held at Fort McIntosh, it was reported the general gave the Laredo captain full permission "to cross to the Mexican side of the Rio Grande when necessary."[59] The exact circumstances under which Benavides would be allowed to cross the river would cause both the Confederate and Mexican governments much agony in the months to come.

Ford, knowing Benavides' reputation for entering Mexico at the least provocation, agreed that such measures were necessary, but appeared apprehensive about the agreement. If such a crossing became necessary, Benavides was to be "very particular to avoid molesting peaceable citizens." The Laredo captain was to go "as a friend to Mexico and as an enemy to the followers of Cortina and Ochoa." Ford was fearful that Cortina would ambush Benavides in Mexico and "get revenge for the beating" Benavides had given Cortina at Carrizo.[60]

Although Cortina did, at least on one occasion, cross to the north bank of the Rio Grande, the so-called Second Cortina

War, was reported by Ford to be over by July, 1861. Ford felt the agreement between Garcia and Benavides "did much to tranquilize the frontier and prevent a war."[61]

As late as September, however, Juan Ortiz, a leading citizen from Laredo, brought reports that Cortina was near Mier, enlisting men to invade the Texas frontier again. Cortina, it was rumored, was not only carrying a commission from Benito Juarez but one from Abraham Lincoln. A force of Mexican Regulars had been sent upriver to arrest Cortina, but when the soldiers encountered the bandit chieftain near Mier, they were shown Cortina's commission from Juarez and had retreated downriver. Benavides had no doubt that Cortina had a force of from fifty to two hundred men but felt the rumors of Cortina having the commissions to be totally false. The captain, nevertheless, moved with most of his command to Carrizo again to "watch any movement Cortina should make and be ready to meet him should he attempt to cross the river." Benavides had no doubt that Cortina would "rob and murder the frontier settlers and perhaps burn the towns on the Rio Grande," if the opportunity arose.[62]

By October, 1861, with Cortina in retreat into the Mexican interior, the six months' enlistment of the soldiers from Laredo had expired, and many of the men began to make preparations for a return to civilian life. Confederate high command in Houston, realizing the value of the Laredo force, asked Benavides and his men to muster into the regular Confederate service for three years. The prominent Danish lawyer from Corpus Christi, Charles Grimus Thorkelin de Lovenskiold, was appointed by the governor of Texas as a special commissioner in hopes of reenlisting the Laredoans under the Stars and Bars of the Southland. Even before arriving on the border, Lovenskiold heard that the Laredo force was refusing to join for three years which the generals in Houston were insisting upon. Such rumors were verified when Captain Benavides wrote Governor Clark that his force had "not been received in the C.S. service, the men having refused to muster in." "Gen'l. Van Dorn and Col. H. E. McCulloch have refused to receive my company except for the war. I have written Col. Ford . . . to appoint some person to muster us out of the service and receive the property but he has not done so," the captain continued.[63] Since other companies in Ford's command had been allowed to muster into the Confederate Army for one year, why was an exception being made for the Laredo force? Benavides queried. There was also no doubt in Lovenskiold's mind that the Laredo force was being singled out for unfair treatment. The commissioner, acting through Lieutenant Charles Callaghan, who acted as Benavides' interpreter, reported that Benavides could persuade the Laredoans to muster into the service for one year but certainly not for three.

The Laredoans, poorly equipped at the beginning of the war, had recently been supplied with "100 Hall's Carbines, 100 pair of Holster Pistols, 50 muskets, some wagons and mules, and a large amount of powder and fixed ammunition."[64] Lovenskiold was apprehensive that Benavides and his men, since they had not been paid in more than seven months, might attempt, if mustered out of the service, to retain their arms. The new governor of Texas, Francis R. Lubbock, also appeared concerned about the armaments, even more so than the status of the border Tejanos. The Texas Legislature reflected many of the governor's views. Tejanos were expendable, but not their arms. The legislature, somewhat ignorant of the mechanization of modern warfare, even gave considerable thought to providing for a regiment of Mexican-Texans to be armed with nothing but lances.[65]

As the controversy over reenlistment continued, Benavides sent Lieutenant Callaghan to Corpus Christi to confer with Lovenskiold. Callaghan told the inspector that supplies were running low in Laredo, and if the men were not mustered out soon, there would be no alternative but to disband the company. "I had better be on hand to muster them out properly before they disband themselves, or otherwise the officers could not guarantee the security of the arms and public property," the commissioner wrote of his meeting with Callaghan.[66]

Back in Laredo, Callaghan wrote Lovenskiold that "Captain Benavides has been able to get his company to consent to muster into the service of the Confederate States for 1 year."[67] Benavides, who was absent from Laredo scouting for Indians, appeared happy about the prospect of continued military service.

In December, Lovenskiold wrote Governor Lubbock on the subject again:

> The company has done the state good service; in fact, more effective than any of the other mounted companies on the frontier, they have kept that section clear of Indians, and prevented, and are preventing, a second 'Cortina' War by lawless Mexicans. A company of this kind is needed at that point... If the Benavides company is not mustered into the service of the C.S. now, they will of course disband, and it will be impracticable hereafter to get any Mexican citizen to enlist or form another company, while the state, as well as the Confederate Government, will be blamed and rendered unpopular about it, as in their ignorance of matters they will attribute their non-acceptance to prejudice against their nationality or origin.[68]

Finally Lovenskiold was able to pressure Charles Russell, State Representative from Webb County, to confer with Governor Clark, who in turn was able to persuade Brigadier General Paul O. Hebert, commanding the Department of Texas, to allow the Laredoans to muster in for one year. Lovenskiold rode to Laredo during the second week in December, 1861, to meet with Benavides and hopefully muster the men out of state service and into the Confederate Army.

In late December General Hebert agreed to allow Benavides' company to be mustered in for one year. Governor Francis R. Lubbock immediately wrote the Laredo captain of Hebert's decision. One week later Benavides wrote Austin thanking the governor "in my own name and in the name of the people of this section of the country for the interest you have taken in the company."[69] On the first day of the new year, Lovenskiold was to muster in the Laredo men.

While on the border Lovenskiold wrote a glowing tribute to the Tejanos from Laredo:

> The history of the past year bears testimony, miscontrovertible to the fact that you have... rendered the state and country much efficient and

> important service in crushing out the Rebellion in Zapata County, in expelling the outlaw Cortina and his followers, and in giving ample security to the lives and properties of your fellow citizens within your jurisdiction. While thus engaged, you have upheld the laws of our common country, supported and sustained its officers and government, and making subordination and obedience your watch word. Not a single complaint has been preferred or raised against you for any usurpation of power, and violation of law and trespass on private rights, or any misconduct. I have passed several weeks amidst your company, and sobriety, good behavior, and excellent discipline characterize them at all times and in all places.[70]

In more than nine months only four men had deserted from the Laredo company, Lovenskiold compared the Laredoans to other troops he had inspected in other areas of the state. "My inspections of other troops . . . composed of citizens, claiming the exclusive right of calling themselves 'Americans' and having among their officers many who were experienced as commanders, and who claimed a reputation for high abilities as chiefs and disciplinarians . . . for the sake of history and truth, that with very few exceptions, they were void of discipline, self-esteem, or espirit de corps."[71]

In conclusion, Lovenskiold wrote, " . . . history and posterity may bear witness to your deeds of valor and patriotism in the Southern cause, and refute as false slander . . . the insinuation that because citizens of Mexican origin you neither could be trusted as far nor fight as well or as valiantly as those of your fellow citizens who have only Anglo-Saxon blood coursing through their veins."[72]

A study of Lovenskiold's correspondence reveals that while the Dane was laudatory in his comments to Benavides, his official reports to Governor Francis R. Lubbock present a contradictory picture. It is quite obvious that Lovenskiold was indulging himself in some form of politics and it is difficult to deduce which of his opinions represent the true state of affairs at Laredo. The Dane reported to Governor Lubbock that "a very strong under current is running among the Mexican population on both sides of the river, against the Confederacy." According to the commissioner, disloyalty to the Confederacy was being promoted in Laredo "by a few northern-born Americans," whom Lovenskiold called "secret enemies to the south."[73] A meeting, under the leadership of Garner W. Pierce and Refugio Benavides, had been held at which numerous soldiers and civilians were said to have been present. The object of the meeting, according to the commissioner, "was to dissuade the soldiers from enlisting in the Confederacy."[74] According to Lovenskiold, the anti-Confederate instigators were passing rumors "that our revolution is simply the result of a 'pronunciamento' by a military leader, one Gen'l. Davis; that the North will soon overwhelm us; and every person found with arms in his hands will be hung and his property confiscated."[75] Lovenskiold insisted that Santos Benavides and the military authorities arrest the leaders, including the captain's brother, throw the leaders in the guard house, and disperse the crowd. When the authorities arrived, however, the instigators could not be found.

One reason for the turmoil was that many of the Laredoans were destitute. For nine months the soldiers had not been paid. Many of the men in the military had large families to support and had been forced to sell off goats and sheep from their small herds. Rumors that the men were threatening to refuse service in the Confederate Army and keep their arms if they were not paid were indeed true. Realizing the situation in Laredo to be critical, Lovenskiold had approached the Webb County Commissioners and proposed that the county release to the military some $3,000 dollars in school funds. When the commissioners refused, Lovenskiold next proposed that the county pay each man thirty dollars, the county to be reimbursed by the state at an undisclosed later date. The commissioners remained adamant, however. Regardless, Lovenskiold was determined to muster the men into the service, fearing "the failure to organize one company for the Confederacy, from among the population of Mexican origin, would have a most injurious effect on the whole Rio Grande Country."[76]

Although thirty-two men refused to reenlist, Lovenskiold, with the assistance of Captain Benavides, was able within two weeks to reenlist eighty men. The commissioner had achieved the objective for which he had been sent to the border.

In April, 1862, Refugio Benavides mustered in a company of his own at Ringgold Barracks. With the exception of First Lieutenant Gardner W. Pierce, whom Lovenskiold had previously accused of treason, all eighty-five men in the company were Tejanos. Pedro Trevino and Eugenio Garza were listed as lieutenants with Ramon Gamboa, Jacob Salinas, Bartolo Moreno, Martin Ramon, and Ildefonso Garcia as sergeants.[77]

Downriver at Brownsville there was a large scale desertion of Mexicans from the Confederate Army. The desertions came in the companies of F. J. Parker, Buquorand, and James R. Marmion. Parker's company was made up entirely of Mexicans, while the other two companies were composed mostly of Anglos. Many of the men who deserted at Brownsville were not Tejanos but Mexican nationals who had been born in Mexico and had only recently crossed the river to join the Confederate Army. They were therefore different in the sense, unlike Santos Benavides' men at Laredo, that they were motivated largely by economics and not by a sense of patriotism. Colonel Augustus Buchel, commanding Fort Brown, felt the Mexicans were "susceptible to bribes and corruption" and could not "be depended upon." Fourteen men from Parker's company had "deserted and passed over the river into Mexico" to take "part in the difficulties . . . existing in Tamaulipas."[78] Buchel, disgusted with his command, reported, however, that some of the desertions were not Mexicans but "old soldiers and deserters from the old Federal Army" who were "a class of men in whom no dependence whatever can be placed." "A few dollars," Buchel wrote, "and a little whisky is quite sufficient to corrupt and entice them away." The commander asked department headquarters for "men of character and intelligence, who have an interest in the success of our cause and country, and who can not be bribed or enticed to desert.[79]

By November, 1862, the Confederate forces along the Rio Grande, part of the Sub-Military District of the Rio Grande, had grown to 917. The troops on the river were attached to the command of Colonel P. N. Luckett. The Tejanos of Santos Benavides were stationed at Carrizo and Laredo; Refugio Benavides' men were at Ringgold Barracks; J. M. Penaloza's and Antonio Navarro's forces at San Antonio and in Atascosa County.

When Ford was relegated to a desk job in Austin, General Hamilton P. Bee came to command the Rio Grande Frontier. Bee, who had served as State Representative from Webb County in the 1850's, had come to Laredo with Captain Mirabeau B. Lamar during the Mexican War and had stayed on to become one of the town's leading merchants. During his political tenure in Austin, Bee had lobbied enthusiastically for better protection for the Rio Grande Frontier and in the process had become a close friend of the Benavides family, especially of Santos Benavides with whom Bee had fought Indians. Mutual respect between the two officers added greatly to the effectiveness of the Confederacy on the Rio Grande during the early stages of the war. Bee's daughter, Lamar, named for his Mexican War commander, was to marry Cristobal Benavides in 1867.

In December, 1862, the guerrilla war along the river flared into the open again. It started when three of Refugio Benavides' men were killed while riding on an express near Roma. Again in December a train of three wagons escorted by five soldiers from Fort Brown was attacked at the Rancho Soledad, about fifteen miles below Rio Grande City. The wagons were set upon by an armed band of Mexicans estimated to number from fifty to 150. The Confederates, who were caught completely by surprise, made no attempt to resist except for one soldier who blazed away at the Mexicans with his revolver, killing two in the process. The Mexicans then proceeded to open fire on the teamsters, killing all except one man who was able to escape and reach Ringgold Barracks safely. The provisions were carried off and the wagons taken to the river bank, possibly for passage into Mexico.[80] Another party of 200 Mexicans crossed into Zapata County, rode to the ranch of Ysidro Vela, seized the judge, hanged him to a tree, and "posted a placard on the body that the penalty of death would be inflicted on any person who dared to take the body down for burial."[81] A company of Confederates from Ringgold Barracks went to the Rancho Soledad, where some of the stolen property was found in the jacales of

Mexican-Texan families living in the vicinity. For revenge the soldiers burned the homes of those Tejanos thought to be implicated in the raid on the supply train, and rode triumphantly back to Ringgold Barracks.

General Bee, in a protest to Governor Albino Lopez of Tamaulipas, asserted that the Mexicans who crossed from Guerrero into Zapata County were carrying the flag of the United States, a flag Bee swore had "no right on the soil of Texas."[82] Zapata, Bee claimed, was part of the First Regiment of Union Cavalry. Bee felt Zapata and his men had been recruited into the Union Army by Leonard Pierce, United States Consul in Matamoros. The general demanded that Zapata and his partisans be arrested and delivered to Brownsville for trial.

Refugio Benavides, with fifty-four of his men, went in pursuit of the Mexican raiders. The captain did not hesitate when reaching the river but continued into Mexico, tracking the Mexicans to near Camargo where they were found camped in a large corral. Benavides, with little hesitation, ordered his men to the attack. With the captain in front, the Tejanos were said to have boldly stormed" the enclosure "tearing down the gate amid a hail of bullets, in the midst of which three horses were killed and two men wounded."[83] In the fight eighteen of the bandits died, fourteen were wounded, and several were taken captive. With the raiders in complete flight, one of Benavides' men stopped to pick up a saddle abandoned by the fleeing Mexicans, at which time the captain raised his sword and ordered the soldier to "fight first and plunder afterwards."[84] Fifty-eight horses, fifty-four saddles, and papers implicating Pierce in the organization of the raid were seized during the battle. Benavides lost two men in the battle as well as twenty-five horses. The captives taken in the fray were said to have "escaped" but had "probably relinquished thieving in this world on their own or anybody else's."[85] It is assumed the prisoners were either hanged or shot as had been the case following Cortina's defeat at Carrizo.

In the months to come, Bee continued to complain of the large numbers of desertions from the Confederate Army at Brownsville. The general wrote Lopez that he would "either take my men back by force or submit to the mortification of seeing my command demoralized."[86] Bee had lost fifteen men in three days, all fleeing across the low waters of the Rio Grande to find refuge with Pierce in Matamoros.

By March it was Governor Lopez's turn to bombard Bee's headquarters with complaints. At Laredo, Santos Benavides, in preparation for a march to Carrizo, had allowed two of his men to cross the river to visit relatives living on the south bank. In Nuevo Laredo the Tejanos were bluntly told by the town alcalde "that if they wished to pass about the town they must leave their pistols which they had in their belts with him until they were ready to return."[87] According to Benavides, the men complied with the request but were fired upon and one of the men, Encarnacion Garcia, was killed in the confusion. According to the Mexican authorities, the men "committed some disturbances" at which time the Nuevo Laredo authorities had attempted to arrest the pair, but the Laredoans resisted by drawing their pistols, and the fighting broke out. One of the soldiers escaped the fracas, fled across the river, and immediately reported the incident and the shooting of Garcia to Santos Benavides. Benavides "immediately crossed and went to the alcalde."[88] While the captain was in Nuevo Laredo, word that Garcia had been killed spread among the Mexican-Texans on the north bank. Within minutes forty of the Confederates were in the saddle and splashing across the muddy waters of the Rio Grande prepared to revenge the death of their comrade. Captain Benavides met the force at the river bank and ordered the men not to enter Nuevo Laredo until he had completed his consultation with the alcalde.

In blunt language Benavides demanded that the alcalde arrest those responsible for the death of Garcia. The alcalde replied that he had no force to make the arrest, which irked Benavides to reply that he did have such a force and would help the alcade make the necessary arrests and furthermore he was authorized by treaty to use force if necessary. The alcalde, obviously intimidated by Benavides' threats, issued an order for the arrest of those responsible for the shooting. By this time, however, the "assassins had all fled." For several hours Benavides searched the town and surrounding countryside, but no sign of the assailants could be found. The alcalde agreed to give Benavides additional time to look for the assailants, but after three days of frantic searching, Benavides was forced to admit that he had no "clue of the direction they had taken."[89]

Downriver at Matamoros, Governor Lopez saw the entire incident in a different light than the Laredo Captain. To Lopez, Benavides was trampling on the civil and military authorities, and committing other outrages."[90] The situation had indeed become explosive. On March 15, 1863, several of Bee's Confederates crossed the Rio Grande into Mexico and captured Edmund J. Davis and four other Texas Unionists who were recruiting Tejanos and Confederate deserters into the Union Army. Davis, who had served as state judge in South Texas prior to the war, had been at one time a close friend of the Benavides family as well as of General Bee. Although Bee disavowed any knowledge of the incident, Governor Lopez was furious. "Mexico is a neutral territory," the governor warned in terse language. To Lopez the invasion of Mexican soil at Boca del Rio and Nuevo Laredo were "one of the most serious crimes against international law."[91]

"Attacks like those made by Santos Benavides will produce bitter feelings; the slightest motive may render fruitless all efforts of the chief authorities to settle the existing differences," Lopez wrote.[92] Bee, in an apologetic mood, promised Lopez that "the conduct of Capt. Santos Benavides at Nuevo Laredo will be officially inquired into as soon as I receive his report."[93] Bee also assured the governor that Davis would be released and "sent to the right bank of the river."[94] Four days later, with Benavides' official report of the Nuevo Laredo disturbance arriving in Brownsville, Bee forwarded the report to the governor. "From my long acquaintance with Captain Benavides," Bee wrote, "and high appreciation of him as a man of prudence and discretion, I am satisfied that the authorities on both sides of the line may equally confide in him as not likely to do any act to comprise the relation which should exist."[95]

About this same time another explosive incident involving the Laredo Tejanos erupted on the border. Ben Thompson, a noted gambler, outlaw and thug, had joined the Confederate Army at Eagle Pass. A usually calm individual, Thompson often became violent when drunk and during one of his wild drinking escapades, deserted from the army, shot up the village of Piedras Negras, across the river from Eagle Pass, killed several individuals in the process and fled downriver.

In Nuevo Laredo a friend staked the Confederate renegade to $300 at a monte game, and in a few days Thompson had won $1,200. Pressing his luck, Thompson crossed into Laredo where the town was full of Santos Benavides' Confederates, many of whom, it was reported, would be paid in a few days. There the noted gambler organized a monte game at a saloon owned by Dick Miller. The first night, with the paymaster not yet arrived, Thompson won twenty-one colt revolvers, valued at $20 each, besides seven Remingtons and three self-cocking pistols. The next night, with most of the troops having been paid, Thompson won $1,900, but when he attempted to close the game, a fight broke out in which Thompson drew a derringer and killed Lieutenant Martin Gonzales and Sergeant Miguel Zertuche. Although the adventurer swam the Rio Grande to find temporary safety in Nuevo Laredo, Benavides' Confederate troops made it so hot for Thompson on the border that he later fled northward through the brush country to continue his murderous life elsewhere.[96]

No sooner had the diplomatic tension along the border quieted than another incident, with Benavides as the focal point, sent couriers scurrying across the Rio Grande with messages from Lopez to Bee. News reached Benavides, who had set up camp at Carrizo, that a party of raiders had stolen some cattle from below Carrizo and driven them into Mexico. Benavides, with thirty of his men, found the trail and went in pursuit. Paying no attention to the international waterway, the Confederates followed the thieves to near Guerrero, where upon reaching the Salado River, Benavides sent a messenger into town to insist on the arrest of the cattle thieves. The Guerrero commander instead ordered the Tejanos back across the Rio Grande, warning that he "would not on any account allow any armed body of men within the limits of his command."[97] Benavides, not satisfied with the officer's reply, in bold defiance rode into Guerrero to confer with the alcalde and the comandante. In the heated, tension-packed confrontation, Benavides informed the Mexican leaders that they were bound by a treaty negotiated between the states of Tamaulipas and Texas which allowed Confederates to pursue bandits into Mexico. The comandante in response argued that such an agreement was not binding on him and that he was "obeying private instructions from Governor Lopez."[98] The alcade admitted, however, that he had no such instructions from Lopez. Benavides had no doubt that the military officer was lying and was to blame for harboring the thieves since he had personally witnessed Mexican authorities order the comandante to arrest the "noted robber" Jose Maria Salinas, but Salinas had frequently been seen in Guerrero "on the streets in company with this same military officer."[99] Benavides was especially angered that it was the Guerrero comandante who had reported his occupation of Nuevo Laredo to Governor Lopez.

Benavides, with only thirty men, not wishing for another military confrontation so soon after the Nuevo Laredo episode, returned to the east bank of the river when the comandante threatened to use force to expel the Tejanos from Mexico. Back in Carrizo, Benavides, in obvious retaliation, issued an order forbidding the residents of Guerrero to carry arms on the east bank of the river. Since many Mexican ranchers kept stock on the Texas side of the river, Benavides was thus placing the Guerrero citizenry "entirely at the mercy of the banditti they are harboring" and forcing the Guerrero populace to get rid of the thieves out of economic necessity.[100]

As excepted the incident brought an adverse and threatening response from Governor Lopez. According to the governor, Benavides was completely ignorant of the treaty between Texas and Tamaulipas. "It stipulates that only in cases of absolute necessity the Texas troops should pursue the evildoers into the territory of the Republic." Lopez wrote Bee.[101] Furthermore, Benavides had crossed the river a second time in an attempt to capture the thieves. "Captain Benavides should have limited himself to giving information in order to institute the necessary investigation," and in failing to do so he had "kept up a deep distrust against him—a distrust which has some real foundation." Lopez argued.[102] The incidents at Nuevo Laredo and Guerrero had created "the utmost want of confidence in the towns, because they were actually contrary to the agreement, and however much Santos Benavides may disguise them, they were a violation against the Mexican authorities," Lopez further charged.

As expected, Bee sided with Benavides. "The act of Captain Benavides seems to me to have been in conformity with the spirit of our agreement," since Benavides' only objective was to "punish thieves," Bee argued.[103] Although Bee claimed that at the time Benavides crossed the river "the stolen property was even then in the streets of Guerrero," he agreed to issue "Instructions . . . to Captain Benavides which will prevent a recurrence of such acts."[104]

The Confederate legislature in Austin saw the border heroics of Santos and Refugio Benavides in a different light than Governor Lopez. In a joint resolution the legislature thanked "Capts. Santos Benavides and Refugio Benavides and the officers and men under their command for their vigilance, energy, and gallantry in pursuing and chastising the banditti infesting the Rio Grande frontier."[105]

Civil rights, severely abused and forgotten in both North and South during the Civil War, were non-existent in relation to Mexican-Texans. This became especially true when the Richmond Congress, realizing that the Confederate Army could not survive long without additional men, passed in April, 1862, a controversial conscription act. All white men between the ages of eighteen and thirty-five, excepting those holding positions in government, industry, transportation, education, or jobs considered critical to the Confederacy, were subject to the draft. Draftees were to serve for three years. In Texas, Governor Francis R. Lubbock, after some legal stammering, agreed to go along with the Confederate Congress and ordered implementation of the law. Five months later another conscript law was passed raising the age of draftees to forty-five. Later yet, men as young as seventeen and as old as fifty were included as potential draftees.

Without hesitation, conscription agents employed by the state were ordered into South Texas to conscript Mexican-Texans. When Tejanos vigorously resisted in certain areas of South Texas, the draft took on a harsh and bitter nature. Indiscriminately Tejanos were forced into the army and in some instances treated more like animals than soldiers of the Southland. As General Bee had previously predicted, the draft in South Texas only served to send hundreds of Tejanos fleeing across the Rio Grande to safety in Mexico.[106]

In Brownsville a guard had to be posted around town to prevent those eligible for the draft from fleeing. The conscription officer, Captain F. J. Parker, was said to have "overlooked or neglected nobody," and drafted "big and little alike." Conscription was reported to be "the order of the day in Brownsville."[107]

Three hundred conscripts, mostly Tejanos, were enrolled in the Corpus Christi area when agents even went as far as to search the town. Many, "appraised in advance of the search," were said to have fled southward and "crossed the river."[108]

So desperate were the state and Confederate authorities for men that one "Tiger" Ware was sent to various ranchitos deep in the brush country south of the Nueces River in search of conscripts. At Agua Poquita a watering hole on the road from the Nueces to the Rio Grande, Ware and another enrolling officer named Trimmer actually contemplated lying around the water hole to ambush conscripts. Ware even jokingly considered drafting an elderly Tejano lady, the only resident of Agua Poquita.[109]

Many Tejanos attempted to avoid the draft by claiming to be citizens of Mexico. I. W. Engledow, enrolling officer for Nueces County, on a visit to the villages of Los Olmosito, Concepcion, San Diego, and Armagosa, reported "nearly every other man I met claimed to be a citizen of Mexico and, therefore, exempt from conscription."[110] In most instances, however, Mexican citizenship did not stop the Confederate agents, and citizens of Mexico were drafted without hesitation. So many Mexican carreteros were drafted that vital commerce between Texas and Mexico became seriously curtailed and General J. Bankhead Magruder, commanding the Department of Texas, was forced to issue an order prohibiting the enrollment of the freightmen. "Mexicans engaged in the transportation of government supplies to and from the Rio Grande will not be interfered with by enrolling or other officers, but all officers are hereby required to afford them ample protection while so engaged," Magruder wrote.[111]

The conscription of Mexican-Texans became so controversial, tumultuous, and unenforceable that Confederate authorities finally gave up the idea of drafting large numbers of Tejanos. At Brownsville General Bee found the conscription laws "useless whenever enforced." To Bee the continued "enforcement of the law on this frontier would have had but the effect of driving the Mexicans across the Rio Grande and making them our enemies." "I have sought other means of enlisting the services and sympathies of these people, who are useful to us and would be dangerous against us," the General wrote.[112] "I have initiated a course . . . toward the Mexicans on this frontier by which I seek to protect them in their rights and immunities as citizens and thereby attach them to our cause," the general continued.[113] Three companies of Tejano militia volunteers, recruited for four months and serving under Captains Spencer, Thomas, and Justo Trevino, had all performed well, according to Bee.

In March, 1863, a nasty incident at Los Persenos in Nueces County, resulted in a full-scale massacre of innocent and helpless Tejanos. The massacre was sparked by one William Adamie who attacked a shepherd working for a Mr. McClain, Adamie "fired at and wounded the shepherd in the head, then beat him with a club and left him for dead."[114] Half alive with blood streaming from his battered body, the shepherd, nevertheless, managed to stagger to a nearby sheep camp. Angered at Adamie's brutality, several of the shepherds went to Adamie's Ranch and fired into his house. Adamie, with rifle in hand, chased the Tejanos back to their camp but was suddenly set upon and, although his rifle was seized, was able to escape and spur his horse to a military camp on San Fernando Creek where a company of Confederate soldiers was encamped. Reporting that "his family were all about to be murdered," a detail of soldiers were dispatched at daylight the next morning to punish the sheepmen. Entering "the shepherds' camp in two parties, one from above and one from below" the Confederates "commenced to murder and shoot until five unoffending and defenseless men had fallen."[115] Even the racist and secessionist editor of the *Corpus Christi Ranchero*, H. A. Maltby, demanded an "energetic and prompt investigation by the civil authorities" into the massacre.[116] Other episodes and incidents of Tejanos being gunned down for no reason except that they happened to be Mexican-Texan and in some way considered a threat to the Anglo power structure fill the pages of those chronicles which recorded the war in South Texas.

The racism of the Anglo-Texan against the Mexican-Texan was exemplified by a hotly contested election for state representative from the counties of Nueces and Webb in 1863. The Anglos of Corpus Christi threw their support behind S. Kinney, while the Laredo Mexican-Texans favored Charles Callaghan, who had served as lieutenant under Santos Benavides. Kinney beat Callaghan in Nueces County 150 to ten, but lost Webb County by a vote of 180 to five, making Callaghan the winner. "The returns of the election," wrote Maltby in the *Corpus Christi Ranchero*, "show that Mr. Kinney is the choice for representative over Mr. Callaghan by fifteen voters out of every sixteen in every place where the English language is spoken; but, over yonder, where the Mexican language is spoken, the tables were turned, and Mr. Callaghan is the choice almost unanimously. We think American men in an American country should have a fair showing in shaping the destinies of the country.[117] In reference to the Laredo vote, the *Ranchero* queried: "Who were they and where did they come from?"[118] The Brownsville *Fort Brown Flag* joined Maltby in editorializing on the subject: "The vote at Laredo may be defended, but morally and politically it is a disgrace. We are opposed to allowing an ignorant crowd of Mexicans to determine the political questions in this country, where a man is supposed to vote knowingly and thoughtfully."[119]

Although Laredo had furnished hundreds of Confederate recruits, perhaps as many as any area of Texas in proportion to its size, the *Flag*, in obvious ignorance, reported that "one-half of the Laredo vote was cast by practical abolitionists, and not only abolitionists, but amalgamationists, for the lower order of Mexicans not only consider a nigger equal with themselves, but they actually court the company of the negroes. A negro can marry with a Mexican, and he can hold office with them, and they always assist a runaway slave to escape from his master. It is inconsistent with our laws or our institutions that Mexicans should have the same political rights in this state as Americans," the newspaper continued.[120]

Undeniably, as in Laredo, the patron system did control large blocks of votes. By the time of the Civil War, and even more so in the late nineteenth century and into the twentieth, the Anglo immigrant in Laredo, Carrizo, Roma, Rio Grande City, Brownsville and elsewhere on the border had come to play a large role in the political destinies of the Tejanos. Many of the Anglos who first came to the area in large numbers during the Mexican War stayed on after the Treaty of Guadalupe-Hidalgo to become some of South Texas' leading political figures. Generally speaking, these Anglos had the economic and political power to destroy the harsh patron system, but instead intensified the system for their own selfish purposes. Other immigrants who arrived on the border came directly from Europe and do not appear to have possessed a background of political democracy, common to other areas of the American frontier. They too came to use the patron system to build their own economic empires based on the brains of corrupt Anglo lawyers and the sweat of hardworking but illiterate campesinos. The Anglo then, in reality, was more responsible for the corrupt politics in South Texas than the Tejano. The Anglo, as exemplified by the attitudes of the Corpus Christi and Brownsville newspapers, only seemed perturbed about the corrupt politics of South Texas when it did not serve their self interests.

In May, 1863, orders came from department headquarters

calling for the creation of a new regiment of Texas Confederates to be called the Thirty-Third Texas Cavalry. The regiment was to be made up of seven companies presently commanded by Lieutenant Colonel James Duff as well as the companies of Santos Benavides (now promoted to major), Refugio Benavides, and T. Breckenridge. Cristobal Benavides, a dashing mustached figure, was promoted to captain and given command of brother Santos' old company. The company, numbering ninety-eight, including officers Jose Maria Garcia, Dario Gonzales, and Martin Gonzales, was the largest in the Thirty-Third Cavalry.

As expected the regiment was retained on the Rio Grande for border defense. The men serving under the Benavides Brothers were stationed on the upper Rio Grande while the remainder of the regiment was to hold the line from Rio Grande City to the gulf. On the first day of September, 1863, while Santos Benavides was stationed at Carrizo, a dispatch rider carrying a letter from the alcalde of Guerrero excitedly spurred his horse into the village. Mexican troops had been ambushed and routed by a raging band of desperados under the leadership of Octaviano Zapata. Major Benavides, taking part of Cristobal's Company H, went to the Clareno Ranch where he joined with part of Captain Thomas Rabb's Company D and within minutes splashed across the Rio Grande into Mexico. Finding the location where the attack had occurred, the Tejanos easily picked up the trail of Zapata and his men, which led downriver in the direction of Mier. Early on the morning of September 2, the camp of the bandits was spotted. Although Zapata and his men were gathered in thick chaparral, Benavides directed that the non-commissioned officers of Company H, many of whom evidently knew several of the desperados, pick out the leaders and "without delay attack the scoundrels." With the bandits camped "in the bottom of a ravine," the Tejanos "were obliged to enter in single file, under a sharp fire from the thieves."[121] The sudden, startling charge caught the desperados off guard, however, and within minutes the sound of gunfire had slackened, and the only sound which could be heard was the whimpering and groaning of the wounded. Although large numbers of Zapata's men were able to escape into the thick chaparral, several of the bandits, including all of the leaders, were dead, their blood staining the soil of their native Mexico. Corporal Natividad Herrera of Company H was praised by Benavides for his "courage and gallantry." During the wild charge into the arroyo, Herrera had emptied his rifle at the bandits and, although out of ammunition, killed Zapata "with the butt of his gun, although Zapata had a loaded pistol and was firing at the corporal all the time."[122] Monico Salmas, who was said to have claimed the rank of captain in the Union Army, and Manuel Villarreal as well as Guillermo Vino, who held the rank of lieutenants, were also killed in the fray.

Bee, as usual, blamed the border trouble on Texas Unionists, especially Edmund J. Davis, who had continued to recruit men into the Union Army from the Mexican side of the river. In reference to Zapata, General Bee seemed exhilarated that he would have "no more trouble with this emissary of the Lincoln Government." "Should E. J. Davis ever invade the Rio Grande with his regiment of refugees and outlaws, he will miss his friend Zapata, who had the power to do us great injury," Bee bragged.[123] General Bee seemed especially pleased with Benavides' quick action. "I especially recommend Major Benavides for his untiring energy and patriotism, and would respectfully suggest that the general commanding recognize officially the distinguished services of Major Benavides, and the firm, unyielding support which the companies of Laredo, commanded by Captains Refugio and Cristobal Benavides, all Mexicans, have ever given to our cause."[124] With the sometimes effective leadership of General Bee, assisted by the gallant Benavides brothers, the Confederate defense of the Rio Grande appeared to be strong. Plans in far-off Washington were soon to bring General Bee's occupation of the lower valley to a quick halt, however.

Harper's Weekly (June 15, 1861)

Bivouac of Texas State Troops on Las Moras Creek near Fort Clark with Mexican-Texans "hauling wood, drawing water...smoking cigarritos,...and drinking Pat's favorite."

Daughters of the Republic of Texas Library

Main Plaza, San Antonio, 1861

Frank Leslie's Popular Monthly (June, 1878)

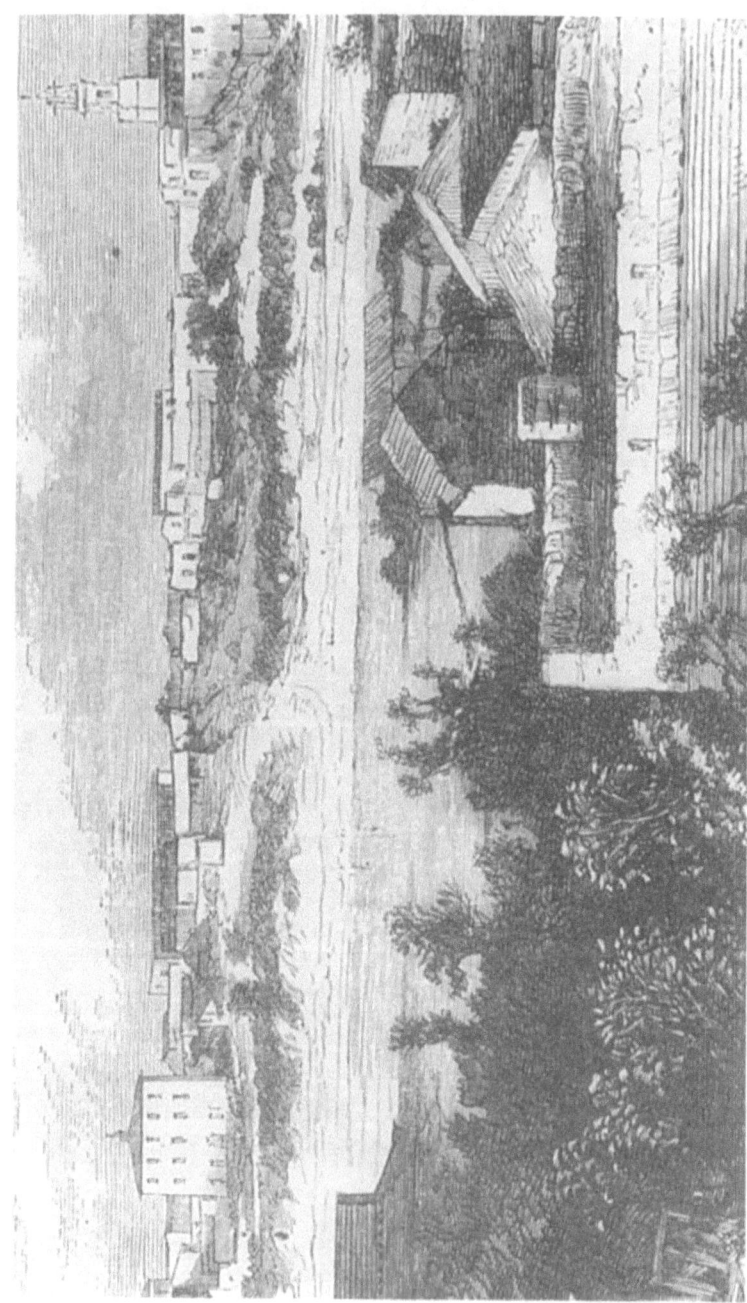

Laredo, Texas around 1878

U.S. and Mexican Boundary Survey.

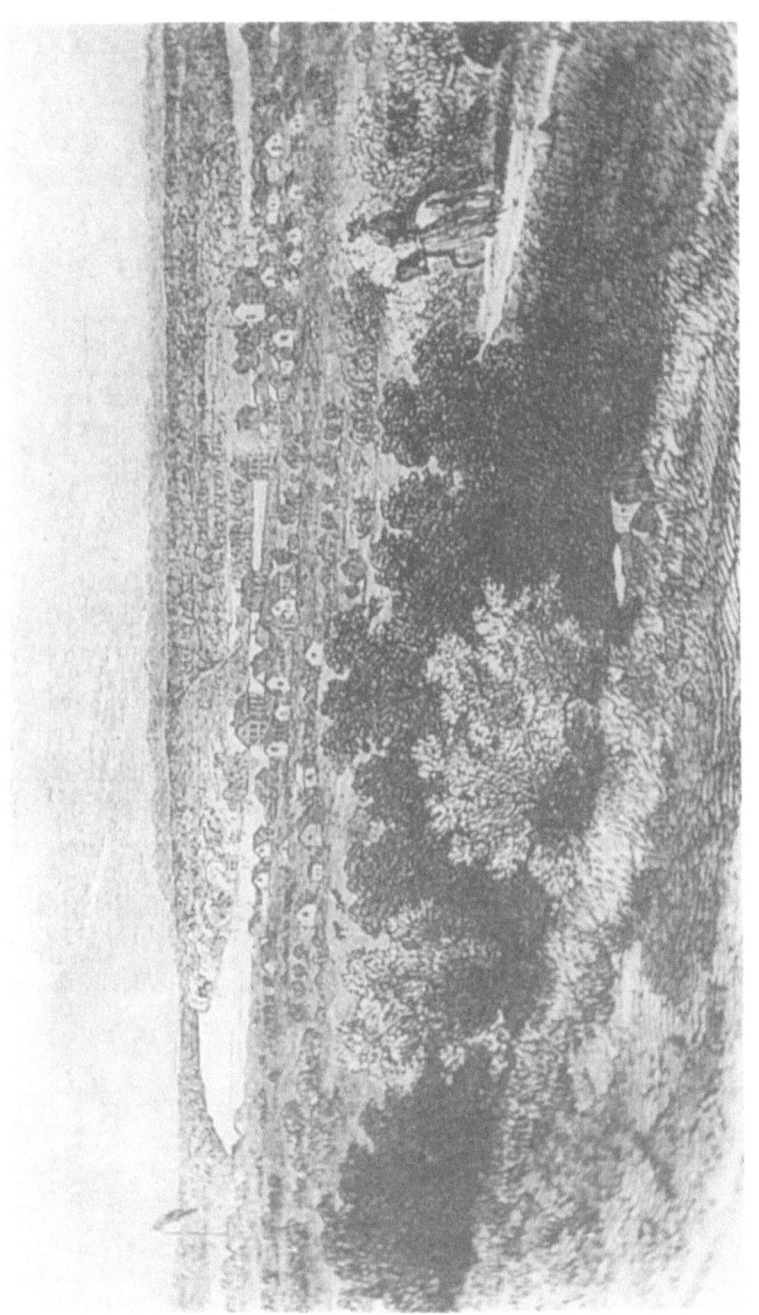

Ringgold Barracks and Rio Grande City

U.S. and Mexican Boundary Survey.

Fort Duncan, near Eagle Pass

U.S. and Mexican Boundary Survey.

Roma, Texas

Harper's Weekly (February 13, 1864)

Confederate evacuation of Brownsville, November 2, 1863.

Harper's Weekly (December 16, 1865)

Union Soldiers on Elizabeth Street, Brownsville.

5

Vidal

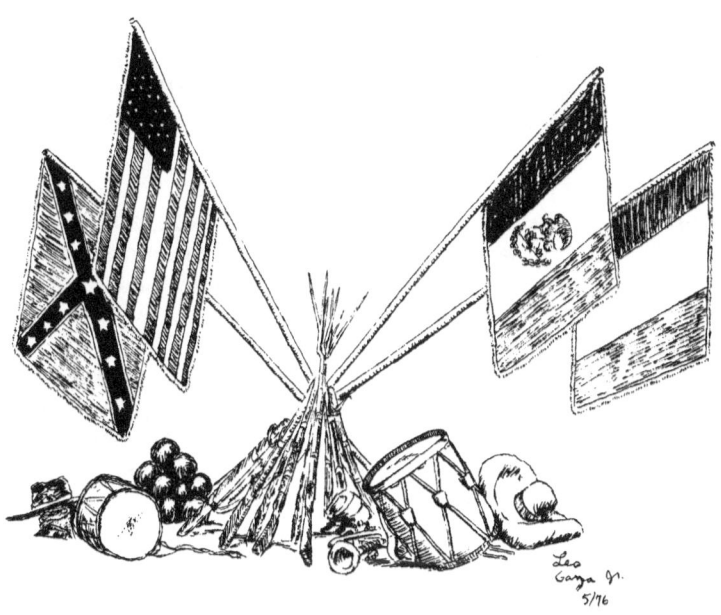

One of the strangest sagas of the Civil War centered around a Mexican-Texan named Adrian J. Vidal. Vidal, born at Monterrey, Mexico, came to Mier, Mexico, following the Mexican War. In 1852 the boy's mother, Petra Vela de Vidal, married Mifflin Kenedy, a wealthy partner of Richard King and Charles Stillman.[125] Vidal, who was only seventeen when the Civil War erupted along the Rio Grande, was said to have been dark complected with hazel eyes and black hair.

The young Mexican-Texan first enrolled as a private in Captain James Duff's company of Partisan Rangers at San

Antonio in October, 1862. He was described by a fellow Confederate as "a vain, trifling fellow without any experience, who cared for nothing except gambling and drinking."[126] When Duff was given command of the Thirty-Third Texas Cavalry, Vidal remained in Company A, now commanded by Captain Richard Taylor. Duff had taken a liking to the young private, however, a friendship which appears to have been partially due to the influence of Vidal's stepfather, the wealthy Kenedy. The young Vidal was soon to wear the bars of a lieutenant.

Vidal, who within a few months was promoted to captain, was given command of a militia company stationed at Boca del Rio with orders to guard the mouth of the Rio Grande. In June, 1863, Vidal reported his company "entirely destitute" of camp necessities and asked headquarters in Brownsville for "kettles, iron pots, and spades." Five days later, he asked for one Sibley tent complete with pole and tripod. For his men, who were in rags, Vidal requested hats, shirts, pants, and fifty pair of shoes. In July, 1863, while on duty at Boca del Rio, Vidal was praised for his bravery in the capture of a Federal gunboat and its crew.[127]

Ever since General Hamilton P. Bee had assumed command of the Confederate Army at Brownsville in January of 1863, the fortunes of the Confederates on the river had slowly deteriorated. General "Prince John" Magruder, commanding the District of Texas, nevertheless ordered Bee to hold the Rio Grande at all costs. By winter, 1863, however, Union forces were deep in Louisiana and threatening East Texas. Bee watched one company after another leave Brownsville for Houston and deployment in Louisiana.

On the morning of October 28, 1863, companies B, E, and F, of the Thirty-Third Texas Cavalry departed Fort Brown and took up the line of march for the Nueces and Houston. Except for a hastily organized militia company, Bee and James Duff found themselves protecting millions of dollars in valuable supplies and cotton with only nineteen men. Quite apprehensive about the situation, Bee and Duff, on the afternoon of the 26th, dispatched two of their men, D. H. Dashiell and a young private named Litteral, to Boca del Rio to order back to Brownsville the militia company commanded by Vidal.[128]

Bee had no reason to doubt Vidal. The young captain had always obeyed orders and performed his sentinel duties on the Rio Grande admirably. Just as darkness crept over Fort Brown and through the narrow streets of Brownsville, information reached Bee that Vidal with his entire company had mutinied and with the help of Unionists and renegades from Matamoros was planning to attack Brownsville during the night. Bee, still not doubting Vidal's loyalty, dismissed the report as a malicious rumor. Two hours later, however, Private Litteral, bleeding and frightened, came racing his horse into Fort Brown. The private, who had been shot through the mouth, motioned for pencil and paper and proceeded to scribble an incredible story. The two privates had met Vidal and his company about fourteen miles outside of town on the road to Boca del Rio. The two privates, who knew Vidal quite well having served in the same company earlier in the war, had delivered their message to Captain Vidal as they had been ordered to do, and the entire party had set out for Brownsville. Two miles down the road, Vidal had dismounted and ordered his company to prepare supper. A fire was started for the evening meal and the captain invited the two privates to share a drink. Suddenly, Vidal and several of his men opened fire on the two privates killing Dashiell, the son of the Texas Adjutant General, and wounding Litteral through the face.[129]

Bee, upon reading Litteral's hastily scribbled notes, and having only a few men with which to protect Brownsville, was panic stricken. Lieutenant Jack Vinton and ten men were sent down the road toward the gulf to locate Vidal and determine if possible his motives for the apparent mutiny. Vinton proceeded only a few miles outside of town when he ran into Vidal's company, reported to number over 100 and advancing toward Brownsville. Vinton began to skirmish with Vidal's company but was driven back to within one mile of town.[130]

Bee, along with General James Slaughter, Colonel James Duff, Major George A. Magruder, Jr., and Captain Winston, immediately held a council of war. It was thought that Brownsville could be defended if the services of the civilians could be enlisted and a local militia company mobilized. Two large artillery pieces were hastily pulled into position.

Couriers were sent out to order back to town the three companies of the Thirty-Third Cavalry which had been ordered to Houston but were thought to be encamped on the Palo Alto prairie. Bee, thinking Vidal to be in alliance with the Unionists from Matamoros, theorized that Brownsville would be attacked not only from downriver but from Mexico as well. Every available man that could be found was armed and placed into position in preparation for the defense of the town. The regulars were placed on the outskirts of town as skirmishers. All through the night the men awaited the attack they knew was imminent.

The expected attack did not come, however, and the night passed without incident. Vidal had decided to bypass Brownsville.[131]

What Vidal's motives in mutiny were are somewhat vague. It is generally thought that the captain had formed an alliance with the Unionists across the river in Mexico. Several Confederates, especially General Bee, blamed Juan N. Cortina for the mutiny. Although "Cheno" Cortina may well have been in contact with Vidal, the elusive "Robin Hood of South Texas" had long been blamed for every crime committed on the Rio Grande from Laredo to the Gulf and may thus have proven to be an easy scapegoat. There seems no doubt, however, that Vidal was intent upon plundering Brownsville, and would have done so had not Private Litteral been able to escape and sound the warning.

Raising the cry of "Muerte a los Americanos," Vidal and his men passed within a mile of Brownsville about three o'clock on the morning of the 29th. From the vicinity of Brownsville they continued up the Rio Grande for about nine miles plundering every ranch in the vicinity. Several unoffending citizens were killed by the Vidalistas for no apparent reason, among whom were a man named King; a Mr. Barthelow, former sheriff of Cameron County; a Mexican-Tejano named Cruz; besides Private Dashiell and six others.[132]

When the three companies of the Thirty-Third Cavalry arrived in Brownsville at daylight on the 29th, they were immediately ordered out in pursuit of Vidal. One of the companies commanded by Captain Richard Taylor reached the ford upriver from Brownsville only minutes after the

Vidalistas crossed into Mexico. Captain Taylor reported a large body of Texas Unionists on the opposite bank of the Rio Grande waiting for Vidal. Taylor conjectured that Vidal had been in contact with the Unionists all along. The Confederate captain, deciding it unwise to cross the river against such odds, returned to Fort Brown.[133]

Bee, frustrated and furious at the strange turn of events, wrote Governor Manuel Ruiz of Tamaulipas claiming that Vidal was acting under orders of the U.S. Consul in Matamoros and had formed an alliance with the Texas Unionists in Mexico. Bee asked Ruiz for his assistance in capturing Vidal. "I at once gave orders that all the troops on the line should unite in pursuing the insurrectionists, and from this city will immediately set forth two detachments of cavalry to reconnoiter the left bank of the Rio Grande," the governor wrote Bee in return.[134]

Although Bee later became convinced that Cortina was assisting Vidal, the general wrote department headquarters on October 31, 1863, that Cortina, under the orders of Ruiz, had captured twenty of the Vidalistas and that Vidal himself was in hiding at Matamoros.[135] Within days, however, events of a greater magnitude came to affect the destinies of Hamilton Prioleau Bee and Adrian J. Vidal.

They came out of the grey dawn from New Orleans. Black men came. White men came. And Mexican-Texans came. From Illinois, from Iowa, from distant Maine, from Missouri, and from Texas, in all, 6,998 men came through a terrible storm in twenty-six ships. They came to cut the Texas cotton trade and strangle the Confederacy. On November 2, 1863, they went ashore and raised their flag on Brazos Island. On November 5 they crossed to the mainland and began marching on Brownsville. Reporting his arrival in Texas, the commander of the Union Rio Grande Expedition wrote a very simple message to Abraham Lincoln: "The flag of the

Union floats over Texas today."[136]

In Brownsville General Bee faced the greatest crisis of his military career. With less than 100 men it would be senseless to attempt a defense of the town. Chaos was the order of the day. Bee sent out Captain Taylor with fifteen men to report on the advance of the Yankees. Taylor reached the mouth of the river and reported thousands of Yankees disembarking. Captain Henry T. Davis, who was sent to Port Isabel, climbed the light house and reported more Yankee landings on Brazos Santiago. In haste Bee wrote headquarters: "The enemy are in force. Brazos Island is covered with tents; six regimental flags were counted; twenty-six vessels, some of them very large."[137]

As Union forces advanced on Brownsville, a long train of forty-five wagons carrying valuable Confederate suplies hastily departed for the Nueces. Confederates, acting on orders, set fire to Fort Brown. All "cotton which was liable to fall into the hands of the enemy," was also burned. The fire quickly spread from the fort to Brownsville, and within hours a whole block of buildings in front of the ferry was ablaze. Several hundred bales of cotton which were not burned were thrown into the river. More than 400 Unionists lined the Mexican side of the river to hiss and curse the panic-stricken Confederates. Eight thousand pounds of powder at Fort Brown exploded, adding fright to the already terrorized townspeople. The residents of Brownsville, despite the efforts of the pro-Confederate Mayor, realizing that their immediate future lay with the Union and not Hamilton P. Bee, seemed more concerned with the raging inferno and did little to assist the Confederates in their hasty evacuation. "Peril was around me on all sides," General Bee wrote.[138]

At ten o'clock on the morning of November 6, the Federals marched into the streets of Brownsville. The Ninety-Fourth Illinois Volunteers, advance guard of the Union Thirteenth Army Corps, led the way, followed five hours later by the First Missouri Light Artillery and the Thirteenth Maine Volunteers. The Union Army had arrived at Brownsville in time to witness a revolution in Matamoros with the pro-Juarista Cortina emerging victorious.

Less than three weeks after the Federal Army occupied

Brownsville, a young man appeared at the enrolling office and identified himself as Adrian J. Vidal, late of the Confederate Army. He was prepared to raise a company for the Federals, and on November 26 he was mustered into the service of the United States and commissioned a captain. In November and December hundreds of Mexican-Texans, many influenced by Vidal, also joined the Union Army. Vidal's company attached to the Second Texas Cavalry (Union), was known simply as Vidal's Independent Partisan Rangers. General Napoleon Jackson Tecumseh Dana, commanding the Union Army in the valley, reported that "Vidal's command has been mustered in, armed and equipped to the number of 89 men for one year."[139] Many of Vidal's men, having served with their captain in the Confederate Army, continued their rough and rowdy ways in the Federal ranks. In early December, 1863, a brawl broke out in the company in which a private was mortally wounded. General Dana promised "to make an example of the murderer."[140]

In May, 1864, a party of Vidal's company struck across the river into Mexico to attack a train of cotton carts near Camargo. The force was repulsed by Mexican soldiers guarding the train and in the process seriously wounded one of Vidal's lieutenants in the face.

In April, the captain's fifteen-year-old sister, described by a Federal officer as "a handsome fascinating and rich young Mexican lady," was married to Lieutenant Fred E. Starck, post adjutant at Fort Brown.[141]

The Vidalistas, acting as the eyes of the Union Army, frequently scouted deep into the South Texas brush country. What frustrated Vidal was not the endless hours in the saddle but the constant paperwork required of a company commander. Vidal, who could not speak English, found such Army bureaucracy alien to his individualism and totally unnecessary.

On May 30, 1864, Vidal dictated a letter to regiment headquarters in which he asked to resign his commission. "I find myself incompetent to carry on the company books as I do not understand nor have anybody in my company to understand the English language for this purpose," Vidal wrote. He continued, "I find myself incompetent to command the company under the Army Regulations." Vidal also complained of not having time to visit his family in Brownsville.[142]

As commander of the Second Texas Cavalry, Colonel John L. Haynes of Rio Grande City, the moving force behind the recruitment of Mexican-Texans for the Union Army and one of the few Anglo-Americans to understand the Mexican-Texans, recommended that Vidal's "resignation be accepted for the . . . reasons given."[143] One day later General F. J. Herron, agreeing with Haynes' recommendations, forwarded the request to department headquarters in New Orleans. On July 9, 1864, by Special Orders No. 184, Vidal's request was approved and the captain issued an honorable discharge. The orders came too late, however. Vidal, impatient at army rules and regulations, deserted from the United States Army on June 19, 1864, before his discharge could reach Brownsville. By another set of special orders the captain's honorable discharge was later revoked.[144]

In the weeks preceding Vidal's desertion, most of the Partisan Rangers had already fled across the river to Mexico. In the four months prior to Vidal's desertion, a total of fifty-three men had deserted from the company. On July 28, five weeks after Vidal's flight, another eighteen men left the company while on a march from Brownsville to Brazos Santiago. Only twenty-three men of Vidal's Partisan Rangers served for the remainder of the war.[145] Benjamin F. McIntyre, an officer in the Union Army, wrote in his diary what was probably the typical Anglo view of Vidal. "Report today is that Capt. Videlle of the 2nd Texas Cavalry has been absent several days without leave and it is supposed he has deserted. Of the last I presume there is but little doubt and the gay fancy little Mexican after raising a company from his countrymen and seeing them properly paid, armed and equipped and nearly half the number desert concluded to desert also. It is a great pity that the country ever accepted these men for soldiers but a much greater pity that they should have been paid the large amount which good men should have received and still a pity that every 'yaller belly' of them has been permitted to desert."[146]

Two weeks after his desertion, rumors reached Union headquarters that Vidal was spending the night at his sister's house in Brownsville. A guard from Fort Brown was sent to search the premises but reported that Vidal had "vamoosed the city." Orders were issued that if found, Vidal was to be shot on sight.[147]

In Mexico, Vidal joined the Juaristas but was captured, court-martialed, and executed by the Imperialists in 1865.[148] The young captain had served both the blue and the gray, deserted from both armies, joined a third and was shot by a fourth. Vidal, although despised and hated by many, had compiled one of the most unusual records in the annals of Civil War history.

As it is I have to fight to the last, though hardly able to stand I shall die fighting. I won't retreat, no matter what force the Yankees have—I know I can depend on my boys.

        Santos Benavides, March 19, 1864

6

Union Tejanos

An estimated 2,550 Mexican-Texans served the Confederacy. Not all Tejanos fought for the Southland, however. An estimated one-third of all Mexican-Texans who saw action in the epic struggle marched under the Stars and Stripes. These included Adrian J. Vidal's Partisan Rangers, guerillas operating from Mexico and along the lower Nueces River, as well as the First and Second Regiments of Texas Cavalry. In all, 958 Mexican-Texans are thought to have fought for the Union, most of whom served in the Second Texas Cavalry, which, excluding officers and a few enlisted men, was exclusively Mexican-Texan.[149]

By the summer of 1862, large numbers of Texas Unionists had gathered at Matamoros, Mexico, many having fled from the interior of the state fearing for their lives. A large percentage of the Unionists were German-Americans from the Texas hill country. Others were veterans of the U.S. Army who had been taken prisoner at San Antonio but had managed to escape and make their way southward to the Mexican border. A few were Mexican-Texans. Many were hoping to reach relatives in the north but did not have the necessary funds for transportation. The men were "destitute of means to proceed further," Leonard Pierce, United States Consul in Matamoros, wrote Secretary of State, William H. Seward.[150] Many of the veterans were reported to be on the verge of starvation. According to Pierce, Matamoros was "fast filling up with them." Pierce took many of the men into the consulate, fed them, gave them clothes, and attempted to procure funds for their passage to the north. At Fort Brown, little more than a stone's throw across the Rio Grande, the Confederate commander, Hamilton P. Bee, complained that Pierce was openly recruiting men for the United States Army in the streets of Matamoros, many of whom Bee asserted were deserters from the Confederate Army.

Among those arriving at Matamoros was the influential Unionist Andrew J. Hamilton. Hamilton, with fifteen men, had escaped from Austin on horseback and had successfully crossed the Rio Grande near Laredo, arriving in Matamoros on July 29, 1862. Pierce within days had booked Hamilton passage on an English schooner bound for New York, but upon hearing rumors that a band of seventy-five Confederates were planning to capture Hamilton near the mouth of the river, waited for the arrival of an American ship.[151]

Another Unionist and Matamoros refugee was Edmund J. Davis. Davis, who had spent several years as a state judge at Laredo, Brownsville, and Corpus Christi, was described as "a tall, slender, graceful sort of man, measuring six feet two and a half inches, of fair complexion and possessing a rather fine face and delicate blue eyes suggesting a generous character."[152] Davis was undeniably the driving force behind Texas unionism.

A near riot broke out in Matamoros in September, 1862,

when one of the Unionists was killed by the Mexican military. Most of the Texans were arrested by the Mexican authorities and thrown in jail where they remained until Pierce was able to obtain their release.[153] At about the same time news reached Matamoros of the massacre of a band of Texas Unionists on the Nueces River, about twenty miles from Fort Clark. Nineteen Unionists, mostly Germans, were killed in the initial attack on the west bank of the river while nine others who were wounded in the ambush were ruthlessly executed. Six others were killed eight days later while fleeing across the Rio Grande into Mexico.[154] Along with his German comrades, one Mexican-Texan, Pablo Diaz, died in the Nueces Massacre. Diaz's epitaph, along with that of his comrades, can be found on a white, weather-beaten monument in the rural German village of Comfort, north of San Antonio. Only seven of the German-Americans were successful in reaching Matamoros.

On October 27, 1862, seventy-two Texas Unionists arrived in New Orleans, Louisiana, having sailed from the mouth of the Rio Grande on the schooner *Planet*.[155] The very afternoon the men arrived in the Crescent City, they enlisted in the Army of the United States. The Texas Union Army was born. Davis, who had been commissioned a colonel, assumed command. Company A was mustered into the service on November 6, 1862, and Company B shortly thereafter. The men were quartered at the military barracks in New Orleans where they anxiously awaited orders which they hoped would carry them back to Texas. Many of the men had bitter memories of their flight from the Lone Star State and awaited with considerable anticipation any opportunity for retaliation. On December 31, the men embarked on the steamer *Cumbria*, destined for Galveston. Arriving in Galveston Harbor, the *Cumbria* anchored and, due to a dense fog, sent a row boat with six men ashore to obtain a pilot. When the boat failed to return, it was accurately conjunctured that Galveston had fallen into Confederate hands. Narrowly escaping being captured, the expedition hastily returned to New Orleans.

Early in 1863 more Texas Unionists arrived in New Orleans to enlist in the Federal ranks, and a third company was added to the First Regiment of Texas Cavalry. In May, with the three companies numbering about 240 men, orders came for the men to make camp at Carrollton, north of New Orleans, where they were mounted and re-equipped.[156] From Carrollton, the men were ordered across the Amite River to attack a Confederate company in possession of the railroad at Independence. Here the Texans easily overran the Rebels, taking twenty-one prisoners in the process. From their captives the Texans were able to learn that a larger force of Confederates were stationed at Camp Moore on the Jackson Railroad north of Independence. By a forced march, the Texans were able to outflank the enemy and force a Rebel retreat. On the return trek to Carrollton, the Texans were ordered to "destroy everything on the route that was serviceable to the enemy."[157] The First Texas Cavalry remained at Carrollton until late May when they were ordered back to New Orleans where a fourth company was organized from more Texas refugees.

In June, as a large Federal force lay seige to Port Hudson, the Texas Cavalry remained on duty in New Orleans. Without a sizeable force to garrison the city, the prosecessionist or "rebellion element" would openly revolt against the Federals, Union leaders felt.

In August, September, and October, 1863, the Texans participated in General Nathaniel P. Banks Bayou Teche campaign. As Banks' advance guard, the men of the Texas Cavalry saw action at Brashear City, Franklin, New Iberia and the Vermillion River before returning to New Orleans in late October. At the same time, another detachment of the Texas Cavalry participated in a Union expedition against Sabine Pass.

Ordered again to Texas, the First Cavalry set sail from New Orleans on October 25, 1863, arriving at Brazos Santiago, near the mouth of the Rio Grande, ten days later. The voyage down the coast was through a storm and proved to be a disaster for the Texans. Several of the vessels carrying the men's horses ran short of water and many of the valuable mounts had to be shoved overboard. Other horses were thrown into the gulf to prevent the boats from foundering in the high seas. At Brazos Santiago still other horses were lost when it was erroneously thought the animals could swim over the sand bar. In the storm the Texans also lost a large portion of their clothing, regimental and company books, as well as other public property, all of which was said to have greatly embarrassed the command.

General Hamilton P. Bee, with only a token Rebel force at Fort Brown, chose wisely not to resist the Union occupation of the lower valley, and on November 6, 1863, the Ninety-Fourth Illinois Volunteers, advance guard of the Union Army, proudly marched into Brownsville. Not having recovered from the storm off Brazos Santiago, it was several weeks before the Texas Cavalry was prepared to take to the field. On November 21, 1863, Davis and his Texans were ordered upriver to Rio Grande City, which fell without resistance, Major Santos Benavides, with a small Confederate force, having fled across the river into Mexico. When Davis retreated downriver to Brownsville with captured Confederate cotton, Colonel John L. Haynes with a smaller force of 200 pushed upriver to occupy Roma. From Roma, Haynes began to recruit Mexican-Texans into the Union Army. Handbills offering the Tejanos bounty to enlist under the Stars and Stripes were circulated up and down the Rio Grande from Boca del Rio to the various ranches below Carrizo. From their camp at Ramerino, near Rio Grande City, newly commissioned officers of the Second Regiment were reported to be vigorously recruiting men in December, 1863. A handbill signed by Lieutenant Antonio Abad Dias promising prospective recruits a bounty of one-hundred dollars twenty-five dollars upon enlistment and seventy-five at the conclusion of the war was widely circulated. Recruits were also offered a blue jacket, pants, shirts, underwear, a raincoat, boots, shoes, and thirteen dollars a month.[158]

It was thus that the Second Texas Cavalry was born. John L. Haynes was largely responsible for the creation of the unit and was the ideal man to command the new regiment.

Haynes, who could speak broken Spanish, knew many of the recruits personally. For several years he had been one of the few Anglo-Americans to understand the problems of the Mexican-Texans of the Rio Grande Valley. Born in Virginia in 1821, Haynes grew up in Mississippi and after serving as a lieutenant in the Mexican War, settled at Rio Grande City, where he married Angelica Wells, became county clerk in 1850, and was elected to the Texas Legislature in 1857 and again in 1859. During the Cortina War which ravaged the lower valley in 1859-60, Haynes vigorously rejected the anti-Mexican feelings of the Anglos of the valley as well as the majority of the Texas Legislature. Forced to admit that the vast majority of Mexican-Texans in Cameron, Hidalgo, and Starr Counties were in sympathy with Cortina, Haynes nevertheless asserted that the outbreak of violence was not a "war of races" as many Anglo-Texans viewed the conflict. In the legislature, Haynes argued for a thorough investigation of the entire revolt. Haynes thought that the rebellion was "caused by a settled belief on the part of the citizens of Mexican origin" that "a deliberate attempt by certain persons to defraud them out of their lands" was being made. He further asserted that the fraud was sustained by persons holding "high official positions in the Federal court," thus agreeing with Cortina's assertion that a "few speculators, assisted by a multitude of lawyers," were endeavoring to "rob the Mexicans of their lands."[159]

For his unpopular stand on the Cortina War, Haynes was condemned and ridiculed by several leading Texas newspapers, especially the Austin *State Gazette* and the *Galveston News*.[160] The Brownsville *American Flag* went as far as to jokingly boast "Juan Nepomuceno Cortina, the Hero of la Bolsa" for President and J. L. Haynes for Vice-President.[161] The Brownsville newspaper also wrote of Haynes:

> With his honor bright, and with Keen insight
>   Among his Peers he stood,
> His soul in the land, of that greaser band
>   Who shed his country's blood.
>
> There's a fraud he cries: with my own good eyes,
>   I see the record plain;
> Let the Gringos bleed. For the wicked deed
>   They lie among the stain.

> Johnny Haynes was right in the bandit's sight,
>   He loved the story well,
> And he drew his knife, for the white-man's life,
>   And pray'd his soul to hell.
>
> The fierce north-wind blew, and the tidings flew,
>   To rouse the slumbering town;
> A greaser came by, with a tear in his eyes,
>   And beg'd he might come down.[162]

During the fight over secession, Haynes had aligned himself with Sam Houston, a leader whom he admired deeply, and whose views he translated into Spanish and presented to the residents of Starr County. "The Lone Star Flag is the only one that will ever supplant the Stars and Stripes in the empire state of Texas," Haynes wrote.[163]

"I was born and have lived always a citizen of the United States and to its Government I owe allegiance," Haynes assured the citizens of Starr County. Although possessing no love for Abraham Lincoln, whom Haynes called an "obnoxious man," secession was nevertheless "as heretical as it is dangerous."[154] Just as his stand on the Cortina War had been unpopular, so was Haynes' views on secession, with editorial criticism coming from the Brownsville *Rio Grande Sentinel*, *Paris Press*, and the *Indianola Courier*.[165] When Texas joined the Confederacy in 1861, Haynes, like Hamilton and Davis before him, crossed the Rio Grande to find refuge in Matamoros and passage to New Orleans. From New Orleans, Haynes, along with A. J. Hamilton, sailed for Washington where both attempted to persuade President Lincoln and Secretary of State Seward of the validity of a plan to land 5,000 Federals at the mouth of the Rio Grande. Haynes also presented a letter outlining what he called the "Rebel Plan" to Lincoln's General in Chief, Henry Wager Halleck. The letter reflected an accurate understanding of Jefferson Davis' ideas for a Southern victory.

Arriving at Brownsville in November, 1863, with the Rio Grande Expedition, Haynes was given permission for the recruitment of the Second Regiment of Texas Cavalry. Many of Haynes' recruits were enlisted in Mexico, having fled across the river because of the Confederate occupation of the lower valley. Several of the men had either fought with Cortina in 1859-61 or were in sympathy with the elusive

"Cheno." Ironically as it may seem, the United States Government was now recruiting men into its ranks which the Army had previously fought in 1859-60.

The Tejanos did not join the Union Army because of some great loyalty to the Union as did Davis, Hamilton, and Haynes. They fought not because of some great desire to preserve the Constitution or abolish slavery, but rather to defeat many of their old political enemies in Texas. The promise of money also helped fill the Federal ranks, as many of the poorer classes of Mexican-Texans rallied to the Stars and Stripes.

A large percentage of the Second Cavalry had been born in Mexico, and came from Mier, Reynosa, Monterrey, Victoria, and Montemorelos. Most of the men were listed on company records as either laborers or herdsmen, although some claimed to be shoemakers, farmers, or fishermen. One man, a saddler from Spain, also enlisted. A few Anglos, mostly German-Americans, served in the Second Cavalry. The Anglos included a sailor from Nova Scotia, a farmer from Alabama, as well as men born in Delaware, Ireland, Prussia, Scotland, and Baden. James Sanders, age fourteen, certainly the youngest in the regiment, was the pride of Company B.[166]

Company A of the Second Regiment was mustered into the service at Brownsville in December, 1863. The company was commanded by Captain George Trevino with Cecilio Vela, Henry Lochte, and John Cuellar as lieutenants. Company B was commanded by fifty-year-old Clemente Zapata from Zapata County with Santos Cadena of Starr County as a lieutenant. Cesario Falcon, a resident of Nueces County, was captain of Company C, while Ramon G. Falcon from Wilson County was listed as a lieutenant. Company D, mustered into the service a few weeks later, was commanded by Monico de Abrego. Jose Maria Martinez was commissioned to command Company E in January, 1864, but the company was never completed, and Martinez was later transferred to a regimental staff position.[167] Adrian J. Vidal's Partisan Rangers enlisted at Brownsville in November and December, 1863, and were attached to the Second Regiment.

Two years later, when the morale of the Texas Union Army had deteriorated considerably, charges were preferred against Haynes for recruiting "about two hundred Mexicans who were ignorant of the English Language."

With the Union Army in possession of the lower Rio Grande Valley, the Second Regiment of the Texas Cavalry, scouted northward into the Nueces County and upriver to Roma and beyond. In March, 1864, the Second Cavalry and attached partisans fought a Confederate force at Los Patricios, southwest of Corpus Christi, and attacked Laredo.

From the beginning of their enlistment, the Second Regiment had problems. The Tejanos, when not on scouting duty, were camped near Brownsville in the big bend of the river above the town. Health conditions here were appalling and several men died of pneumonia. In December, 1863, Davis complained to Haynes that the Second Regiment was cutting down all the trees in the vicinity for fire wood and ordered a stop to the practice.[168]

In early 1864, word reached the Mexican-Texans that George W. Paschal, an Austin refugee, was about to be appointed lieutenant colonel of the regiment. Writing from their forward camp at Ramireno, upriver from Rio Grande City, officers Trevino, Abrego, Martinez, Zapata, Dias and Falcon protested the action. The officers assured Haynes that they were all "desirous to contribute personally in the destruction of the Confederacy," but did not want Paschal as their commander. Paschal did not speak Spanish and had not "accompanied the men in the short period of their campaign."[169] Regardless of the desires of the Tejanos, Paschal was appointed lieutenant colonel in April, only adding to the deep discontent already running through the entire regiment.

The lack of discipline in the Second Regiment became the talk of the Union Army at Brownsville. Much of the rowdiness was due to the fact that the men had not received the clothing they had been promised and were going around camp almost naked. Furthermore, the Second Regiment had not been paid or received the bounty money they had been promised. Haynes protested to department headquarters in New Orleans, but his plea did little to alleviate the men's lack of money and clothing.[170] The inability and unwillingness of the Union Army to pay and clothe the Second Regiment seriously curtailed the number of Mexican-Texans joining the Federal ranks. According to Davis, further recruitment would be extremely difficult if regular payments were not made to the men. Davis and Haynes had hoped to continue their recruitment of men from Mexico, but found their efforts frustrated. Admitting "that the Mexican recruits have not been as numerous as was expected" Davis blamed the lack of recruits on "the difficulties on the other side of the river" which had "driven into the ranks of the contending parties most of the available men."[171] In reference to the Second Regiment, Davis wrote: "They soon become dissatisfied with our manner of making payments, and being of Indian blood and nature, the discipline and restraint of this camp, and the value of their horses, arms and equipments proving too much of a temptation, they take an opportunity to desert and carry them into Mexico, in some cases deserting from off picket."[172]

During the first six months of 1864 more than 200 men deserted from the Second Regiment. With few exceptions, Captain Adrian J. Vidal's entire company, along with their commander, deserted. On May 20, Captain Monico de Abrego and Lieutenant Cecilio Vela also left their regiment to seek refuge in Mexico. Another reason for the high desertion rate was the rumor, which later proved to be true, that the Texas Cavalry was about to be transferred to Louisiana. The news angered the Mexican-Texans who had been promised that they would only serve for the "campaign in Texas." A near riot broke out in at least two companies when word of the Louisiana transfer began to spread. The disturbances caused Davis to post a regular guard around the Texan camp to prevent flight into Mexico.

Other more severe measures were also undertaken by the Union commanders. In May, Private Pedro Garcia, Company E, First Regiment, deserted while on picket duty at Punta del Monte in Cameron County. Garcia was caught, ordered court-martialed, and was charged with desertion and attempting to join the enemy. The officers who heard Garcia's case decided that because of "the great number of desertions from the Texas Cavalry Volunteers and the large amount of government property thereby lost" that an example be made of the young private.[173] Found guilty on two of three charges, Garcia was sentenced to be "shot to death with musketry."

Benjamin F. McIntyre, a lieutenant in the Nineteenth Iowa Infantry, vividly recorded the inglorious execution of Private Garcia in his diary.

> We had been in this position but a short time when the solemn notes of the Dead March fell upon our ears and soon a squad of soldiers was observed slowly approaching followed by a band of music. Behind them was a coffin carried by four men and immediately followed the dead cart with its victim, near whom walked a priest who had been the constant companion of the doomed man since his execution had been made known.
>
> The cart and its victim passed within our lines, each band playing a most melancholy air and after passing around our entire line halted beside an open grave by the side of which the coffin was placed.
>
> A bandage was placed over his eyes to screen the manner of his death from him but he pushed it from his eyes and gazed around with seeming indifference upon the armed squad who stood awaiting the word to end his existence.
>
> The word was given. Make ready. Aim. A dozen rifles were aimed at his breast. It was a moment of painful suspense and was felt by the vast throng—a moment and a human life would be ended. I would not ask to know his feelings as kneeling upon his burial casket beside his open grave he so soon must fill. Each one who gazed upon the spectacle I doubt not felt the cold blood curdling in his veins and would prefer never again to witness an alike exhibition.[174]

The sentence and execution was said to have caused so much turmoil among the Mexican-Texans, both soldiers and civilians, that news of the execution caused a stir among the Confederate forces at Rio Grande City.

Prejudice and scorn toward the Second Regiment was rampant at Brownsville. "The 2nd Texas Cavalry which have been enlisted here are almost entirely of Mexican origin. I consider them dishonest, cowardly and treacherous and only bide their time to make good their escape," one Union lieutenant asserted.[175]

Besides Davis, the only man to defend the men of the Second Regiment was John L. Haynes. Haynes was forced to admit that the Second Regiment had a "disproportionately large number of deserters," but nevertheless tried to explain to General Francisco Jay Herron, Commander at Brownsville, the reasons for the desertions. "The men are near their families," Haynes wrote, "they live an inactive life in camp, no furloughs given them, and many desert simply to visit their homes and fear to come back." "Others," Haynes argued "are no doubt instigated by the Mexican authorities to desert to join their ranks with the superior arms they receive in this service, high prices being paid for such arms, which causes greatly increase the ordinary proportion of desertions."[176] Haynes had deliberately recruited from among the "twenty-five thousand inhabitants of this state of Mexican extraction" and assured General Herron "that they will make good soldiers with a little drill, and properly officered." The commander of the Second Regiment was confident of his men's "courage and good conduct."[177]

Against the desires of his men, Colonel Haynes urged that the Second Regiment be ordered to Louisiana so the men would not be so close to their homes and would not desert. Herron, believing Haynes to be "a good officer and a valuable man," approved the request and asked Department of the Gulf Headquarters in New Orleans to transfer the regiment.[178] Herron, confident that Haynes could "make a fine regiment out of the Mexicans," asked that special attention be given to the transfer request.

With General Nathaniel Prentiss Banks approving of the transfer, all of the Texas Cavalry Brigade, except Companies A and C of the First Regiment, were ordered to New Orleans. Just before the Texans sailed for New Orleans, Captain George Trevino was given a leave of absence to visit his new bride in Reynosa but told Haynes he was afraid to do so for fear that many of his men would refuse to leave Texas without him.

Company A and C of the First Texas Cavalry, mostly Anglo-Americans, were overrun by Confederates under Colonel John S. Ford at Las Rucias near Brownsville in June. The men who surrendered to the Confederates were later reported to have been treated in a "very inhuman manner and would have been murdered on the ground since they were Texas Renegades had it not been for Colonel Ford."[179] The prisoners were marched through a searing July sun to

Houston and then to Hempstead where they were confined in a stockade. Because of the bad health conditions at Hempstead, eleven of the men died within four hours. The remainder, reported to be in a "prostrate and emancipated condition," were exchanged a few months later.[180]

Sailing from Brazos Santiago on the steamer *Crescent* the men of the Second Regiment reached New Orleans the latter part of June, 1864, where they were immediately marched to Morganza, Louisiana. At Morganza, on the east bank of the Mississippi, upriver from Baton Rouge, the Second Regiment found themselves in a strange land. The swamps, bottomlands, and bayous of Louisiana were quite different from the flat arid plains of South Texas. The men could not speak English, much less the French widely spoken by many of the natives of Louisiana. At Morganza, Captain Trevino requested a leave of absence to visit his wife in Reynosa, Mexico, as well as the families of many of his men who were reported to be destitute, having been forced to flee across the Rio Grande by the Confederate Army. Trevino was hoping to make some arrangement through a commercial house in Matamoros to ship food to the families. With Paschal, Haynes, Davis, and others approving Trevino's request, the captain departed for Mexico, but returned to serve out the remainder of his enlistment and was honorably discharged at New Orleans in July of the following year.[181]

In August, 1864, the First and Second Regiments were consolidated. Captain Trevino's Company A became Company I of the First Regiment; Clemente Zapata's Company B became Company K; Captain Cesario Falcon's Company C became Company L; Company D, now commanded by Gustave H. Radetzki, since the desertion of Captain Abrego, became Company M.[182] With the consolidation, several officers of the Second Regiment including Clemente Zapata, were mustered out of the service. Since the Tejanos spoke no English, Haynes accompanied the officers to New Orleans to help the men in procuring their pay and obtain transportation to Brazos Santiago. Since the men had "contributed largely to the recruiting of the 2nd Texas Cavalry," and "had served faithfully," the commander was reluctant to see his men go.[183] Haynes had by this time been given command of the regiment. Davis had been promoted to brigadier general with command of six regiments, mostly of Blacks, all comprising the District of Morganza.[184]

At Morganza the Texas Cavalry received rumors that Confederates had crossed the Atchafalaya River with artillery at Simmesport. Driving north from Morganza, the regiment reached Simmesport to find no artillery but a strong picket of Texas Confederates. In several skirmishes three Rebel prisoners were taken and several flat boats and a ferry destroyed before the Texans retreated to Morganza.[185]

A twenty-seven-year-old private, Flario Cantu, was the first Mexican-Texan to die in Louisiana, pierced by a Confederate musket ball at Tshavalavo, near Morganza, July 28, 1864.[186]

In October, the Texans were sent eastward across the Mississippi to Bayou Sara and Saint Francisville toward Clinton as a diversionary force to hold Confederate troops in the area while a larger Union force drove eastward against Woodville in southern Mississippi. The men left Morganza at daylight on the morning of October 3, 1864, with 100 rounds of ammunition and five day's rations for each man. Upon crossing Bayou Sara, the expedition separated with parties pushing northward toward Woodville and eastward against Clinton. Before reaching Jackson, more than half way to Clinton, one party overran several Confederate pickets and took six prisoners before falling back to Bayou Sara and the Mississippi.[187]

In camp at Baton Rouge, Captain Cesario Falcon blamed the Louisiana climate, his bad health and "not being sufficiently acquainted with the English language" for his inability to perform his duties.[188] Shortly thereafter, Captain Falcon, who was having to "depend on others for the proper interpretation of orders," submitted his resignation to regimental headquarters. Falcon had also received the tragic news that his father had been murdered by Confederates back in Texas. The captain's family had also been forced to flee to Mexico and without provisions were dependent on the captain for support. The captain's desire to leave Louisiana was perhaps encouraged by the death of his first lieutenant, Ramon G. Falcon, who expired of fever at Baton Rouge, January 30, 1865.[189] While at Baton Rouge written charges were brought against Colonel Haynes. The colonel was accused of passing "the evenings and often the greater part of all of the night, gambling with subordinate officers," besides making "no effort to suppress public gambling" among his men.[190]

From Morganza, three companies of Mexican-Texans were marched eastward 159 miles to West Pascagoula, Mississippi, which they occupied in November, 1864. The men were then countermarched westward to Greenburg, Louisiana, east of Morganza, where they set up camp on Christmas Day.

Early in 1865, the men were on the march again this time to Baton Rouge where they were reunited with the other companies of the First Regiment. Disease and fever took its toll at Baton Rouge. More than fifteen Mexican-Texans died in the cold winter dampness of Louisiana, never again to see the sunshine of their native Texas.

On May 29, 1865, Captain Trevino's Company embarked on a steamer for Natchez, Mississippi where the company remained until late June. In July, with the surrender of the Confederate Trans-Mississippi Department, the regiment was marched overland to Houston. Although the war was over, several men continued to desert. Others were placed in confinement in Houston for rowdiness while one Tejano was killed "while engaged in marauding near Houston."[191]

Early in 1865 the Second Regiment had been revived with the enlistment of three companies at New Orleans. Some thought was even given to recruiting Texas refugees at St. Louis and other points on the Mississippi. Unlike the old Second Regiment, the new unit was comprised almost entirely of Anglos with only ten Mexican Americans serving in the three companies. The three companies, along with other Union regiments, were overrun at Palmito Hill near Brownsville, in the last land battle of the war. Many of the Texans were executed after they had surrendered.[192] Those who survived the carnage at Palmito Hill, along with the Sixty-Second Colored Infantry, marched into the central Rio Grande Valley in the summer of 1865.

From Houston the First Regiment was marched to San Antonio where on October 31, 1865, Colonel Haynes stood before his men to deliver a farewell address: "For nearly four years you have been exiled from your homes, driven forth by the intolerance of a rebellion which could permit neither discussion or opposition because it was based upon slavery: the highest crime against the rights of man." The colonel asked the Texans "to cultivate peace and harmony and to show respect for law and order" and not to "indulge in feelings of hate or revenge."[193] Although more than 200 Mexican-Texans remained with the regiment, only two officers, Lieutenants John C. Cuellar and Eugenio Guzman, were in San Antonio to see the formal end of a war that had begun for Mexican-Americans some four years, six months, and seventeen days earlier with a skirmish in Zapata County, Texas.

A. J. Hamilton was now Governor of Texas. E. J. Davis became governor in 1870. Davis even dreamed of giving Union veterans from Texas 160 acres of Lone Star soil. John L. Haynes, besides being appointed Collector of Customs at Galveston, became a leader in Texas Republican politics, even journeying to Washington for a visit with President Ulysses S. Grant. The Mexican-Texans who had fought for the Union did not achieve political power as their Anglo commanders did. They did not receive any free headright land. They lived much as they had before the war, clustered in small villages along the muddy waters of the Rio Grande, many in poverty, and many others suppressed economically and politically by the Anglo in whose war they had fought, died, and helped win.

7

The Rio Grande Expedition

From their base at Brownsville, Union forces hoped to seize the upper Rio Grande. In November, 1863, Colonel Edmund J. Davis with a force of 1,500 men, including the First and Second Texas Cavalry, accompanied by infantry on the steamboat *Mustang*, began a movement upriver. Without a shot being fired, Davis marched into Ringgold Barracks and Rio Grande City, Colonel Santos Benavides with less than thirty men having fled across the river to Reynosa a week before. General N. J. T. Dana was disappointed that Benavides would not stand and fight. "Is he a Mexican or a

Texan?" the general queried. Obviously frustrated, Dana wrote the American consul in Matamoros: "I am not disposed to play hide and seek with such cutthroats as he is. If he is a Texan, I shall demand him, as a renegade, for punishment. If he is a Mexican, it must be looked to that he answers properly to the Mexican authorities for his outrages against our laws."[194]

From Rio Grande City a smaller detachment of the Texas Union Cavalry pushed upriver to Roma but found the Confederates gone there also. After recruiting numerous Mexican-Texans into the army, the force retreated downriver to Brownsville leaving two hundred men of the Tejano Second Cavalry at Roma under the command of Colonel John L. Haynes.[195]

Union commanders at Brownsville, New Orleans, and Washington now turned their thoughts to outfitting a larger expedition which would drive up the Rio Grande to form a junction with a similar expedition of Union troops from the Territory of New Mexico.

General James H. Carleton, with his California Column, would march to El Paso; cross the Rio Grande into Mexico; draw the necessary beef, flour, corn and vital supplies from Mexican sources, march across Mexico to Piedras Negras and cross into Texas. From Eagle Pass the Bluecoats would drive toward San Antonio and link up with the Union force moving inland from the Gulf. Although Carleton was anxious for the implementation of such a plan, the lack of supplies in Mexico and a growing problem with the guarding and feeding of 6,000 captured Navajo Indians forced a cancellation of the plan.[196]

The First Texas Cavalry, the only mounted unit brought from New Orleans, with the newly organized Second Cavalry continued to operate deep into the Nueces country. In many ways the Civil War on the Rio Grande had become a civil war within a civil war. It was now Texan against Texan, Tejano against Tejano. It was a vicious, no-holds-barred guerrilla war that ravaged the land and left hundreds dead and thousands starving.

In November, 1863, Santos Benavides was promoted to colonel for "gallant and distinguished services" and given permission to raise a regiment of "Partisan Rangers in West

Texas." The regiment was to be named for its commander, and according to General E. Kirby Smith, commander of the Trans-Mississippi Department, it mattered not whether the recruits were of "conscript age or not."[197]

General Magruder was also impressed with Benavides' continued loyalty to the Confederacy. Although the men in Benavides' command had not been paid for more than six months and the soldiers' "families were in a destitute and starving condition," the colonel and his men had not waivered in their loyalty to the Southern cause. Magruder had authorized Benavides to impress 250 bales of cotton from which to pay his men. Another 250 bales were to be sold and the money placed in a credit account in Monterrey. Yet another 1,000 bales were to be sold in Monterrey from which Magruder hoped to realize $150,000 with which Benavides was to "buy arms from the Federal soldiers and deserters and offer such inducements as would probably bring to his standard the whole of the border population of Mexico, and thus entirely defeat the plans of the enemy there."[198] Magruder was convinced that the successful implementation of such a plan was the only way the cotton trade with Mexico could continue. Furthermore, Magruder promised to make Benavides a brigadier-general.

In December, 1863, shocking news reached Texas that Patricio Milmo, acting in behalf of P. Milmo and Company, and through his brother-in-law, Santiago Vidaurri, Governor of Nuevo Leon, had seized seven chests at Monterrey containing $16,000,000 in Confederate funds bound for San Antonio and Shreveport, Louisiana. Jose Augustin Quintero, Confederate agent in Monterrey, tried unsuccessfully to persuade Milmo to release the funds. Milmo threatened to hold the funds until the Confederate government paid its debts to his company. Simon Hart, quartermaster along the Rio Grande, reported the claims to be largely fraudulent and blamed Charles Russell, another Confederate quartermaster, for revealing the sources of the chests to Milmo. Hart charged that at the time the Federals had moved into the lower valley the money owed to Milmo only amounted to $56,289, and since that time Milmo had received from 600 to 800 bales of cotton, more than enough to cover the indebtedness.[199] The entire matter, after reaching the highest echelons of the Confederate government, was not settled until January of 1864, when General Kirby Smith halted all trade with Mexico and sent a special agent to Monterrey to confer with Governor Vidaurri. By February the flow of cotton and other goods along the Rio Grande had resumed.

Many of the river towns—especially Brownsville, Rio Grande City, Roma, Laredo, and Eagle Pass—flourished at one time or another during the war due to the flow of goods to and from Mexico. Many Texans were able to amass small fortunes from the Rio Grande trade. Principal among these was the trio of Mifflin Kenedy, Richard King, and Charles Stilman, who were given a contract for supplying the Confederate forces on the river. Jose San Roman, a millionaire Spanish merchant owning stores in Brownsville and Matamoros, also prospered during the war. Brownsville merchants Roman, Francisco Yturria, and Jeremiah Galvan were even able to procure guns and medical supplies from New York. Several Tejano ranchers owning vast expanses of land in the lower valley appear to have also benefited financially from the war. These included J. N. and Juan Cavazos, Dorotea Alameda, E. E. Cortina, and A. G. Ureste. At Laredo Jesus Gutierrez, Yldefonso Gonzales, Augustin Trevino, David Sada, as well as Antonio Gamboa, Augustin Salinas, Hipolito Garcia, and J. M. Garcia carried on a lively mercantile trade. Even the old Mexican-Texan warrior Juan N. Seguin was listed as importing "457 lbs. of sugar, 277 lbs. of coffee, 1 box of brandy, 1 box of candles, and 2 sacks of flour" in January of 1864.[200] Perhaps the largest Laredo merchant was Raymond Martin, a French immigrant who had married into the native population. In January, 1864, Martin was listed as importing 8,535 yards of cloth, over 500 gallons of whiskey, besides cigars, shoes, quinine, knives, and hundreds of lesser items.

The most extensive export item was of course cotton. So

extensive was the cotton trade on the Rio Grande that a special Texas Cotton Office operating under the Confederate Cotton Bureau was organized to regulate the trade. It was in the cotton trade that corruption on a grandiose scale abounded. Leading Texas newspapers cried that the Cotton Bureau was rotten with corruption and demanded reform of the bureau. Leading military figures, like Bee and Magruder for example, were accused of having their hands in the till and involved in wide-scale improprieties.

Perhaps the most open corruption was at Laredo in the office of the secretary of the Cotton Bureau, C. W. Thompson. Santos Benavides accused Thompson of passing cotton illegally and accumulating $2,000 in bribes. On the night of April 3, 1863, Thompson, with $7,000 in treasury funds, attempted to flee Laredo purportedly to cross the river at Rio Grande City and join the Federals at Matamoros. A squad of Benavides' cavalry caught Thompson a few miles outside of town on the road to Carrizo. Benavides wrote Magruder urging that an example be made of Thompson. "The abstraction of government money by agents of the government is said to have become so frequent, that government agents are now looked upon as little better than highway robbers," Benavides claimed. Laredo citizens were asking "why a wholesale robber should escape while he who steals a cow or a horse meets with the just punishment of death."[201] Despite Benavides' complaints, corruption at Laredo continued, so much that Laredo was officially closed as a port in August, 1864.

It was early in 1864 that a familiar face once again appeared on the frontier. Old Rip Ford, not content with a desk job in Austin, had come to fight again. Ford, with the assistance of Benavides, would drive the Yankees from Texas. "I am confident you and myself can drive the enemy from the valley of the lower Rio Grande," Rip wrote

Benavides.[202] Ford envisioned himself as the Confederate David who would march into the Rio Grande Valley and either slay the Union Goliath or drive him into the Gulf of Mexico. With General Magruder approving the plan, Ford set out to recruit men for what came to be called the Rio Grande Expedition.

As before, Benavides was vital to Confederate fortunes on the river. But Rip was not the only one to realize the strategic geographical and political position of Benavides at Laredo. E. J. Davis, who knew Benavides personally, at the insistence of Colonel Haynes journeyed up the Mexican side of the Rio Grande to Nuevo Laredo in an attempt to lure Benavides to the Federal cause.[203] Benavides would be commissioned a brigadier-general, Davis said. Benavides is said to have offered to discuss the situation with Davis and agreed to a meeting at Fort McIntosh, but Davis, fearful of crossing to the east bank, possibly remembering his near death at Brownsville earlier in the war, refused.

In early February, 1864, Benavides rode northward through the brush country to confer with Ford and finalize plans for the expedition. Arriving at Ford's headquarters in San Antonio on February 7, the Laredo colonel warned of problems in the Nueces country and on the Rio Grande. Because of the lack of water and grass, the proposed route of the expedition would have to be changed. A march from San Diego straight south to the Rio Grande would "render all our horses unserviceable and incapacitate us for active operations for weeks," Benavides told Ford.[204] The two leaders also appeared worried about the possible advance of a large Union force from West Texas.

Benavides was not only to act as Ford's eyes, spying out the Federals in the lower valley, but was to provide the expedition with provisions. Ford was hoping to move against the Federals by way of Fort Merrill, San Diego, Sal del Rey, and then into the lower valley. "I do not wish to approach the Rio Grande and enable the Mexicans on the other bank to telegraph my movements to the enemy from hour to hour."

The winter of 1863-1864 proved to be one of the coldest and driest in memory and did, as expected, produce problems for the expedition. The winter rains, common to South Texas, did not appear, and even the Nueces River ran dry. "You cannot imagine how desolate, barren, and desert-like this country is; not a spear of grass, nor a green shrub ... nothing but moving clouds of sand to be seen on these once green prairies," a Confederate wrote Ford.[206] Plans called for Benavides to stockpile flour, coffee, and breadstuffs for the expedition near the Sal del Rey. The Laredo colonel was also to prevent the Mexican-Texan ranchers from driving their cattle and hogs to the Mexican side of the river. No property of any kind was to be carried into Mexico. Any Mexican-Texans caught doing so would have their possessions confiscated.[207] Benavides reported to Ford that supplies could not be found at Laredo, but "9,000 lbs. of flour, 500 lbs. of rice, 160 lbs. of flour, 500 lbs. of rice, 160 lbs. of coffee, and 2,500 pounds of powder," had been stored at Camargo.[208] Beef was reported to be plentiful in the Laredo area. No money was available in Laredo to buy additional subsistence supplies, however. In fact, Benavides had been forced to seize eighteen bales of cotton, which he sold for $1,258, to buy forage for his regiment's horses which were reported to be starving. The new route for the expedition would be to follow the San Antonio-Laredo road straight south to Old Fort Ewell on the Nueces, thence to Los Angeles, Los Ojuelos, San Antonio Viejo and finally to the Rio Grande. Hopefully such a march would not attract the attention of Federals who were using Nuevo Laredo to spy on the movements of Benavides' Regiment as well as Unionists at Piedras Negras who were also reporting on the strength and movement of various Confederate commands.

About this same time a Unionist named Bill Cannon arrived at Nuevo Laredo with a dispatch for Federal troops in far West Texas. Cannon paid a Mexican vaquero $200 to carry the letters to Union forces thought to be at Fort Lancaster. Benavides, learning of the transaction, sent a courier of his own to Piedras Negras to demand that the vaquero be arrested as a horse thief. The Mexican commander at Piedras Negras, a friend of the colonel, ordered the apprehension of the messenger who upon resisting arrest was shot and seriously wounded. Benavides assured Ford that he would attempt to obtain the dispatches.[209]

Benavides was sure that a large force could not move from Brownsville without his knowing it. At the time the Laredo colonel arrived in San Antonio, a twenty-five man reconnaissance force from Laredo, commanded by Lieutenant Martin Gonzales, had moved into the lower valley and was able to learn that the Federals had moved their cavalry horses from Brownsville to the Como se Llama Ranch, north of Brownsville, for lack of forage.

Leaving San Antonio on the morning of February 9, Benavides arrived at Eagle Pass four days later. The colonel reported that renegades from across the river in Piedras Negras were preparing to attack Eagle Pass and Fort Duncan. Texas Unionists and Confederate deserters were reported to be arriving at Piedras Negras daily. Learning from brother Refugio, stationed on the river below Laredo, that the enemy had "not made any forward movement" from the lower valley, the colonel was determined to stay in Eagle Pass since the town was in "considerable danger."[210]

The "danger" was a rambunctious Unionist named T. P. McManus. McManus had been sent to Piedras Negras to raise men for the First Texas Cavalry and to "operate against the Rebel trains on the San Antonio-Eagle Pass route."[211] From his dispatches to Federal Headquarters in Brownsville, it appears that McManus knew more about the movements of Confederates in the interior of Texas than Benavides knew about the Federals in the lower valley. "To prevent me from sending you an express," McManus wrote his commander, "every mesquite in the state would have to be garrisoned with rebel bayonets."[212] Much of McManus' information was coming from "reliable gentlemen" in San Antonio, Austin, and Houston.

The same day Benavides arrived on the river, a party of 100 Unionists recruited by McManus had started for Brownsville. From his base opposite Eagle Pass, McManus was hoping to join Colonel Haynes whom he thought to be on the Nueces or General Carleton whom McManus felt was advancing from West Texas. McManus had sent a messenger to Carleton, but the courier had been overtaken on the river forty-five miles above Eagle Pass and shot three times by four Mexicans whom McManus asserted the "Christ killing Jew[ish] cotton speculators" had hired.[213]

Benavides, learning of the departure of the 200 Unionists for Brownsville, crossed the river and with a handful of men went in pursuit. The colonel realized he did not have sufficient men to attack the Unionists but was hoping to steal their horses.[214]

Upon hearing other rumors of an impending attack on Eagle Pass, Benavides returned to Fort Duncan where he remained until February 26. Finally riding downriver to Laredo, Benavides was taken so ill from exhaustion that for days he was unable to rise from his bed. "For three years he has been in the field constantly without a tent or bed and often without blankets, without food . . . without water and almost all the time riding through the country," a Confederate wrote of Benavides.[215]

In Laredo, Benavides remained apprehensive about a possible Federal advance from Brownsville. From a Rebel sympathizer in Matamoros, the colonel learned that a large cavalry force under Colonel Haynes had left the lower valley for Corpus Christi. Another force was reported to be on the march for the Nueces county where they were to recruit men for a move westward against Eagle Pass. Other rumors told of a Union force advancing up the Mexican side of the river for an attack on Laredo or Eagle Pass.[216]

With seemingly insurmountable problems at Eagle Pass, General John B. Magruder decided to change the route of the cotton being transported into Mexico. Laredo was to replace Eagle Pass as the major port of entry. If possible, Benavides was to go in person to see the new Governor of Tamaulipas to explain Magruder's decision. Unable to travel because of his illness and not overly excited about visiting with his old enemy Juan N. Cortina, now Governor of Tamaulipas, Benavides instead sent three "respectable and confidential persons."[217] The colonel assured Magruder that the Laredo-San Antonio route was safe and that he would do his utmost to keep it that way.

Two months later Benavides, in a strange turn of events since the battle at Carrizo in May, 1861, completed an agreement with Cortina to protect the Confederate cotton crossing the border at Laredo. In a letter addressed to "His Excellency Juan N. Cortina," Magruder congratulated the red-bearded Cortina on his willingness to cooperate with Confederate authorities.[218]

On March 17, Old Rip proudly marched out of Alamo Plaza

in San Antonio with his ragged Confederate Army of conquest. Before Ford could reach the Rio Grande, however, Federal guerrilla activities had interrupted his plans. Deep in the South Texas chaparral country the advance units of the Confederate force had run into Union guerrillas.

Captain Mat Nolan, acting as Ford's left flank, had been sent far to the east and south. On Sunday, March 13, at 7:30 A.M., near Los Patricios, about fifty miles southwest of Banquete, Nolan had run headlong into the Union guerillas. The Federals, all Tejanos, were commanded by Cecilio Valerio and his son Juan and were loosely attached to John L. Haynes' Second Calvalry. Cecilio Valerio, who knew the Nueces country of South Texas as few others, in the words of Ford, "was an active officer; well acquainted with the country; brave and vigilant."[219] Nolan reported the guerrillas to number 125 and to be well armed with "Burnside carbines, revolvers, and sabers."[220] Although Valerio's force was "posted in a dense mesquital," Nolan did not hesitate but fiercely charged into the thicket with his sixty-two men. A furious fight developed.

Nolan reported that Valerio and his son at the head of eighty men "charged and fought us most gallantly, and could only be repulsed after a desperate fight and at the cost of much blood and property."[221] After fifteen minutes of fighting, the guerrillas drew off and retreated into the mesquite. Nolan lost three men in the frantic struggle. Five of Valerio's men were found dead in the thicket. Several ghastly pools of blood, indicating that several of the guerrillas had been severely wounded, were also found. Besides the five bodies in the thiicket, Nolan felt that twelve to fifteen more guerrillas were either killed or wounded.

In the frenzied fray Confederates captured thirty-one horses, forty-two saddles and bridles, twenty-five sabers, 107 blankets, six Colt revolvers, and five Burnside carbines. Papers were also found in the equipment abandoned by the Tejanos, indicating that Colonel Haynes had left the Rio Grande with intentions of reinforcing the guerrillas.[222]

Because of the density of the mesquital thickets and a fear that Haynes might be within striking distance, Nolan hastily retreated back to his camp on San Fernando Creek, south of Banquete. Four days after the battle at Los Patricios, Nolan turned eastward to attack a Federal force which had seized Corpus Christi.

In Laredo, Benavides, although still seriously ill, began preparations for his juncture with Ford. With scouts reporting almost daily, the colonel was confident that a Union advance against Laredo or Eagle Pass was impossible without his knowing it. Suddenly, however, on the afternoon of March 19, 1864, an excited vaquero named Cayetano de la Garza, a relative of the colonel, thereafter known as the Paul Revere of Laredo, came racing his horse into San Agustin Plaza and reported that a large Union cavalry force was approaching Laredo from downriver. Benavides at first questioned the validity of the report. How could such a force, reported to number 1,000, get by his scouts at Carrizo, at Los Ojuelos and in the brush country? Surely they would have detected such a large force. The young vaquero insisted his story was true, and Colonel Benavides sounded the alarm. Hurriedly men raced about town and across San Agustin Plaza, preparing for the impending attack.

From his bed Benavides rose to meet the Union onslaught. A small cavalry force was deployed along the road leading downriver in an attempt to delay the Federals. An urgent call was sent to bring in more than 100 men who were camped about twenty-five miles north of town and who were grazing their horses. Another express was hurriedly sent upriver to Eagle Pass to bring down what men were available there.[223]

All Benavides had to defend Laredo with was forty-two men from the companies of his brothers Refugio and Cristobal and thirty men from Captain Chapman's company of militia which had fortunately arrived on the river only a few days prior to the Union attack. Several citizens volunteered to help defend the town and were deployed as sharp shooters on top of the buildings around the plaza. Although the Federal force was reported to outnumber Benavides' force more than ten to one, the colonel was determined to fight. Benavides told a fellow Confederate, Thomas Dwyer: "This would not have happened had I not been confined to bed for some days. I would have known all about their advance and would have gone below and attacked them. As it is I have to fight to the last; though hardly able to stand I shall die fighting. I won't retreat, no matter what force the Yankees have—I know I can depend on my boys."[224] Santos gave specific orders to his brother Cristobal in the event that he should be defeated: "There are five thousand bales of cotton in the plaza. It belongs to the Confederacy. If the day goes against us fire it. Be sure to do the work properly so that not a bale of it shall fall into the hands of the Yankees. Then you will set my new house on fire, so that nothing of mine shall pass to the enemy. Let their victory be a barren one."[225]

It was later learned that two Unionists, Jim Fisk and Paten Smith, operating from Nuevo Laredo had reported to Haynes of Benavides' bad health and of the fact that only a small Confederate force was protecting thousands of dollars in Confederate cotton, neatly stacked in San Agustin Plaza.

With the streets leading into the town plaza barricaded with the cotton and with snipers in place on the rooftops around the plaza, Benavides rode out of Laredo to meet the foe. The Federal force, now estimated at 200, one-half of which were Mexican-Texans, was thought to be commanded by Cecilio Valerio and Jim Fisk. After his defeat at Los Patricios, Valerio had apparently retreated to the Rio Grande, made a junction with a portion of the Second Texas Cavalry, and moved upriver to attack Laredo. Since the battle at Los Patricios was fought on the morning of March 13, Valerio had ridden hard to attack Laredo on the afternoon of March 19. It was later learned that the Federals had evaded Benavides' scouts by crossing into Mexico downstream from Carrizo and continuing up the west bank until they were within a few miles of Laredo where they recrossed to the east bank.

On the outskirts of Laredo and near the banks of Zacate Creek, just east of town, Benavides made his stand. His forty-two men were ordered to dismount and take a position in and around a large corral from which they could easily fire on the advancing Federals. One-half mile from town the Yankees also dismounted, formed into groups of forty, and charged the Confederate position. Three times the Federals advanced, and three times they were driven off. An eyewitness reported that "Benavides and his men fought with the coolest bravery."[226] Juan Ibarra and Major J. S. Swope were singled out for their heroism in the battle. Swope, mounted on a "magnificent sorrel," charged the Yankees and emptied his pistol into their ranks before retreating, his horse hit three times. Juan Ibarra also charged the Federals and fought bravely before his horse was killed. No Confederates were reported killed. Several Yankees were seen to fall and were carried off by their comrades.

The battle lasted for about three hours. Benavides reported that the Bluecoats were "repulsed by the vigorous fire of my gallant men."[227] The Union version of the battle, if it exists, is yet to be found.

As darkness fell upon the tired and weary men, Union and Confederate alike, the sniping slackened, and the Federals were seen to draw off into the chaparral. The Union retreat did not stop until the men were about three miles below Laredo where they camped for the night.

The inhabitants of Laredo, soldiers and civilians, were kept on constant alert. Benavides expected another attack, if not during the night, certainly on the morrow. The eerie stillness was suddenly broken at two o'clock in the morning when pickets north of town reported a sizeable cavalry force to be advancing rapidly. As death and darkness gathered all about, the men quickly prepared themselves for another attack. The anxiety turned into jubilance, however, when the force was discovered to be Confederates arriving from their camp north of town. "A general rejoicing took place among our little force," the colonel later wrote.[228] Trumpets were sounded. Soldiers and citizens cheered. The bell atop San Agustin Church sounded into the crisp March evening and was easily audible in the Federal camp southeast of town.

As daylight crept through the narrow dusty streets of the still frightened town, Colonel Benavides sent brother Refugio with about sixty men to report on the location of the enemy. As the captain crossed Zacate Creek, numerous trails of blood could be seen in the sand along the creekbed. Bloody rags were also visible here and there in the tall grass and in the scrubby mesquite. The Federal camp, three miles downriver, was found vacated. Refugio reported that the Federals had left in a hurry, probably encouraged in their departure by the timely arrival of Confederate reinforcements the night before. Clothing was found scattered about the camp. Five horses, all branded U.S., were also found.

Again, on the morning of the 21st, Refugio Benavides was sent out as a scout. The trail of the Federals was followed further downriver. The Captain reported that the Yankees had broken up into small squads and were in full retreat toward Carrizo.

On the third day after the battle, a report reached the Laredo colonel that a large force of Federals was again approaching the eastern outskirts of Laredo. Dwyer reported that "Benavides . . . being very much exhausted . . . again got into his saddle and galloped out at the head of a body of his men to give them a fight."[229] One of the Confederate scouting parties had mistakenly been reported as a Union attack. Benavides, although determined to fight again, was so weak that he fell from his horse and received a serious head wound. Dwyer wrote an urgent letter to Ford reporting Benavides to be "wholly exhausted and very unwell."[230] W. W. Camp, a surgeon attached to Benavides' Regiment, reported that "fatigue and exposure" had confined the colonel to his room and only "at the hazard of his life" was he able to rise.[231] Camp, like Dwyer, urged that Benavides be relieved.

"You have added to the reputation you and your command have already acquired," Rip wrote Benavides of the battle for Laredo.[232] Ford urged Benavides to allow some "officer in rank . . . to take charge of the troops." Upon hearing of the attack on Laredo, Rip set out for the Rio Grande. Pausing briefly at Los Ojuelos, where Ford had hoped Benavides would have supplies stored, the Rio Grande Expedition reached Laredo on the 15th of April.

Ford was surprised to find Governor Santiago Vidaurri at Benavides' Headquarters. Rip seemed somewhat perturbed at the Laredo colonel's involvement in Mexican political affairs, although the involvement had come at the direction of General James Slaughter, Ford's superior, who knew Benavides well, having served at Fort McIntosh in 1856 as a lieutenant in the artillery. Vidaurri — high riding caudillo, Governor of Nuevo Leon, Confederate sympathizer, and friend of Benavides — had been driven out of Monterrey by partisans of Benito Juarez. In Houston, General Slaughter had learned through Jose Agustin Quintero, Confederate agent in Monterrey, that Vidaurri had large quantities of arms, cannon, and ammunition which he was willing to sell at "reasonable rates."[233] Benavides had been directed "to write or send someone to Monterrey" to buy the badly needed arms. The entire mission was to be of "great secrecy," and Benavides was directed not to "breathe a word of it to anyone."

Vidauri was able to leave Monterrey ahead of the Juaristas with "eighteen pieces of light artillery, a large quantity of ammunition, a number of Sharp's carbines, and 15,000,000 percussion caps."[234] The governor's intention was to deliver the war materials to Benavides at Laredo but was overtaken by 1,600 Juaristas at Villa Aldama in the foothills of the Sierra Madre, half way between Laredo and Monterrey. Vidaurri was badly beaten, and most of his men surrendered. Before the surrender, however, the war materials were hidden in the homes of political friends of Vidaurri. With the state archives and treasury, Vidaurri, accompanied by "a party of faithful friends," escaped the defeat at Villa Aldama to reach Benavides at Laredo. Colonel Benavides immediately dispatched Nicolas Sanchez with letters from Vidaurri to the parties with whom the arms and caps had been secreted. Juarez' partisans, however, had found the war materials, and when Sanchez attempted to procure the supplies, he was almost caught and executed.

Shortly after the battle for Laredo, Benavides and Ford received information that the Union forces in the lower valley were attempting to persuade Juarez to allow the Federals to advance on Laredo from Mexican soil. From the sketchy facts it appears that Colonel Haynes and several other high-ranking and influential Union officers had gone to Monterrey to confer with Juarez. Juarez was reported to have stated that "Mexico was too small and weak a nation to wage war against either the United States or the Confederate States."[235]

Both Ford and Benavides felt that a movement against the upper Rio Grande from Mexico "would be tantamount to a declaration of war by the Juarez government" and were even willing to "be placed side by side with the French" against Juarez if necessary.[236]

Although Refugio, Cristobal, and most of Benavides' Regiment departed Laredo with Ford, Colonel Benavides, because of his continued indisposition, was unable to do so. From Laredo the Rio Grande Expedition turned eastward to Los Ojuelos. One day's march beyond the springs where the road turned abruptly to the southeast the column went into camp near the village of Las Animas. Colonel Ford directed that the campsight be named Camp Benavides in honor of the Laredo Colonel. Advancing through spring rains, the column reached Ringgold Barracks on May 2.

With Santos Benavides seriously ill in Laredo, command of Benavides' Regiment was passed to Captain Refugio Benavides. Captain Benavides was directed by Ford to impress as many horses as possible, all badly needed for the final push against Brownsville.

Twenty-five miles upriver from Ringgold Barracks, Lieutenant Garza of Benavides' Regiment, acting as Ford's advance guard, ran into a party of Mexican bandits. Garza and his men fired on the party and killed the bandit chief. The party, some thirty in number, had left their horses on the west bank and had waded across the river on foot. Near Rio Grande City Lieutenant Garza and his men were able to pass themselves off as Yankees and were able to learn that Federal scouting parties were only a few miles downriver. Garza did not stop in Rio Grande City but continued on downstream. The lieutenant was within site of the village of Las

Cuevas, twelve miles beyond Rio Grande City, when cannon shots were heard upriver near Ringgold Barracks. Believing Ford's entire column to be under attack, Garza wheeled his detachment and raced upriver. Much to Garza's surprise the attack turned out to be a noisy fiesta across the river in Camargo.[237]

The occupation of Rio Grande City completed the first phase of Ford's plan. Here he paused to regroup and prepare his men for the all important advance against Brownsville. Captains Navarro and Alderete of Ford's command were ordered to bring their companies downriver from Laredo where they had arrived from duty on the Nueces. Although Ford was able to obtain a considerable amount of supplies from Mexico, many of the companies were still in need of equipment and arms. A serious dispute erupted when Captain Pedro Cervallos of Benavides' Regiment stopped a train being escorted downriver by a detachment of Captain Gidding's company and took percussion caps and leather to make cartridge belts.[238] Ford was furious at Captain Cervallos and demanded that all the seized items be immediately returned.

Although on good terms with his old friend, Alcalde Rafael Lopez of Camargo, Ford was still fearful that a Union force might complete an agreement with either Juarez or Cortina and by using Mexican soil successfully envelop his army. Peaceful relations with residents on the west bank of the Rio Grande as well as with the Mexican-Texans on the east bank were vital to Ford's plans.

Due to their knowledge of the terrain, those units detailed for scouting duty were almost exclusively Tejano. Men of Benavides' Regiment were able to scout within twenty miles of the coast and as far north as the Nueces. Lieutenant Cerento Flores with Ceiste Domingo as guide was ordered to proceed downstream along the river road and recruit as many Mexican-Texans as possible. "I have invited the Mexicans to return to this bank and peaceably pursue their vocations," Ford wrote.[239] Many men fleeing from the war in Mexico ironically joined the Confederates.

Almost daily, scouts and spies arrived at Ringgold Barracks bringing information on the movement of the Federal forces. From such reports Ford was even able to construct a crude map of the fortified positions around Brownsville and of the new fort the Federals had built in the bend of the river above the town. Although Federal forces in the lower valley were reported to number 7,000, Ford, with his 1,500 Texans, was determined to force a confrontation.

In late June, Ford decided upon a reconnaissance in force to feel out the Yankees. Rip was especially interested in asserting the validity of rumors that the Federals were evacuating Brownsville. Sending Lieutenant Daniel Showalter and Captain Refugio Benavides to the Como Se Llama Ranch on the Arroyo Colorado north of Brownsville, Ford moved with Giddings along the river road before turning north to form a junction at the Como Se Llama Ranch. Ford reached Showalter and Captain Benavides on June 23, 1864. The combined forces, subsisting entirely on jerkey, then moved toward the Rio Grande, reaching the river road at the Carricitos Ranch below the village of Las Rucias. Learning from captured Mexican-Texans that a large Union picket was stationed in the village of Las Rucias, Rip, by using "an obscure trail through the chaparral," advanced on the Federals and was able to "get within a few hundred yards of the enemy without being discovered."[240]

The Federals at Las Rucias were part of the First Texas Cavalry commanded by Captain Philip G. Temple. Finally detecting Rip's advance, the Federals took a position in a large brick building, in several small jacales, and behind several piles of brick and rubble. The Federals were greatly outnumbered with the Confederates having 400 men of which 250 were deployed before the village.

The battle opened with Ford sending Captain James Dunn and Cristobal Benavides forward. Dunn charged upon the Federal position and was killed instantly. Cristobal Benavides had his horse shot from under him as did Sergeant Higinio Sanchez. Ford next sent Refugio Benavides in a flanking movement "behind a fence to the bank of the laguna [to] turn the right flank of the enemy and command the ground in [the] rear of the houses."[241] Refugio evidently misunderstood the order and moved to the extreme right and attempted to turn the enemy's left flank instead. The Laredo Captain twice charged on horseback but was stopped both times by a small lagoon. Refugio ordered his men to dismount, and they joined the remainder of Ford's command in a final assault against the Federal position.

Outmanned, the Yankees fled, many across the lagoon, others into the cane and underbrush near the muddy banks of the Rio Grande. Several were successful in reaching safety in Mexico. Ford estimated that twenty of the enemy were killed, ten or twelve wounded, and thirty-six taken prisoner. Several of the wounded drowned while attempting to cross the lagoon. The Rebels captured two wagons and teams, twenty-eight horses, a number of saddles, as well as a considerable amount of "commissary and quartermaster stores."[242]

Three Rebels were killed and four wounded. In his official report of the battle, Ford reported that Refugio Benavides "acted well," and that Cristobal Benavides deserved "credit for [his] gallant conduct."[243]

Rip was able to learn from the captured Yankees that no Federals were west or north of Arroyo Colorado and that a large number of Davis' Union Cavalry had left for New Orleans. Furthermore, the Union Texans remaining in Brownsville were badly demoralized. The Federal prisoners, many of them Germans from the Texas Hill Country, had been told by their commanders that if they were captured they could expect no quarter from the Confederates and would certainly be executed.

Unable to carry the captured Union supplies, Ford thought of burning the goods, but the jacales of the local Mexican-Texans in which the supplies were stored would have to be fired. Feeling the support, or at least the neutrality of the Mexican-Texan population of the lower valley to be indispensable, the supplies were left as they had been found.

After the victory at Las Rucias, the Confederates advanced through a pouring rain to within five miles of Brownsville and were successful in temporarily disrupting all Federal communications to the coast. Rip wanted to stay on the Arroyo Colorado but did not have the necessary supplies to sustain his men. After five days the Rebels broke camp and retreated upriver to Ringgold Barracks.

Back at Rio Grande City Ford heard of more trouble upstream at Eagle Pass. McManus, champion of the Union guerillas operating along the upper Rio Grande, had intensified his raids across the Rio Grande into Texas. In the eyes of the Union leaders at Brownsville, McManus could never hold Eagle Pass, but by raiding across the river, could force Ford to divert men to the upper Rio Grande, men which the Confederates badly needed for operations in the lower valley. On April 3, the Union partisans operating from Piedras Negras had robbed the San Antonio stage outside of Eagle Pass, cut the eight horses loose and fled across the river to Mexico. The guerrillas were reported to be constantly taking mules and wagons on the San Antonio road. General F. J. Herron was hoping that McManus might even raid as deep into the Texas interior as Fort Inge and prevent the "killing of Union men on their way out."[244]

During the first week of April, 1864, Captain J. B. Weyman, commanding Fort Duncan, reported that he had chased three separate squads of Unionists across the river into Mexico. Weyman complained that Francisco Garcia, comandante at Piedras Negras who had promised to help stop the raids, would "not deliver the thieves up." Weyman bitterly charged that McManus held a "Yankee commission to burn, murder, and destroy . . . the people and ranches of Western Texas."[245]

On June 17 a band of forty guerrillas crossed into Texas five miles above Eagle Pass, "unfurled the United States flag" and during the next day were reported to have "received a considerable augmentation to their numbers from the Mexican side of the river."[246] The new commander at Fort Duncan, Captain James A. Ware, having only thirty-four men at the post, called out a home-guard militia company. Ware placed guards in the post hospital, at the customs house, the quartermaster's store house, several business houses below the town, and sent fifteen men north of town to patrol the countryside in the direction of the expected approach of the enemy. A few minutes past noon, just as the soldiers and citizens had finished barracading the street with cotton, the guerrillas attacked, forced Ware's pickets to retreat, and succeeded in capturing Captain Ware and several other Confederates. The Union attack was stopped at the post hospital, however, and after releasing their prisoners and carrying off what arms they could, the guerrillas retreated into Mexico, unsuccessful in destroying the valuable cotton.[247]

At Ringgold Barracks, Ford continued to consolidate and

build his army. Cristobal Benavides was appointed provost marshal charged with not only policing the army but regulating the flow of civilians across the river. Benavides was to arrest and turn over to civil authorities "persons charged with political and other offenses." Furthermore, the captain was to "arrest officers, soldiers, and other persons guilty of riotous or disorderly conduct, . . . prevent the sale of intoxicating spirits when in his opinion the same is detrimental to discipline and good order in the army."[248]

All Mexican-Texans and Mexican nationals who joined the Rebels at Ringgold Barracks were placed in Benavides' Regiment. Santos Benavides, still indisposed at Laredo, hoped to join the expedition before the final push on Brownsville. On July 11 the colonel was able to rise from bed and with a small escort set out downriver. Before reaching Carrizo, however, Benavides became too ill to continue, and after ordering his squad to continue their trek downstream, returned to Laredo.[249] Benavides was a fighter, however, and wrote Ford that in a few days he hoped to recover enough to join his men.

At the same time Benavides seemed alarmed about the defenses of his hometown. Ford wanted almost all of the Laredo detachment to join his command at Ringgold Barracks, but Benavides was reluctant to release the soldiers. The colonel's only hope of defending Laredo was a few men of Cristobal Benavides' and Julian Garcia's companies. To complicate matters, Garcia's men were without arms. Benavides, still seriously ill, not only refused to send more men downriver but asked Ford to send Cristobal Benavides back to Laredo, leaving the captain's company in charge of Sergeant Eugenio Garcia.[250] Because of his sickness the colonel was placing more and more reliance on his adjutant, Lieutenant T. A. Rodriguez.

In July, 1864, as larger numbers of Federals departed Texas for Louisiana, Ford began to apply more pressure on Brownsville. On July 30 the Rebel advance guard surprisingly rode into Brownsville to find the Yankees gone, having evacuated Fort Brown and the town two days earlier. Confederate sympathizers from Matamoros, under the leadership of E. W. Cave, had crossed the Rio Grande to restore order when anarchy seemed imminent. As the Rebels gathered at Brownsville, several companies of Benavides' Regiment succeeded in driving the Federals back toward the gulf where the Yankees had set up defenses at Brazos Santiago.

Within hours of the Rebel occupation of Brownsville, couriers brought word that a sizeable Federal force was still in camp below Brownsville and another larger force was continuing to fortify Brazos Island. Ford, who was sick and unable to mount his horse, ordered out a regiment to attack the Bluecoats. Finding the Yankees still in camp about eighteen miles outside of town on the road to Brazos Island, Colonel Showalter sent Captain Refugio Benavides forward as a reconnaissance to determine the strength of the Federal force. Benavides instead impetuously charged into the Federal camp, scattering Yankees in all directions. For some reason which was never explained, Showalter failed to follow up the attack. Benavides later reported to Ford: "We captured a number of wagons and fixed them to move off. We expected Colonel Showalter every moment. All at once we saw a heavy column of the enemy moving upon us. I then looked for Colonel Showalter, and saw his command going the other way, about a mile and a half off. The carajos came, and took all our wagons away from us."[251] Benavides and his company had been forced to flee for their lives.

Two weeks later Ford sent Showalter to attack the Federal encampment at Point Isabel. Refugio Benavides with his usual daring attacked a force twice his size and drove the Yankees into their works on nearby Brazos Island. Lieutenant Eugenio Garza was also singled out for bravery in driving a force of 100 Yankees from a "good position."[252]

By late 1864, as the war in the lower valley became stalemated, the desertion rate in the Confederate forces began to grow steadily. Refugio Benavides reported that large numbers of his command were simply "going off."[253] The captain attributed the desertions to the fact that Colonel Benavides had told the wives of his men that their husbands "were at liberty to go whenever they want." According to Captain Benavides, there was little he could do to stop the men from leaving.

Writing from Rancho de las Palmas, Captain Benavides reported to his confidant Felix Blucher that he too wanted to return to Laredo since his wife was seriously ill with fever. His wife had also received a false report that the captain had been killed in action. Captain Benavides confessed to his German compatriot, whom he appeared to admire greatly, that he would serve his country to the very end, but felt it senseless to advance across the salt flats for an attack on the enemy camp at Boca Chica.

In late August, Cristobal Benavides was reported to be absent without leave and was ordered to report back to Brownsville. Ford, alarmed at the growing desertion rate and hearing the same rumors that Captain Refugio Benavides had reported to Blucher, demanded to know from Santos Benavides why he was allowing his men to "return to their homes."[254] Colonel Benavides was "causing trouble and insubordination," and Rip demanded that he direct his men to return to their units.

In early September the squabbling between the two officers erupted into a full-fledged feud. Benavides had ordered the men being recruited in the vicinity of Rio Grande City by Captain M. Weisenger to report to Laredo. He was attempting to fill up his regiment as a prerequisite to being commissioned a brigadier-general. Ford, like Benavides, was not in the best of health, and the temper of both commanders seems to have been on edge. On September 2, 1864, Ford sent two threatening letters to Benavides. In the first he warned the Laredo Colonel that if the new recruits were not ordered downriver to Brownsville, Benavides would be reported for "disobedience."[255] In a second letter, Ford demanded to know "by what authority" Benavides had given "Capt. Weisenger permission to visit Laredo in the face of orders" to report to Brownsville.

Two days later, Lieutenant W. L. Newsom, assistant adjutant general, obviously influenced to a large degree by Ford, levied serious charges against Benavides and demanded that he be arrested.[256] Newsom accused Benavides of taking money by force from the custom house officials in Laredo, using the property of civilians without their permission, endeavoring to defeat the successful accomplishments of Ford's expedition, seizing cotton and selling it after the Cotton Bureau had already sold it, and crossing cotton into Mexico at night. In more specific specifications Newsom accused Benavides of leaving Laredo for Houston without orders, reprimanding Cristobal Benavides for obeying Ford's orders, failing to send troops to Ford when ordered to do so, and allowing the men at Laredo to sleep in their own houses. Furthermore, the Confederates at Laredo, according to Newsom, were not attending roll call or dress parade, and were performing little or no duty. Among those listed as witnesses against Benavides were Santos' uncle Basilio, brothers Refugio and Cristobal, Tomas Trevino, the collector of customs and the agent of the cotton bureau at Laredo, as well as several others. General E. Kirby Smith was also furious at Benavides' unorthodox behavior. If Benavides could not satisfactorily explain why he had seized the cotton at Laredo, an order for his arrest was to be issued.[257]

Rip was also angry with Nolan for taking men from Ford's command whose term of service had expired and remustering them into Benavides' Regiment. The seriousness of the dispute brought Colonel Benavides riding downriver from Laredo. The colonel went to Ford's headquarters and in a rather heated discussion attempted to make reconciliations. Benavides told Ford that he already had enough men in his regiment and did not need any of Fords. Rip challenged Benavides to show on paper "more than 500 men in actual service."[258] Although Generals Bee, Slaughter, and Magruder had previously promised Benavides a commission as brigadier general, Ford was set against such a decision since such a promotion would in many ways upstage Rip's Rio Grande exploits. Ford argued that if Benavides were given his way, the army in the lower valley would simply cease to exist. Years later Ford wrote sarcastically of the confrontation: "If a bee of brigadier general species got in Benavides' hat and stung him, and caused insanity, he deserves our sympathy."[259] Although the two men appear to have parted from the Brownsville parley on good terms, it is interesting to note that years later Benavides refused to correspond with Ford, yet continued his pre-war friendship with Edmund J. Davis, who commanded the Texas Union Army and became Radical Reconstruction Governor of Texas.

General Slaughter, realizing that the Benavides-Ford dispute was threatening the future of the Confederacy on the Rio Grande, alleviated the problem by dividing the Rio Grande frontier into two sub-districts. Ford was to command the lower valley while Benavides was given command of the area from Rio Grande City upriver to Eagle Pass.[260]

On December 1, 1864, Colonel Benavides appointed his brother-in-law, John Z. Leyendecker, as assistant quartermaster of his regiment. Leyendecker, who had come to Lareado from Germany after the Mexican War, had married Andrea Benavides in 1857. When Andrea died at the beginning of the war, Captain Leyendecker had married Julianita, elder sister of his first wife.[261]

As the war in the lower Rio Grande Valley dragged into its final year, the morale of the Confederate Army continued its already rapid deterioration. The morale problem was partially due to the inability of the Confederate government to supply the troops in the valley. Many of the men had little if any ammunition. Refugio Benavides even sent a note to headquarters refusing to "send a single man to the front" until he received ammunition.[262]

In January many of the Tejanos were reported to be "without pants" and were "going about camp in their drawers."[263] When the winter of 1864-1865 proved to be terribly cold, even for the lower valley, the men began to make "application to go home after clothing." Over 100 men in Benavides' Regiment simply rode out of camp and headed for home. On January 31, 1865, ten men deserted from Captain Trevino's Company, taking with them the best mounts in the company. The men were reported to be on their way to their homes near San Antonio. Captain T. E. Carter wrote Ford of the desertions: "I have done the best Col. that I know how with this Mexican Company and thought that I had them pretty near satisfied until recently. The prime cause of this dissatisfaction is their Capt. being gone. They have also suffered from lack of clothing."[264] Many companies, due to the large number of desertions, were consolidated and in some instances reconsolidated. By February, 1865, General James E. Slaughter, who had moved his headquarters to Fort Brown, reported, however, that ten of Benavides' companies were still in the field.[265]

The only entertainment the Tejanos were granted came with their visits to Brownsville. Here in the saloons the men gambled, drank, brawled, and frequently whored. In November, 1864, Private Francisco Gomez of Captain Trevino's company, while drinking in one of the gambling houses on the main plaza, became involved in an argument with a Lieutenant Ransom. From the available evidence it appears that both men were drinking heavily. The drunken lieutenant was standing at a Monte table when Private Gomez for some undisclosed reason shoved the lieutenant. "God damn you! If you run against me anymore, I will shoot you!" Ransom screamed at the private.[266] The private strode to within a few feet of Ransom and pounded his chest as if to challenge the lieutenant. Ransom, who had already drawn his pistol, without hesitation shot Gomez in the left side. The private fell upon the dirty floor of the gambling hall and within minutes expired.

A board of officers was called to investigate the incident. The shooting and subsequent inquiry appear to have had racial overtones, so much so that the incident was said to have thrown the entire community into confusion. All of those who testified at the hearing were Anglos as were those who sat on the board of inquiry. At the hearing it was reported that Gomez "was a gambler, a very overbearing man and quarrelsome."[267] The court, finding "that the killing of the deceased" resulted from an "assault made upon him," set the lieutenant free.

In May a near riot broke out in the Confederate command at Rio Grande City. Part of Benavides' regiment had gathered around the commissary warehouse at Ringgold Barracks "demanding clothing and making threats." Captain Cristobal Benavides, in command of the post, strode onto the scene, assured the men that they would get their clothing if they would remain calm, and quietly turned to Captain Callaghan and ordered that the clothing be disbursed in an orderly manner.[268]

Many of Benavides' officers were forced for financial reasons to impress cotton and other supplies. The seizure of hay from the numerous Tejano ranchitos in the Ringgold Barracks vicinity caused considerable tension and mistrust between the civilians and the military. Further trouble came when the mutilated bodies of two Confederate soldiers from Captain Davis' company were found outside of Rio Grande City. In a revengeful reprisal three soldiers from the company angrily shot two Tejano boys suspected of the crime. An investigation of the incident failed to prove who had committed the bloody crime although three soldiers of Captain Davis' company were held under suspicion. Colonel Santos Benavides admitted that he was "so incensed . . . upon hearing of the barbarous act" that had "he discovered the guilty party" he "would have hesitated in giving them a trial."[269] Answering a letter critical of his leadership, Benavides admitted that large numbers of his men were indulging in "gambling and drinking" but argued that the men were greatly in need of food, clothing, and forage for their animals. The lack of clothing continued to be one of the most serious problems facing the regiment. One company on the Rio Grande was said to have been "almost naked" and in bad need of shirts, drawers, socks, and particularly pants. Many of them were simply refusing to do service in their "nude condition."[270]

The end of the war came late to South Texas. More than a month after General Robert E. Lee surrendered his Army of Northern Virginia to Ulysses S. Grant at Appomattox Court House, Virginia, the last land battle of the war was fought in the lower valley. On May 13, 1865, in the Battle of Palmito Ranch, some sixteen miles east of Brownsville, Ford attacked and routed a Federal force who, upon hearing of the news from Virginia, had come to take possession of Brownsville. Some say that it was from his prisoners that Ford first learned of the events in far-off Virginia. A few Tejanos fought on both sides in the Battle of Palmito Ranch. Almost all of Benavides' regiment, however, were upriver.

Despite the Confederate victory at Palmito Ranch, hopes of holding Brownsville were futile. A pessimistic realization that the end had come at last descended over the Brownsville Confederate command. Only General James E. Slaughter dreamed of keeping the army intact, even in Mexico if feasible. Slaughter crossed into Matamoros where he sold the Confederate cannon to Imperialist General Tomas Mejia for $20,000 in silver pesos, money badly needed for the army. Furious at Slaughter, Ford had the general arrested when he recrossed into Brownsville and refused to release him until the money was turned over to Ford, $4,000 of which Rip kept for himself.

In the few days that remained before the Federals entered Brownsville, matters became even more chaotic. The once proud Confederate Rio Grande Army now melted away. The Rebels, many of them hungry and in rags, began to desert in groups of twenty or thirty and make their way northward through the brush country to the Nueces River and eventually home.

General Slaughter, with a small group of Mexican-Texans as a body guard, fled upriver to join Santos Benavides at Rio Grande City. General Slaughter brought word that the Federals had entered Brownsville and had put a large part of the Mexican-Texan populace to cleaning the streets under heavy guard of the Sixty-Second Colored Infantry.

Benavides, loyal to the end, was determined that conditions in his regiment did not become as anarchic as they had at Brownsville. From Rio Grande City the colonel wrote his brother-in-law, Captain John Z. Leyendecker: "Undoubtedly our war is already terminated. I am doing all I can here in order to protect the interests of the government and also of my soldiers. Have brother Refugio keep all in order; that he not permit the soldiers to rob under any circumstances, that they leave the poor ranchers to sell their calves to earn a living; that they do not obstruct order and justice; that I will do the same as the only one in command of the line."[271] With what little money that was left, Benavides gave each of his officers thirty pesos, said good bye, and watched as many of his men departed for points north. Colonel Benavides, too, left for home, riding upriver to Laredo to prepare for a new life which would come with the inevitable arrival of Federal bayonets.

Finally in July, 1865, Santos, who at the time was on a scouting expedition against Indians, received a polite letter from Union officers in Brownsville directing that he sign and forward his parole papers. The end of the Civil War had come to Santos Benavides, his two courageous brothers, and the Mexican-Texans of the Lone Star State. Tejanos had been among the first to take up arms for the Confederacy and were among the last to surrender. Even in defeat a sense of dignity and honor abounded.

Helen Yturri.

Gravestone of Capt. José Rafael de la Garza
San Fernando # 1, San Antonio, Texas.

Appendix A

CONFEDERATES

Very little is known about many of the *Tejanos* and *Mexicanos* who fought in the Civil War. This irreplaceable historical gap exists because much of the relevant data has been lost, is confusing and contradictory, never existed, or is in disarray. Even when individuals can be identified, they may appear on only one set of records. Often this lone reference, especially in militia units, is too vague to even determine the soldier's exact name. To complicate the work of researchers, many of the Anglo recruiting officers and regimental adjutants during the war were totally ignorant of Spanish. The fact that a large number of the *Tejanos* and *Mexicanos* were illiterate further complicated accurate record keeping. In many of the records, an individual's name may be spelled several different ways. For example, Emilio Cabello or Caballero, a private in Company A of Col. Samuel G. Ragsdale's Battalion of Texas Cavalry, is listed as Carello, Carbele, Corbello, Corvello, and Cordello. With little or no knowledge of Spanish, Anglo recruiting officers tended to spell the names of *Tejanos* and *Mexicanos* phonetically. If there appeared to be a consistent spelling of a soldier's name throughout the records, that spelling has been retained here. When names were obviously misspelled, the soldier's name has been corrected.

Much of the information relating to *Tejanos* and *Mexicanos* that follows is from the National Archives in Washington, D.C., and the Texas State Archives in Austin. A large part of the information from the National Archives has been consolidated into "Compiled Service Records of Confederate Soldiers Who Served in Organizations From the State of Texas," which is part of Record Group 109 and available on 445 rolls of microfilm. These compiled service records contain personal papers as well as data extracted from muster rolls, lists of deserters, promotions, hospital records, court martial charges, furloughs, medical certificates, orders, pay or clothing records, enlistment papers, discharge certificates, prisoner of war records, and various other records including lists of killed and wounded that are also part of Record Group 109. Individuals seeking a particular individual, but not knowing the unit in which the soldier served, may want to first consult the forty-one rolls of microfilm, "Index to Compiled Service Records of Confederate Soldiers Who Served in Organizations From the State of Texas," which is also available from the National Archives. Among the most valuable records relating to Confederate *Tejanos* and *Mexicanos* at the Texas State Archives are some 1,500 muster rolls, many of which contain the names of *Tejanos* and *Mexicanos* who served in militia units not found in the Compiled Service Records. Some records, especially muster rolls, give the soldier's age and even the individual's place of birth. This information, if known, is provided in the data that follow.

The following compilation contains the names of all known *Tejano* and *Mexicano* soldiers who served the Confederacy. All non-Spanish surnamed individuals, 85,000 or more, have been omitted. Soldiers are listed alphabetically, followed by a brief service records that includes the soldier's rank, company, and regiment or battalion in which the soldier served. In instances of reduction in rank, the man's highest rank is listed.

If it is certain that a soldier served in two or more companies, regiments, battalions, or brigades, that information is also provided. For example, many of the *Tejanos* and *Mexicanos* who enlisted in Col. Alfred M. Hobby's 8th Texas Infantry later served in a regiment commanded by Col. Santos Benavides. Men who joined Col. Philip N. Luckett's 3d Texas Infantry early in the war later enrolled in Benavides' Regiment as well. So did a number of *Tejanos* and *Mexicanos* who were in Col. James Duff's 33d Texas Cavalry. Undoubtedly, in some instances the same soldier may be listed twice. For example, Benino García who enlisted in the militia in Cameron County early in the war may well be the same individual who later enrolled in Company E of the 8th Infantry. Similarly, it is likely that Francisco Leal, who enlisted in Gray's Militia Company from Bexar County, later became a sergeant in Company F of the 3d Texas Infantry. If there is any doubt, however, a separate listing is given. If an individual served in the Texas Militia, the county where he enlisted and, in some instances, the town, is given. If the soldier deserted, that information, including date, if known, is also provided, although in many instances the date reflects the time when the individual was recorded as missing rather than the actual date of desertion. Some enlistment records gave the occupation of the soldier and this information is included also, although a disproportionate number of Hispanic—surnamed soldiers appear to be listed as laborers. It is very possible that *Tejanos* and *Mexicanos* may have given their occupation as "labrador" (an independent rancher or farmer) and were listed as "laborers." Such mistakes in translation were common in Texas at the time, especially in census records.

With reference to Hispanic surnamed soldiers, the sixteen volume *Roster of Confederate Soldiers, 1861-1865* (Wilmington, N.C.: Broadfoot Pub. Co., 1996) contains thousands of misspellings, inaccuracies, and omissions and was of limited value.

Undoubtedly, the names of many *Tejanos* and *Mexicanos* who fought in the war have been lost to history. This loss is especially true in militia units on the frontier where muster rolls and other records were lost and where record keeping appears to have been minimal. In fact, it appears that muster rolls of several companies either did not survive the war or were lost or destroyed afterwards.

ABBREVIATIONS USED:

Pvt	private	Ags	Aguacalientes
Cpl	corporal	Coah	Coahuila
Sgt	sergeant	Gto	Guanajuato
Lt	lieutenant	Jal	Jalisco
Capt	captain	La	Louisiana
Maj	major	NL	Nuevo León
Col	colonel	NM	New Mexico
b	born	Pue	Puebla
k	killed	SLP	Sam Luis Potosi
d	deserted	Tamps	Tamaulipas
POW	prisoner of war	Chi	Chihuahua
Co	company		
Reg	regiment		
Brig	brigade		
Batt'n	battalion		
Inf	infantry		
Cav	cavalry		
Cty	county		
Mus	musician		
Pct	precinct		
TST	Texas State Troops		
TM	Texas Militia		

A

ABITO
  Luciano; Pvt, C, 8th Tex Inf.
ÁBREGO
  A; Pvt, A, 17th Brig, TM, Montgomery Cty.
  A; Pvt, A, 4th Tex Inf.
  Higinio; Pvt, C, Ragsdale's Batt'n of Tex Cav.
ACEVEDO
  Gerardo; 20, Pvt, 3d Tex Inf, b San Luis Potosí, SLP, d April 29, 1862.
ACKES
  Felicito; Pvt, C, Ragsdale's Batt'n of Tex Cav.
ACOSTA
  Atanacio; Pvt, C, Ragsdale's Batt'n of Tex Cav.
  D; Pvt, D, 20th Tex Inf.
  Domingo; 22, Pvt, G, 3d Tex Inf.
  Francisco; Pvt, A, 17th Tex Cav.
  Joseph; Pvt, H, 16th Tex Inf.
  Juan Feliciano; A, 17th Tex. Inf.
  T; C, 2d Inf, TST
ADEX
  Jesús; Pvt, A, Ragsdale's Batt'n of Tex Cav.

AGUILAR
- Agapito; 25, Pvt, C, 8th Tex Inf, d, rejoined, Dec 1863; Benavides' Reg.
- Alejo; Pvt, Zapata's Co, TST, Pct 10 (San Diego), Nueces Cty.
- Doroteo; 8th Tex Field Battery.
- Elijio; 27, Pvt, E, 8th Tex Inf.
- Guadalupe; 22, Pvt, H, 33d Tex Cav; A, Benavides' Reg.
- Jesús; Pvt, A, Ragsdale's Batt'n of Tex Cav; D, Benavides' Reg.
- Librado; 24, Pvt, I, 33d Tex Cav; Cpl, I, Benavides' Reg.
- Luciano; Pvt, C, 8th Tex Inf.
- Nepomuceno; Pvt, Treviño's Co of Partisan Rangers.
- Ramón; Pvt, 14th Field Art.

AGUIRRE
- Juan; Pvt, F, 3d Tex Inf, d May 24, 1862.

ALANÍS
- Domingo: McNeel's Coast Guards.
- Eduardo; 22, Pvt, A, 3d Tex Inf, d December 18, 1861.
- Esteban; 34, Pvt, I, 33d Tex Cav; B, Benavides' Reg.
- Jorge; A, 1st Tex Cav.

ALBIAR
- Juan; Pvt, C, Ragsdale's Batt'n of Tex Cav.

ALCALÁ
- Teodoro; 23, Pvt, C, 8th Tex Inf, b Mex, laborer.

ALCANTAR
- Pedro; Pvt, A, 8th Tex Inf, d Jan 1864 (Indianola), rejoined March 14, 1864.

ALCANTE
- Antonio; Bugler, C, Benavides' Reg.
- Jesús; 1st Sgt, Minute Men, TM, Starr Cty.

ALDAMA
- Dimas; 31, Pvt, G, 3d Tex Inf, d Dec 6, 1862.

ALDERETE
- Ascencio; Jr 2d Lt, 30th Brig, TM, Pct. 5, Wilson Cty.
- Jesús; 1st Lt, 30th Brig, TM, Pct. 3 & 4, Wilson Cty.
- Pablo B; Capt, C, Ragsdale's Batt'n of Tex Cav; H, Baird's Reg, Arizona Brig.
- Rafael; Capt, Jeff Davis HG, 29th Brig, TM, Refugio Cty.
- Trinidad; 1st Lt, Jeff Davis HG, 29th Brig, TM, Refugio Cty.

ALDÓN
- Carlos; 23, Pvt, F, 3d Tex Inf.

ALEGRÍA
- Lucas; 25, Pvt, I, 33d Tex Cav; B, Benavides' Reg.
- Poniciano; 19, Pvt, I, 33d Tex Cav; B, Benavides' Reg.

ALFARO
- Manuel; 38, Pvt, Gray's Co, TM, 30th Brig, Pct 5, Bexar Cty.

ALGUATE
- Luis N; Pvt, A, 8th Tex Inf.

ALEMÁN
- Luis; Pvt, Rhodes' Co, 3rd Batt'n, Tex Cav.

ALMANZA
- [no first name given], Pvt, F, 3d Tex Inf.

ALMENDAREZ (Almendaris)
- Ambrosio; 21, Pvt, F, 3d Tex Inf, b Chihuahua, Chi, discharged May 28, 1862

ALVARADO
- Bacilio; Bugler, I, Benavides' Reg.
- Frank; 25, D, 2d Tex Mounted Rifles, d 4 Jan 1862.
- Nicolás; 4th Sgt, Jeff Davis HG, 29th Brig, TM, Refugio Cty.

ÁLVAREZ
- Luis; Mus, 2d Tex Mounted Rifles (Mesilla, NM).
- Luis; Pvt, I, Benavides' Reg.
- Luis; Pvt, 8th Tex Field Battery.
- Nicolás; Pvt, 21, I, 16th Tex Inf.
- Pedro; Pvt, 15th Field Battery.
- Ponoseno; 20, Pvt, D, 2d Tex Mounted Rifles.
- Teodoro; 18, Pvt, A, Ragsdale's Batt'n of Tex Cav.

AMADO
- Domingo; 18, Pvt, B, 29th Brig, TM, Refugio Cty.

AMADOR
- Enemincir [?]; Pvt, 36th Tex Cav
- Hervacio [Horacio?]; Pvt, E, 32d Tex Cav.
- Hervacio [Horacio?]; Pvt, Maverick's Co, TMV, Wilson Cty; E, 36th Tex Cav.
- J; Pvt, C, Baird's Reg, Arizona Brig.
- Jesús; 30, Pvt, E, 8th Tex Inf.
- Juan; 28, Pvt, E, 8th Tex Inf.
- Ruiz; Pvt, B, 2d Tex Mounted Rifles.

AMAYA
- Anastacio; Bugler, B & D, Benavides Reg.

ANAYA
- Jesús; Pvt, B, Ragsdale's Batt'n of Tex Cav.

ANCIRA
- G; Pvt, Teel's Co, TST.

ANDRADE
- Andrés; 30, Pvt, C, 8th Tex Inf, disability discharge (chronic rheumatism and syphilis) May 15, 1863 (San Antonio), b San Fernando, Tamps.

ANZALDÚA
- Bartolo; 3rd Cpl, Engledow's Co, 29th Brig, TM, Nueces Cty.
- Pablo; Pvt, F, 2d Tex Cav.
- Pedro; Cpl, K, 33d Tex Cav.
- Ramón; 40, Pvt, A, 24th Brig, TST, Victoria Cty.

APODACA
- Valentín; 28, Pvt, D, 2d Tex Mounted Rifles.

AQUINO
- Torsobio; Pvt, C, 8th Tex Inf; 5th Sgt, C, Benavides' Reg.

ARAGÓN
- Juan; Pvt, C, Baird's Reg, Arizona Brig.

ARAIS
- Lorenzo; E, Pvt, 3d Tex Inf.

ARALES
- Juan; Pvt, C, Ragsdale's Batt'n of Tex Cav.

ARÁMBULA
- Faustino; Pvt, F, 1st Tex Cav; Zapata's Co, TST, Pct 10 (San Diego), Nueces Cty.
- Fernando; 21, Pvt, A, Ragsdale's Batt'n of Tex Cav.

ARÁMBULA [continued]
    Lorenzo; 20, Pvt, C, 8th Tex Inf, b Mex, laborer.
    Luis; Pvt, C, 8th Tex Inf.
ARCE
    Pascual; 38, Pvt, Watkins' Co, 3d Frontier Dist, Uvalde Cty.
ARCHULETA
    Ignacio; Pvt, Gray's Co, TM, Pct 5, Bexar Cty.
ARCIAGA
    Juan; Pvt, F, 3d Tex Inf, d Sept 6, 1862.
ARCINIEGA
    Gregorio; Pvt, B, 33d Tex Cav.
ARELLANO
    Cristóbal; 3d Sgt, Bustillo's Co, Bexar Cty; Sgt, F, 3d Tex Inf, disability discharge Feb 1864.
ARENAS
    Martín; 24, Pvt, I, 8th Tex Inf, b Mex.
ARISPE
    Jesús; 18, Pvt, Bustillo's Co, Bexar Cty.
    Ygnacio; 45, Pvt, Bustillo's Co, Bexar Cty.
ARISTA
    Manuel; Pvt, C, 16th Tex Inf.
ARMENDÁRIZ
    Sabino; Pvt, Gray's Co, 30th Brig, TM, Pct 5, Bexar Cty.
ARNICA
    A; Pvt, C, 4th Tex Cav.
AROCHA
    A; Pvt, E, 33d Tex Cav.
    B; E, 33d Tex Cav.
    Alejandro; Pvt, Treviño's Co of Partisan Rangers.
    Benigno; Pvt, E, 33d Tex Cav; C, Benavides' Reg.
    Celso; 24, Pvt, Gray's Co, 30th Brig, TM, Pct 5, Bexar Cty.
    José Antonio; 28, Pvt, Gray's Co, TM, 30th Brig, Pct 5, Bexar Cty.
    Lino; 46, Pvt, Gray's Co, 30th Brig, TM, Pct 5, Bexar Cty.
    Nepomuceno; 18, Pvt, Bustillo's Co, Bexar Cty; B, 2d Tex Mounted Rifles.
ARREDONDO
    Canuto; Pvt, B, Benavides' Reg.
    Cristóbal; Sgt, F, 3d Tex Inf.
    J; Pvt, C, 8th Tex Inf.
    Joaquín; Pvt, D, Benavides' Reg.
    Juan; 23, Pvt, H, 33d Tex Cav; A, Benavides' Reg.
    Juan; Pvt, Zapata's Co, TST, Pct 10 (San Diego), Nueces Cty.
ARREOLA (Ariola)
    Andrés; Pvt, F, 2d Tex Mounted Rifles.
    JE; Pvt, C, 16th Tex Inf.
    John; Pvt, Pedernales Cav, TM, Grooms Springs, Blanco Cty.
    Juan Guadalupe; Pvt, A, 17th Tex Cav.
    Luis; Pvt, B, 2d Tex Mounted Rifles; Pvt, I, Benavides' Reg.
    M; Pvt, K, 16th Tex Inf.
    Máximo; Pvt, Pedernales Cav, TM, Grooms Springs, Blanco Cty.
    Tomás; Pvt, D, 1st Tex Cav; B, 2d Tex Mounted Rifles.

ARTEAGA
   Florencio; 22 Pvt, 3d Tex Inf, b Monterrey, NL.
ÁVALOS
   Gabino; 22, Pvt, H, 3d Tex Inf, d May 8, 1863.
   Juan; Pvt, C, Ragsdale's Batt'n of Tex Cav.
AVEY
   Octavio; Pvt, B, Ragsdale's Batt'n of Tex Cav.
ÁVILA
   Juan; Pvt, F, 3d Tex Inf, d Jan 26, 1862.
   Luciano; 22, Pvt, C, 8th Tex Inf.
AVILÉS
   Benigno; 18, Pvt, D, 2d Tex Mounted Rifles.

B

BACA
   Loreto; 20, Pvt, H, 33d Tex Cav; A, Benavides' Reg.
   Miguel JM; Pvt, I, Benavides' Reg.
   Práxides; 4th Cpl, A, Benavides' Reg.
   Ylario; 24, Pvt, I, 33d Tex Cav.
BALDERAS
   Francisco; Pvt, I, 33d Tex Cav.
   Manuel; Pvt, B, Ragsdale's Batt'n of Tex Cav.
   Rafael; Pvt, Hynes' Co, TM, Bee Cty, ranchero.
   Ygnacio; Pvt, Zapata's Co, TST, Pct 10 (San Diego), Nueces Cty.
BALDEZ; see Valdez.
BALLE; see Valle.
BALLES; see Valles.
BALLÍ
   Juan; 27, Pvt, Thomas' Co of Partisan Rangers.
BALTAZAR
   Carlos; 27, Pvt, Bustillo's Co, Bexar Cty.
   Domingo; Pvt, H, 33d Tex Cav; A, Benavides' Reg.
BALVERDE; see Valverde.
BANDA
   Anacleto; 24, Pvt, G, 3d Tex Inf, d April 2, 1862.
   Juan; Pvt, Treviño's Co of Partisan Rangers.
   Magdaleno; 27, Pvt, Bustillo's Co, Bexar Cty.
BARAJAS
   Claudio; Pvt, E, 8th Tex Inf.
   Juan; Pvt, Engledow's Co, 29th Brig, TM, Nueces Cty.
BARELA
   Alfonso; 30, Pvt, E, 8th Tex Inf, CM, Jan 13, 1863, for neglect of duty,
      b Mex, laborer.
   Antonio; conscript, Pcts 1 & 6, Victoria Cty.
   Marcelino; Pvt, C, Ragsdale's Batt'n of Tex Cav.
   Timoteo; 28, Pvt, C, 8th Tex Inf, b Mex, laborer.
BARRA
   Julián; Pvt, Gray's Co, TM, Pct 5, Bexar Cty.
BARRAGÁN
   H; Pvt, Medina Guards, 40th Brig, TM, Bexar Cty.

BARRALES
   [Uncertain first name]; 18, Pvt, C, 3d Tex Inf, b Zacatecas, Zac.
BARRERA
   AM; Capt, 30th Brig, TM, Pct. 1, Bexar Cty.
   Antonio; 25, Pvt, Watkins' Co, 3d Frontier Dist, Uvalde Cty.
   Carlos; Pvt, F, 3d Tex Inf.
   J; Pvt, K, 33d Tex Cav.
   Jacinto; 37, Pvt, Thomas' Co of Partisan Rangers.
   Jesús; 22, Pvt, A, 3d Tex Inf, disability discharge Sept 7, 1861.
   Jesús; 20, Pvt, C, 8th Tex Inf; C, Benavides' Reg.
   John; Pvt, Duff's Co, Bexar Cty.
   José María; Pvt, A, Benavides' Reg.
   José Ríos; 28, Pvt, I, 8th Tex Inf, b Tex.
   Juan; Sgt, F, 3d Tex Inf.
   Juan E; 30, 1st Sgt, H, 8th Tex Inf.
   M; Pvt, K, 33d Tex Cav.
BARRIENTOS
   Gabino; 18, Pvt, C & F, 3d Tex Inf, b Monterrey, NL.
   L; Pvt, C, 8th Tex Inf.
   Salvador; Pvt, Rhodes' Co, 3d Batt'n of Tex Cav.
BARRIO
   José; Pvt, Arizona Rangers; George's Co, Herbert's Batt'n of Arizona Cav.
   Rafael; Pvt, Coast Guards, 32d Brig, TM, Cameron Cty.
BARRIOS
   Cornelio; Sgt, A, Ragsdale's Batt'n of Tex Cav.
BARRÓN
   Carlos; 33, Pvt, C, 8th Tex Inf.
BASÁN; see Bazán
BAUTISTA
   Juan; Pvt, Teel's Co, TST; B, 2d Tex Mounted Rifles.
BAZAN
   Alejo; Cpl, Thomas' Co of Partisan Ranggers.
   Bernardino; Pvt, Minute Men, TM, Starr Cty.
   Desiderio; Pvt, Minute Men, TM, Starr Cty.
   Francisco; Pvt, Zapata's Co, TST, Pct 10 (San Diego), Nueces Cty.
   Juan; Pvt, I, 33d Tex Cav.
   Juan; Pvt, Engledow's Co, 29th Brig, TM, Nueces Cty.
BECERRA
   Francisco; 2d Lt, C, 3d Tex Inf.
BELA; see Vela.
BELTRÁN
   Aniseto; 25, Pvt, C, 8th Tex Inf, b Mex, laborer.
   Jesus; C, Ragsdale's Batt'n of Tex Cav.
   José; 19, Pvt, C, 3d Tex Inf, d Sept 18, 1862.
   Manuel; Pvt, C, Ragsdale's Batt'n of Tex Cav.
   Stephen; Pvt, 4th Tex Field Battery.
BENAVIDES (Benavídez)
   Atilano; 24, Pvt, H, 33d Tex Cav.
   Cristóbal; 23, 2d Lt, H, 33d Tex Cav; Capt, A, Benavides' Reg.
   D; I, Borden's Reg of Tex Cav.

BENAVIDES (Benavídez) *[continued]*
    David; Pvt, Giddings' Batt'n of Tex Cav.
    F; Pvt, Teel's Co, TST; B, 2d Tex Mounted Rifles.
    Lorenzo; 40, Pvt, H, 33d Tex Cav.
    Luis; 20, Pvt, H, 33d Tex Cav; A, Benavides' Reg.
    Pablo; 16, Mus & Pvt, C, 8th Tex Inf; C, Benavides' Reg, CM Jan 31, 1863 for sleeping while on guard.
    Pedro; 32, Pvt, F, 3d Tex Inf, d Dec 3, 1862.
    Refugio; 35, Capt, I, 33d Tex Cav; Benavides' Reg.
    Santos; 36, Capt, Benavides' Co, Tex Mounted Rifles; Maj, 33d Tex Cav; Col, Benavides' Reg.
BERBÁN
    José María; Pvt, Medina Guards, 40th Brig, TM, Bexar Cty.
    Pascual; Pvt, Medina Guards, 40th Brig, TM, Bexar Cty.
BERNAL
    Jesús; Pvt, D, Ragsdale's Batt'n of Tex Cav.
    Leandro; 19, 1st Sgt, F, 3d Tex Inf.
    Refugio; Sgt, Rhodes' Co, 3rd (Yager's) Tex Cav.
BERNALES
    Eulogio; Pvt, C, 3d Tex Inf, d May 16, 1862.
BLANCO
    Santos; 27, Pvt, B, 2nd Tex Mounted Rifles.
BOCA
    Miguel JM; Pvt, I, Benavides' Reg.
BOCANEGRA
    Longino; 18, Pvt, F, 3d Tex Inf, d Jan 30, 1862.
BONILLA
    Charles L; 24, Sgt, Littleton's Co, Ford's Reg.
BORREGO
    Secundino; 24, Pvt, C, 8th Tex Inf, b Mex, laborer.
BOTELLO
    Antonio; 22, Pvt, H, 33d Tex Cav; A, Benavides' Reg.
    Concepción; 25, Pvt, H, 33d Tex Cav; A, Benavides' Reg.
    Gabino; 26, Pvt, F, 3d Tex Inf, d Oct 7, 1861; H, 33d Tex Cav.
    Joseph; Pvt, B, 2d Tex Mounted Rifles.
    Marcos; 45, Pvt, H, 33d Tex Cav.
    Matildo; 25, Pvt, H, 33d Tex Cav.
    Víctor Jr; 23, Pvt, H, 33d Tex Cav; A, Benavides' Reg.
    Víctor Sr; 25, Pvt, H, 33d Tex Cav.
    Viviano; 25, Pvt, H, 33d Tex Cav; A, Benavides' Reg.
BRISEÑO
    Incarnación; Pvt, Medina Guards, 40th Brig, TM, Bexar Cty.
    Margarito; Pvt, B, Ragsdale's Batt'n of Tex Cav.
BRITO
    Gabino; Bugler, A, Ragsdale's Batt'n of Tex Inf.
    Nepomuceno; 30, Pvt, C, 3d Tex Inf, d Oct 15, 1861.
BUSTAMANTE
    Bensualdo; 19, Pvt, Littleton's Co, Ford's Reg.
    Forbio; 39, Pvt, Bustillo's Co, Bexar Cty; Cpl, C, Benavides' Reg.
    Hilario; Pvt, 3d Batt'n of Tex Cav.

BUSTAMANTE *[continued]*
    Lucas; Pvt, Rhodes' Co, 3d Batt'n of Tex Cav.
    Manuel; 23, Pvt, Bustillo's Co, Bexar Cty.
    Toribio; 31, Pvt, C, 8th Tex Inf.
BUSTILLO
    Clemente; Capt, Bustillo's Co, 30th Brig, TM, Bexar Cty.
    F; Pvt, Teel's Co, TST; B, 2d Tex Mounted Rifles.
BUSTILLOS
    Antonio; Pvt, K, 6th Tex Inf.

C

CABALLERO
    Andrés; Pvt, E, Benavides' Reg.
CABELLO
    Emilio; Pvt, A, Ragsdale's Batt'n of Tex Cav.
CABOS
    Frailan; 33, Pvt, C, 3d Tex Inf, d Dec 5, 1861.
CABRERA
    Magado; 23, Pvt, E, 8th Tex Inf, d Dec 3, 1863 (Victoria).
CABRILLO
    Antonio; Pvt, D, 8th Tex Inf.
CADENA
    Antonio; Pvt, Jeff Davis HG, 29th Brig, TM, Refugio Cty.
CALDERÓN
    Anselino; 20, Pvt, A, Ragsdale's Batt'n of Tex Cav.
    C; Pvt, Teel's Co, TST; B, 2d Tex Mounted Rifles.
    Luis; Pvt, 3d Batt'n of Tex Cav.
    N; Pvt, Teel's Co, TST; B, 2d Tex Mounted Rifles.
    Rafael; Cpl, Bustillo's Co, Bexar Cty.
    Ramón; 32, Pvt, B, 2d Tex Mounted Rifles; Sgt, F, 3d Tex Inf.
CALLAHAN
    Juan; 19, Pvt, A, Ragsdale's Batt'n of Tex Cav.
CALVILLO
    Francisco; 22, Pvt, B, 2d Tex Mounted Rifles, POW, paroled at Fort Union, NM, April 5, 1862.
    Francisco; Pvt, H, 8th Tex Inf, d Sept 12, 1862 (San Antonio).
CALZADO
    Toribio; 27, Pvt, C, 3d Tex Inf, b Matamoros, Tamps, d Nov 9, 1861.
CAMACHO
    Candelario: Pvt, Thodes' Co, 3rd Tex Cav.
CAMARGO
    Pedro; Bugler, I, Benavides' Reg.
    Ynés; Pvt, I, Benavides' Reg.
CAMPOS
    Antonio; Pvt, D, 9th Tex Cav.
    Julián; Pvt, B, Ragsdale's Batt'n of Tex Cav.
    Justo; Pvt, D, 17th Tex Inf.
CANALES
    JM; Pvt, Zapata's Co, TST, Pct 10 (San Diego), Nueces Cty.
    Mateo; 20, Pvt, H, 8th Tex Inf.

CANALES [continued]
　　Santiago; Pvt, Zapata's Co, TST, Pct 10 (San Diego), Nueces Cty.
CAÑAVERO
　　Antonio; 22, Pvt, D, 8th Tex Inf, d Dec 21, 1863 (Columbus).
CANO
　　Andrés; 28, Pvt, C, 3d Tex Inf, b Puebla, Pue, d Dec 11, 1861.
　　Encarnación; 33, Pvt, I, 33d Tex Cav; A, Ragsdale's Batt'n of Tex Cav.
　　José María; Pvt, 3d Batt'n of Tex Cav.
　　P; Pvt, H, 4th Tex Inf.
CANTÚ
　　Aciano; 18, Pvt, C, 8th Tex Inf, d March 28, 1863, rejoined Dec 31, 1863, b Mex, laborer.
　　Augustín; Pvt, F, 3d Tex Inf, d April 6, 1862.
　　D; 28, Pvt, G, 8th Tex Inf, d Nov 20, 1863 (Corpus Christi).
　　Domingo; Pvt, Jeff Davis HG, 29th Brig, TM, Refugio Cty.
　　Félix; Pvt, Jeff Davis HG, 29th Brig, TM, Refugio Cty.
　　Fernando; Pvt, Zapata's Co, TST, Pct 10 (San Diego), Nueces Cty.
　　Hilario; Rhodes' Co, 3d Batt'n.
　　Ignacio; Pvt, Zapata's Co, TST, Pct 10 (San Diego), Nueces Cty.
　　José; Pvt, G, 2nd Tex Mounted Rifles.
　　Juan; Pvt, Minute Men, TM, Starr Cty.
　　M; 29, Pvt, Teel's Co, TST; G, 8th Tex Inf.
　　Narciso; 36, Pvt, Coast Guards, 32d Brig, TM, Cameron Cty; Thomas' Co of Partisan Rangers.
　　Osario; Pvt, C, Benavides' Reg.
　　P; Pvt, G, 8th Tex Inf.
　　Victoriano; 29, Pvt, C, 8th Tex Inf, b Mex, laborer.
CAPO
　　H; I, 15th Tex Cav.
CARBAJAL
　　A; Pvt, E. Waller's Reg of Tex Cav.
　　Antonio; 24, Sgt, Thomas' Co of Partisan Rangers.
　　Francisco; 21, Pvt, E, 8th Tex Inf, disability discharge Dec 12, 1862.
　　Luis; 25, Pvt, B, 2d Tex Mounted Rifles.
　　Mesindo; 27, Pvt, H, 33d Tex Cav.
CÁRDENAS
　　Ceballos; Pvt, A, Ragsdale's Batt'n of Tex Cav.
　　Eluterio; 23, Pvt, C, 3d Tex Inf, d May 2, 1862; A, Ragsdale's Batt'n of Tex Cav.
　　Gabriel; 26, Pvt, I, 33d Tex Cav.
　　José; 38, Pvt, Duran's Co & Tom's Co, FST, Atascosa Cty.
　　Joseph; Pvt, K, 6th Tex Inf.
　　Joseph; Pvt, Medina Guards, 40th Brig, TM, Bexar Cty.
　　Juan; 19, Pvt, B, 2d Tex Mounted Rifles; Sgt, H, 8th Tex Inf; 1st Sgt, E, Benavides' Reg.
　　Nicanor; 18, Pvt, C, 8th Tex Inf.
　　Olegardo; Cpl, G, 37th Tex Cav.
　　Pablo; Pvt, D, Ragsdale's Batt'n of Tex Cav.
　　Rafael; 29, Pvt, H, 8th Tex Inf.
　　Rafael; 28, Pvt, B, 2d Tex Mounted Rifles.

CÁRDENAS [continued]
    Silvio; 23, Pvt, A, Ragsdale's Batt'n of Tex Cav; D, Benavides' Reg.
CARRASCO
    Félix; 22, Pvt, H, 33d Tex Cav; A, Benavides' Reg.
    Juan; Pvt, H. Mann's Reg of Tex Cav.
    Tranquilino; 20, Pvt, H, 33d Tex Cav; A, Benavides' Reg.
CARRILLO
    A; Pvt, F, 5th Tex Inf.
    Antonio; Pvt, D, 11th Batt'n of Tex Vols.
    Antonio; 38, Pvt, I, 33d Tex Cav.
    Joseph; 28, Pvt, B, 2d Tex Mounted Rifles, wounded in arm at
        Cañada Alamosa, NM.
CARRIÓN
    Joaquín; Pvt, C, Benavides' Reg.
    Segundo; Pvt, Zapata's Co, TST, Pct 10 (San Deigo), Nueces Cty.
CASANDRA
    G; Pvt, C, 8th Tex Inf, d Dec 6, 1863 (Victoria).
CASANOVA
    Cristiano; 46, Pvt, Tom's Co, TM, Atascosa Cty.
    Juan Antonio; 19, Pvt, H, 8th Tex Inf.
    Ventura; Pvt, Medina Guards, 40th Brig, TM, Bexar Cty.
CÁSARES (Cázares)
    Antonio; Pvt, A, 3d Batt'n of Tex Cav.
    Cecilio; Pvt, D, 36th Tex Cav.
    Francisco; Pvt, A, 3d Batt'n of Tex Cav.
CASAS
    Estanislado; 25, Pvt, A, 3d Tex Inf.
    Miguel; 30, Pvt, C, 3d Tex Inf, b Nuevo León, d Feb 12, 1862.
CASIANO
    Fermín; Pvt, Duff's Co, Bexar Cty.
    Ignacio Jr; Pvt, A, 33d Tex Cav.
    Simón; 25, Pvt, I, 33d Tex Cav; B, Benavides' Reg.
CASILLAS
    Santiago; Pvt, Medina Guards, 40th Brig, TM, Bexar Cty.
    Santos; Pvt, C, Benavides' Reg.
CASTAÑEDA
    Carlos; Pvt, 3d Batt'n of Tex Cav.
    Desiderio; Pvt, 3d Batt'n of Tex Cav.
    Juan; Pvt, 3d Batt'n of Tex Cav.
    Juan; 38, Pvt, Thomas' Co of Partisan Rangers.
    T; Pvt, Treviño's Co of Texas Cav.
CASTAÑO
    Severo; 20, Pvt, Bustillo's Co, Bexar Cty; A & F, 3d Tex Inf.
CASTAÑON
    J; Pvt, Treviño's Co of Partisan Rangers.
    Juan; Pvt, C, Benavides' Reg.
    Luis; 2d Sgt, Duran's Co, FST, Atascosa Cty.
    Luis; Pvt, Medina Guards, 40th Brig, TM, Bexar Cty.
    Simón; Pvt, Medina Guards, 40th Bri, TM, Bexar Cty.

CASTELLANO
- T; Pvt, Treviño's Co of Tex Cav.
- Tomás; Pvt, F, 3d Tex Inf, d Nov 30, 1862.

CASTILLERO
- B; Pvt, Treviño's Co of Partisan Rangers.

CASTILLO
- Alcario; Cpl, B, Ragsdale's Batt'n of Tex Cav.
- Cecilio; Pvt, Medina Guards, 40th Brig, TM, Bexar Cty.
- Cristóbal; 25, Pvt, H, 33d Tex Cav.
- Faustino; Pvt, Jeff Davis HG, 29th Brig, TM, Refugio Cty.
- John; Pvt, 15th Tex Field Batt'n.
- José; 25, Pvt, I, 8th Tex Inf.
- José María; Pvt, E, 8th Tex Inf.
- Nicomedes; 28, Pvt, Thomas' Co of Partisan Rangers.
- Priciliano; Pvt, C, 3d Tex Inf, d Dec 9, 1861.
- Refugio; 20, Pvt, D, 3d Tex Inf, b San Fernando, Tamps.
- Refugio; Pvt, Engledow's Co, 29th Brig, TM, Nueces Cty.
- Serapio; 22, Pvt, H, 33d Tex Cav.
- Severiano; 19, Pvt, C, 8th Tex Inf; C, Benavides' Reg.

CASTILLÓN
- Severo; 22, Pvt, I, 8th Tex Inf, d Sept 15, 1862 (Corpus Christi), rejoined Dec 17, 1862, d Feb 14, 1863 (Corpus Christi), b Tex.

CASTRO
- Amedio; Pvt, 8th Tex Field Battery.
- C; Pvt, F, 2nd Tex Mounted Rifles.
- F; Pvt, Teel's Co, TST; B, 2d Tex Mounted Rifles.
- JF; 1st Lt, H, Baird's Reg, Arizona Brig.
- Jacob; B, 18th Tex Cav.
- Jesús P; 20, Pvt, C, 8th Tex Inf.
- Jesús T; 20, Jr 2d Lt, C, Ragsdale's Batt'n of Tex Cav.
- José María; Pvt, E, 8th Tex Inf.
- Joseph T; 21, Jr 2d Lt, F, Benavides' Reg, d Oct 16, 1862 (Corpus Christi).
- Miguel; Pvt, F, 3d Tex Inf, d Sept 16, 1862.
- Nepomuceno; Sgt, 3d Batt'n of Tex Cav.
- V; Pvt, Treviño's Co of Partisan Rangers.
- Vicente; Pvt, D, 8th Tex Inf.

CAVAZOS
- Antonio; Pvt, 4th Tex Field Battery.
- Dimas; Pvt, F, 3d Tex Inf, d June 19, 1862.
- Lucas; 35, Pvt, 3d Tex Inf, b Reynosa, Tamps, d May 2, 1862.
- Nepomuceno; Sgt, Rhodes' Co, 3rd (Yager's) Tex Cav.

CEBALLOS
- Antonio; 24, Pvt, D, 2d Tex Mounted Rifles.
- Antonio; Pvt, F, 3rd Tex Cav.

CELESTINO
- Charles D; Sgt, D, 2nd Tex Inf.

CERDA
- Antonio; Pvt, Rhodes' Co, 3d Batt'n of Tex Cav.
- Blas; Pvt, B, 33d Tex Cav.
- Eugenio; 30, Pvt, H, 33d Tex Cav; A, Benavides' Reg.

CERDA [continued]
    Gregorio; Pvt, Coast Guards, 32d Brig, TM, Cameron Cty.
    Jesús; Pvt, Zapata's Co, TST, Pct 10 (San Diego), Nueces Cty.
    José; 24, Pvt, Bustillo's Co, Bexar Cty.
    Ramón; Pvt, Treviño's Co of Partisan Rangers.
CERVANTES
    Casanio; 25, I, 8th Tex Inf, b. Tex.
    Juan; 27, Pvt, H, 8th Tex Inf; Cpl, E, Benavides' Cav.
CERVERA
    Gastón; Pvt, I, 8th Tex Inf.
    Juan; Pvt, Jeff Davis HG, 29th Brig, TM, Refugio Cty.
    Manuel; 24, Pvt, H, 8th Tex Inf, d March 63.
CEVALLOS
    Pedro; 31, Capt, F, 3d Tex Inf, resigned Nov 14, 1863.
CHACÓN
    Carlos; Pvt, Gray's Co, TM, Pct 5, Bexar Cty.
CHAIRES
    C; Pvt, Treviño's Co of Partisan Rangers.
CHAPA
    Bernando; 33, Pvt, Gray's Co, TM, 30th Brig, Pct 5, Bexar Cty; B, Benavides' Reg.
    Francisco; 24, Pvt, H, 8th Tex Inf.
CHARO
    Nicolás; 24, Pvt & Cpl, H, 33d Tex Cav; Sgt, A, Benavides' Reg.
CHAVANA
    Albino; Pvt, C, Benavides' Reg.
    Stephen [Esteban]; Pvt, A, 11th Tex Inf.
CHAVARRÍA
    José M; Pvt, I, Benavides' Reg.
    Manuel; 25, Pvt, Bustillo's Co, Bexar Cty.
CHÁVEZ (Chaves)
    Bernardino; Pvt, I, Benavides' Reg.
    Erasmo J; 27, Bvt 2d Lt, H, 8th Tex Inf; 2d Lt, E, Benavides' Reg.
    Francisco; 27, Pvt, C, 8th Tex. Inf, d Dec 1862.
    Irineo; Pvt, C, Ragsdale's Batt'n of Tex Cav.
    Jesús; 33, Pvt, A, Ragsdale's Batt'n of Tex Cav.
    José M; Pvt, Mitchell's Minute Men, TM, Bexar Cty.
    Manuel; Pvt, 8th Tex Field Battery.
    Mariano; Pvt, C, Ragsdale's Batt'n of Tex Cav.
    Martín; Pvt, F, 3d Tex Inf.
    Pedro; Pvt, 8th Tex Field Battery.
CIPRIÁN
    Cecilio; Pvt, I, Benavides' Reg.
CIPRIANO
    Benigno; 27, Pvt, C, 8th Tex Cav.
    Pablo; 20, Pvt, H, 33d Tex Cav.
CISNEROS
    John; Pvt, Lamar HG, 29 Brig, TM, Refugio Cty.
COLCHADO
    Ylario; Pvt, B, Benavides' Reg.

CONDI
    Pablo; Pvt, 28, Thomas' Co of Partisan Rangers.
CONTRERAS
    Bacilio; 19, Pvt, C, 8th Tex Inf.
    José; 27, Pvt, C, 8th Tex Inf, d Dec 6, 1863 (Victoria).
    Manuel; 20, Cpl, C, 3d Tex Inf, d Jan 7, 1862.
    N; Pvt, 8th Tex Inf.
CÓRDOVA
    JD; Pvt, Eubank's Co B, Nacogdoches Cty.
    Morcal; Pvt, B, 2d Tex Inf.
    Ramón; Pvt, Eubank's Co B, Nacogdoches Cty.
CORONA
    Anastacio; 25, Pvt, Bustillo's Co, Bexar Cty.
    Antonio; Pvt, I, 33d Tex Cav.
    Anastacio; 25, Pvt, I, 33d Tex Cav; Sgt, B, Benavides' Reg.
    Hilario; 27, Pvt, H, 33d Tex Cav; A, Benavides' Reg.
    Paz; 18, Pvt, H, 33d Tex Cav; A, Benavides' Reg.
CORONADO
    Néstor; 35, Pvt, C & F, 3d Tex Inf, b Victoria, Tamps.
    Reyes; Pvt, B, Benavides' Reg.
CORRALES
    Susano; Pvt, Gray's Co, 30th Brig, TM, Pct 5, Bexar Cty.
CORTEZ
    Antonio; 23, Pvt, C & F, 3d Tex Inf, b Brownsville, Tex, d Feb 4, 1862.
    Carlos Hernández; Pvt, C, 3d Tex Inf.
    Eduardo; 16, Pvt, E, 8th Tex Inf, d Dec 3, 1863 (Victoria).
    H; Pvt, F, 2d Tex Inf.
    Jesús; Pvt, Teel's Co, TST; B, 2d Tex Mounted Rifles.
    Julián; 21, Pvt, Teel's Co, TST; B, 2d Tex Mounted Rifles; C, 8th Tex Inf.
    Julio; Pvt, 3d Batt'n Tex Cav.
    Simón; 40, Pvt, E, 8th Tex Inf.
CORTINAS
    JN; Pvt, Teel's Co, TST.
    José; Pvt, F, Benavides' Reg.
    José M; 23, Pvt, B, 2d Tex Mounted Rifles; D, Ragsdale's Batt'n of Tex Cav.
    Juan N; Pvt, F, 3d Tex Inf.
    Manuel; 19, Pvt, E, 8th Tex Inf, d Sept 3, 1862.
COSTA
    Joseph A; Sgt, G, 6th Tex Inf.
COY
    Alex; Pvt, C, 2d Tex Inf.
    Antonio; 30, Pvt, C, 8th Tex Inf; Benavides' Reg, b San Antonio, Tex, laborer.
    Charles P; Pvt, H, 22d Tex Cav.
    Jacob; Pvt, C, Benavides' Reg.
    Juan; 19, Bugler, H, 8th Tex Inf.
CRUZ
    Higinio; Mus, 2d Tex Mounted Rifles (Mesilla, NM).
    José María; Mus, 2d Tex Mounted Rifles (Mesilla, NM).
    JS; Pvt, C, 33d Tex Cav.

CRUZ [continued]
    Miguel; 28, Pvt, E, 8th Tex Inf, d Dec 3, 1863 (Victoria).
    Peter; Pvt, B, Baylor's Reg, Arizona Brig.
    Tomás; Pvt, Treviño's Co of Partisan Rangers.
    Vicente; Mus, 2d Tex Mounted Rifles (Mesilla, NM).
CUÉLLAR
    Cenobio; Pvt, F, 1st Tex Cav; 2d Lt, Zapata's Co, Pct 10, (San Diego) Nueces Cty.
    Concepción; Pvt, F, 1st Tex Cav; 4th Sgt, Zapata's Co, Pct 10 (San Diego), Nueces Cty.
    Matías; 45, Cpl, C, 3d Tex Inf, b. Mexico, Mex, d May 1, 1862.
    Melecio; Pvt, F, 1st Tex Cav; 3d Sgt, Zapata's Co, Pct 10 (San Diego), Nueces Cty.
    Ramón; Pvt, F, 1st Tex Cav.
    Ramón; Pvt, Zapata's Co, Pct 10 (San Diego), Nueces Cty.
    Santiago; 40, Bugler, H, 33d Tex Cav; A, Benavides' Reg.
CUEVAS
    Juan; Pvt, Engledow's Co, 29th Brig, TM, Nueces Cty.

D

DARIÉN
    Joaquín; 42, Pvt, Gray's Co, 30th Brig, TM, Pct 5, Bexar Cty.
    Mariano; Pvt, Gray's Co, 30th Brig, TM, Pct 5, Bexar Cty.
    Vicente; Pvt, Gray's Co, 30th Brig, TM, Pct 5, Bexar Cty.
DÁVILA
    Francisco; Pvt, I, 33d Tex Cav.
DE ALCALÁ
    Manuel; 23, Pvt, Thomas' Co of Partisan Rangers.
DE AQUINO
    Toribio; 20, Pvt, C, 8th Tex Inf, d Nov 16, 1863, rejoined Nov 31, 1863.
DE CÓRDOVA
    HM; Pvt, D. Hardeman's Tex Cav.
    JR; Pvt, A & B, 2d Tex Inf.
DE DÍOS LEÓN
    Juan; Cpl, C, Benavides' Reg.
DE HOYOS
    Leonardo; Pvt, F, 2nd Tex Mounted Rifles.
    Pablo; 28, Pvt, D, 3d Tex Inf, b Monterrey, NL.
    Valentín; Pvt, C, Benavides' Reg.
DE JESÚS
    Pedro; Pvt, I, Benavides' Reg.
DE LA BARBA
    José; 33, Pvt, D, 5th Tex Cav.
DE LA BARRERA
    José; 30, Pvt, H, 3d Tex Inf, disability discharge Dec 31, 1862.
DE LA CERDA
    N; Jr 2d Lt, H, Benavides' Reg.
    Nemecio; Cpl, H, 8th Tex Inf.
    Pedro; Pvt, E, Benavides' Reg.

DE LA CRUZ
    Genaro; Pvt, F, 3d Tex Inf, d May 14, 1863.
    Martín; Pvt, C, 8th Tex Inf.
DE LA GARCÍA
    S; 24, Pvt, G, 8th Tex Inf.
DE LA GARZA
    Emanuel; Pvt, Davis Guards, 24th Brig, Kemper City & Carlos Ranch, Victoria Cty.
    Fernando; 25, Pvt, Neal's Artillery Co.
    Francisco; Pvt, Lamar Home Guards, 29th Brig, Refugio Cty.
    Geraldo; Pvt, Davis Guards, 24th Brig, Kemper City & Carlos Ranch, Victoria Cty.
    H; Pvt, A, Waller's Reg of Tex Cav.
    Ignacio; Pvt, Coast Guards, TST, Cameron Cty.
    José; Pvt, B, 30th Brig, TST, Bexar Cty, d 19 November 1863.
    Joseph R; 23, Capt, K, 6th Tex Inf; 17th Consolidated Tex Dismounted Cavalry, killed April 8, 1864, Sabine Crossroads, La.
    Juan; Davis Guards, 24th Brig, TM, Victoria Cty.
    Juan; 48, Pvt, Winters' Co, 29th Brig, Live Oak & McMullen ctys.
    Justo; 19, Pvt, E, 8th Tex Inf, d July 15, 1863.
    Rafael; Pvt, A, Waller's Reg of Tex Cav.
DE LA ROSA
    Benselado; 25, Pvt, C, 8th Tex Inf, b Mex, laborer.
DELESA (Deleza)
    Clemente; 20, I, 33d Tex Cav; Pvt, B, Benavides' Reg.
DELGADO
    Bartolo; 46, Pvt, Gray's Co, 30th Brig, TM, Pct 5, Bexar Cty.
    Clemente; 34, Pvt, H, 33d Tex Cav; A, Benavides' Reg, interpreter.
    JM; Pvt, Treviño's Co of Tex Cav.
    José de Jesús; conscript, [no other data.]
    Leandro; 27, Pvt, E, 8th Tex Inf, d Dec 3, 1863 (Victoria).
    Macedonio; 35, Pvt, Tom's Co, TM, Atascosa Cty.
    Marcelo; 23, Pvt, E, 8th Tex Inf, d Dec 3, 1863 (Victoria).
    Nicolás; 38, Pvt, Tom's Co, TM, Atascosa Cty.
    Pedro; 37, Pvt, A, Ragsdale's Batt'n of Tex Cav.
    Pedro; 25, Pvt, Bustillo's Co, Bexar Cty; H, 33d Tex Cav; A, Benavides' Reg.
    Severo; Pvt, D, 25th Tex Cav.
    Silverio; 20, Pvt, E, 8th Tex Inf.
    Víctor; Pvt, C, 1st Tex Cav.
DE LEÓN
    Antonio; 28, Pvt, Gray's Co, 30th Brig, TM, Pct 5, Bexar Cty; H, 8th Tex Inf; Pvt, E, Benavides' Reg.
    Frank; Pvt, Ferguson's Co, Victoria Cavalry, Victoria Cty.
    Gervacio; 2d Sgt, I, Benavides' Reg.
    Jesús; Pvt, 8th Tex Field Battery.
    Juan; 46, Pvt, Gray's Co, 30th Brig, TM, Pct 5, Bexar Cty.
    Juan (2d); Pvt, Gray's Co, TM, Pct 5, Bexar Cty.
    S; 4th Sgt, Ferguson's Co, Victoria Cav, Victoria Cty.
    S; Pvt, Gidding's Reg of Tex Cav.
    Silvestre; Pvt, Waller's Reg of Tex Cav.

DE LEÓN [continued]
  Valentín; 24, Pvt, Gray's Co, 30th Brig, TM, Pct 5, Bexar Cty.
DE LOS REYES
  Juan; Pvt, H, 8th Tex Inf.
DE LOS SANTOS
  Martín; 21, Pvt, C, 8th Tex Inf, d, rejoined Nov 2, 1862, b Mex, laborer.
DEL TORO
  Ignacio; Pvt, F, 3d Tex Cav.
DEL VALLE
  E; Pvt, Treviño's Co of Partisan Rangers.
DE MESA
  Abraham R; Cpl, D, 2nd Tex Inf.
DESETA
  Pablo; Capt, Benavides' Reg.
DE ZAVALA
  A; Pvt, A, Madison's Reg, Arizona Brig.
DÍAZ (Días)
  Albino; Pvt, Minute Men, TM, Starr Cty.
  Clemente; Pvt, C, 25th Cav.
  Clemente; Pvt, H, 9th Tex Inf.
  Desiderio; Pvt, I, Benavides' Reg.
  Florentino; 19, Pvt, C, 3d Tex Inf, d Dec 19, 1862.
  G; Pvt, F, 22nd Tex Inf.
  Jesús; 29, Pvt, A, Ragsdale's Batt'n of Tex Cav.
  José María; Pvt, Medina Guards, 40th Brig, TM, Bexar Cty.
  Manuel; conscript, [no other data.]
  Miguel; Pvt, Jeff Davis HG, 29th Brig, TM, Refugio Cty.
  Miguel; 23, Pvt, C, 8th Tex Inf; G, Benavides' Reg, b Mex, laborer.
  Pedro; 40, Pvt, Bustillo's Co, Bexar Cty.
  Pedro; 38, Pvt, F, 3d Tex Inf, d May 6, 1862.
  Reducindo; Pvt, Engledow's Co, 29th Brig, TM, Nueces Cty.
  Victoriano; Pvt, Medina Guards, 40th Brig, TM, Bexar Cty;
    A, Ragsdale's Batt'n of Tex Cav.
  Victorio; Pvt, D, Benavides' Reg.
DOMÍNGUEZ
  Sixto; 50, Pvt, Thomas' Co of Partisan Rangers.
DOVALINA
  Francisco; Pvt, 2d Tex Mounted Rifles, d June 10, 1862 (Ringgold Barracks).
  Juan; 4th Sgt, I, Benavides' Reg.
DURÁN
  Antonio; Pvt, Treviño's Co of Tex Cav.
  BF; Pvt, D, 7th Tex Cav.
  Bartolo; Sgt, C, Ragsdale's Batt'n of Tex Cav; H, Baird's Reg, Arizona Brig.
  JR; E, 19th Tex Inf.
  Joseph A; 1st Lt, Durán's Co, FST, Atascosa Cty.
  LJ; 1st Sgt, 2d Tex Inf.
  Polinario; Pvt, C, Ragsdale's Batt'n of Tex Cav.
  Presente; Pvt, A, Benavides' Reg.

E

ELIZONDO
  Doroteo; Pvt, Minute Men, TM, Starr Cty.
ELUTERIO
  Mauricio; Pvt, B, Benavides' Reg.
ENRÍQUEZ
  Andrés; 23, Pvt, Bustillo's Co, Bexar Cty.
  Felipe; 31, Pvt, G, 3d Tex Inf, d Dec 1, 1862.
  Jorge; 27, Pvt & Musician, C, 6th Tex Inf.
ESCALANTE
  Juan G; Pvt, H, 33d Tex Cav.
ESCALERO
  J; Pvt, Gidding's Batt'n of Tex Cav.
  José M; 2d Lt, Mission Guards, 30th Brig, TM, Bexar Cty.
  José María; Pvt, I, 33d Tex Cav.
ESCAMILLA
  Amalio; 24, Pvt, H, 33d Tex Cav.
  Ángel; 25, Pvt, I, 33d Tex Cav.
  Aniceto; 27, Pvt, H, 33d Tex Cav; A, Benavides' Reg.
  Emilio; 25, Pvt, C, 8th Tex Inf, d Nov 1, 1863.
  Estanislado; 26, Pvt, H, 33d Tex Cav; A, Benavides' Reg, tailor.
  Pablo; Pvt, H, 33d Tex Cav; Cpl, A, Benavides' Reg.
  Ynés; 25, 3d Cpl, H, 33d Tex Cav; 1st Sgt, A, Benavides' Reg.
ESCOBAR
  Félix; 35, Pvt, H, 33 Tex Cav; A, Benavides' Reg.
ESCOBEDO
  Andrés; Pvt, C, Ragsdale's Batt'n of Tex Cav.
  Cesario; Pvt, 3d Batt'n of Tex Cav.
  Justo; Pbt, B, Benavides' Reg.
  Simón; 29, Pvt, C, 8th Tex Inf, b Mex, laborer.
ESPARZA
  Bernardo; 21, Pvt, E, 8th Tex Inf.
  Francisco; 29, Pvt, A, Ragsdale's Batt'n of Tex Cav; D, Benavides' Reg.
  Guadalupe; Pvt, B, Ragsdale's Batt'n of Tex Cav.
  J; Pvt, C, 8th Tex Inf, d Dec 6, 1863 (Victoria).
  Jesús; 27, Pvt, E. 8th Tex Inf, discharged Oct 30, 1863.
  Manuel; 33, Pvt, Tom's Co, 3d Frontier Dist, Atascosa Cty.
ESPINOSA (Espinoza)
  Eligio; 23, Pvt, Bustillo's Co, Bexar Cty; A & G, 3d Tex Inf.
  Elrico; Pvt, A, 3d Tex Inf.
  José M; Pvt, Zapata's Co, TST, Pct 10 (San Diego), Nueces Cty.
  José Maria; Pvt, B, 33d Tex Cav.
  Lino; 30, Pvt, C, 8th Tex Inf, b Mexico, laborer.
  Santa Cruz; Pvt, Medina Guards, 40th Brig, TM, Bexar Cty.
  Valentín; 35, Pvt, Bustillo's Co, Bexar Cty.
  Valentino; 30, Pvt, G, 3d Tex Inf, CM July 23, 1863, found guilty of selling a $5 blanket, sentenced to two months at hard labor with "ball and chain attached to his leg."

ESQUIVEL
> Alejo; Pvt, H, 8th Tex Inf; E, Benavides' Reg.
> Enrique; Pvt, A, 3d Tex Inf.
> Luis; Pvt, A & D, 3d Tex Inf.
> T; Pvt, A, 3d Tex Inf.
> Teodoro; conscript, [no other data.]
> Ysidro; 34, Pvt, Bustillo's Co, Bexar Cty; A & D, 3d Tex Inf.

ESTEBAN
> Juan; Pvt, C, Ragsdale's Batt'n of Tex Cav; B, Benavides' Reg.

ESTRADA
> Antonio; Pvt, D, Ragsdale's Batt'n of Tex Cav, d Feb 20, 1864.
> Francisco; Pvt, I, Benavides' Reg.
> Natividad; 22, Pvt, D, 2d Tex Mounted Rifles.
> Seferino; Pvt, C Ragsdale's Batt'n of Tex Cav; D, Benavides' Reg.

F

FALCÓN
> [no first name given]; Pvt, F, 3d Tex Inf.
> José M; 3d Cpl, Treviño's Co of Partisan Rangers.
> Juan J; 19, Cpl, A, Ragsdale's Batt'n of Tex Cav, d Nov 22, 1862.
> Ramón; Jr 2d Lt, 30th Brig, TM, Pct. 3 & 4, Wilson Cty.
> Ramón; Pvt, 8th Tex Field Battery.

FARÍAS
> Antonio; Pvt, Gray's Co, TM, Pct 5, Bexar Cty.
> Francisco; [no other data.]
> Juan; Pvt, B, Ragsdale's Batt'n of Tex Cav.
> Leocadio; Pvt, Minute Men, TM, Starr Cty.
> Leonardo; 2d Lt, Minute Men, TM, Starr Cty.
> Pablo; Pvt, Gray's Co, TM, Pct 5, Bexar Cty.
> Trinidad; 24, 4th Sgt, H, 33d Tex Cav.

FERNÁNDEZ
> Gabriel; Pvt, Coast Guards, 32d Brig, TM, Cameron Cty.
> Juan; 18, Pvt, H, 8th Tex Inf, b. Guerrero, Gue, d Dec 3, 1863 (Victoria).
> Juan; Pvt, D, 3d Tex Inf, d March 16, 1862.
> Rafael; 18, Pvt, F, 8th Tex Inf.
> Seves; Pvt, 5th Tex Field Battery.

FIGUEROA
> Antonio; 28, Pvt, E, 8th Tex Inf.
> Francisco; 40, Pvt, E, 8th Tex Inf.
> Gerónimo; 32, Pvt, E, 8th Tex Inf, d Aug 17, 1863.

FLORES
> Adiano; Pvt, E, Benavides' Reg.
> Agustín; 27, Pvt, Bustillo's Co, Bexar Cty.
> Andrés; 30, Pvt, H, 33d Tex Cav.
> Antonio; Pvt, A, Benavides' Reg.
> B; Pvt, C, 8th Tex Inf, d Dec 6, 1863 (Victoria).
> BA; Pvt, Benton's Co of Tex Vols, Guadalupe Cty.
> Bartolo; Pvt, Zapata's Co, TST, Pct 10 (San Diego), Nueces Cty.
> Brígido; 4th Cpl, Zapata's Co, TST, Pct 10 (San Diego), Nueces Cty.
> Canuto; 25, Pvt, Bustillo's Co, Bexar Cty.

FLORES [continued]
  Carlos; 20, Pvt, F, 3d Tex Inf, d Dec 1861.
  Casimero; 32, Pvt, I, 33d Tex Cav.
  Cecidro; 48, Pvt, Gray's Co, 30th Brig, TM, Pct 5, Bexar Cty.
  Cenobio; 33, Pvt, Gray's Co, 30th Brig, TM, Pct 5, Bexar Cty.
  Cosme; Pvt, Treviño's Co of Tex Cav.
  Domingo; 21, Mus & Cpl, C, 8th Tex Inf; C, Benavides' Reg.
  Domingo; 25, Pvt, Bustillo's Co, Bexar Cty.
  Felipe; Pvt, D, 1st Tex Cav; H, 33d Tex Cav.
  Felipe; Pvt, H, 36th Tex Cav.
  Félix; Pvt, Medina Guards, 40th Brig, TM, Bexar Cty; H, 33d Tex Cav.
  Félix; Pvt, H, 36th Tex Cav.
  Gertrudis; Pvt, C, Ragsdale's Batt'n of Tex Cav.
  Gregorio; E, Madison's Reg. of Tex Cav.
  HD; Pvt, D, 4th Tex Inf.
  Henry; Pvt, H, 15 Tex Inf.
  Ignacio; 26, Pvt, F, 3d Tex Inf, d April 29, 1862.
  JP; Pvt, A, 11th Tex Inf; 12th Tex Inf.
  Jacinto; 26, Sgt, C, 3d Tex Inf, d Dec 1861.
  Jesús; 24, Pvt, D, 4th Tex Cav.
  Jesús; Pvt, 24th Batt'n of Tex Inf.
  John; Pvt, G, 1st Tex Heavy Artillery.
  Jorge; Pvt, E, Madison's Reg of Tex Cav.
  José A; Pvt, F, 2d Tex Mounted Rifles.
  José María; Pvt, Medina Guards, 40th Brig, TM, Bexar Cty.
  Joseph A; Pvt, A, 11th Tex Inf.
  Juan; Pvt, Treviño's Co of Partisan Rangers.
  Juan; 39, Pvt, F, 3d Tex Inf, d Dec 1862.
  Julián; 26, Cpl, C, 3d Tex Inf, b NL, Mex, d Feb 9, 1862.
  Julio; 26, Pvt, C, 3d Tex Inf, b NL.
  M; Pvt, D, Timmons' Reg of Tex Inf.
  Manuel; 38, Pvt, E, 8th Tex Inf; E, Benavides' Reg.
  Manuel; enrolled & furloughed, Victoria Cty.
  Manuel; 22, Pvt, H, 8th Tex Inf.
  Manuel; 30, Pvt, Bustillo's Co, Bexar Cty.
  Marcos; Pvt, D, 9th Tex Inf.
  Marcos; Pvt & Drummer, D, Timmons' Reg of Tex Inf, Waul's Legion.
  Mariano; 1st Lt, 30th Brig, Pct 5, Wilson Cty.
  Patricio; 35, Pvt, C, 3d Tex Inf, b. NL, d Dec 11, 1861.
  Pedro; 3d Lt, Bustillo's Co, Bexar Cty.
  Pedro; Pvt, Treviño's Co of Partisan Rangers.
  Pedro; 23, Pvt, 2d Tex Mounted Rifles; B, Ragsdale's Batt'n of Tex Cav.
  Pedro; 29, Pvt, G, 3d Tex Inf.
  Peter; Pvt, K, 15th Tex Inf.
  Plácido; 25, Pvt, Treviño's Co of Partisan Rangers.
  R; Pvt, C, 8th Tex Inf, d Dec 6, 1863 (Victoria).
  Ramón; 22, Pvt, Bustillo's Co, Bexar Cty.
  Refugio; 18, Pvt, F, 3d Tex Inf, d Dec 6, 1862.
  Salvador; 19, Pvt, B, 2d Tex Mounted Rifles.
  Santiago; 23, Pvt, Gray's Co, 30th Brig, TM, Pct 5, Bexar Cty.

FLORES [continued]
- Víctor; 26, Pvt, H, 7th Tex Cav.
- Viviano; 46, Pvt, Gray's Co, TM, 30th Brig, Pct 5, Bexar Cty.

FRANCISCO
- James [Santiago] M; Pvt, D, 2nd Tex Mounted Rifles.
- José; Musician, F, 2nd Tex Mounted Rifles.
- Juan; 22, Pvt, F, 6th Tex Inf.
- M; Pvt, A, 1st Tex Inf.

FRAUSTO
- James; Pvt, I, 33d Tex Cav.
- José María; 29, 4th Sgt, C, 3d Tex Inf, b Matamoros, Tamps, d Dec 19, 1861.
- Ramón; Pvt, I, 33d Tex Cav.
- Santiago; Pvt, B, Benavides' Reg.

FUENTES
- Hernández; 25, Pvt, G, 3d Tex Inf, d Oct 7, 1861.
- Luis; 24, Pvt, C, 3d Tex Inf, b Brownsville, Tex.
- Martín; 22, Pvt, H, 8th Tex Inf.

G

GALI
- José Claro; 20, Pvt, Bustillo's Co, Bexar Cty.

GALINDO
- Clemente; 18, Pvt, H, 8th Tex Inf; E, Benavides' Reg.
- Josiano; Pvt, Medina Guards, 40th Brig, TM, Bexar Cty.
- Urbano; 27, Pvt, H, 8th Tex Inf, d Nov 1, 1862.

GALLARDO
- J; Pvt, B, 2d Tex Mounted Rifles.
- Manuel; 17, Pvt, A, Ragsdale's Batt'n of Tex Cav; B, Benavides' Reg.

GALLEGO
- Trinidad; 50, Pvt, A, 3d Tex Inf, b Santa Rosa, Mex, disability discharge March 1862.

GALVÁN
- Dolores; Pvt, F, 3d Tex Inf.
- Jesús; 18, Pvt, C, 8th Tex Inf, d June 1863.
- Ramón; Pvt, F, 3d Tex Inf, d Jan 26, 1862.

GAMBOA
- Antonio; 26, Pvt, H, 33d Tex Cav.
- Bartolo; 32, Pvt, I, 33d Tex Cav.
- Jacinto; Pvt, B, Benavides' Reg.
- Pablo; Mus, 2d Tex Mounted Rifles (Mesilla, NM).
- Prudencio; 30, Pvt, I, 33d Tex Cav; B, Benavides' Reg.
- Ramón; 45, 1st Sgt, I, 33d Tex Cav.
- Sóstenes; 20, Pvt, I, 33d Tex Cav.

GAONA
- Narciso; 43, Pvt, Bustillo's Co, Bexar Cty; Sgt, C, 8th Tex Inf, disability discharge (broken left leg) Sept 20, 1863, b. Mex, laborer.

GARCÍA
- A; 41, Pvt, G, 8th Tex Inf.
- A; A, 24th Tex. Inf.
- Abelino; Pvt, Zapata's Co, TST, Pct 10 (San Diego), Nueces Cty.

GARCÍA [continued]
    Andrés; Pvt, Donelson's Co, TST.
    Andrés; Pvt, Coast Guards, 32d Brig, TM, Cameron Cty.
    Anicito; 18, Pvt, H, 33d Tex Cav; A, Benavides' Reg.
    Antonio; 30, Pvt, H, 3d Tex Inf, d May 3, 1863.
    Antonio; 32, Pvt, E & H, 8th Tex Inf, d Dec 3, 1863 (Victoria),
        rejoined March 26, 1864.
    Antonio; Pvt, 24th Batt'n, TST.
    Benigno; 32, Pvt, E, 8th Tex Inf, d July 21, 1863.
    Benito; Pvt, Coast Guards, 32d Brig, TM, Cameron Cty.
    Bernabé; 22, Pvt, Bustillo's Co, Bexar Cty; D, Benavides' Reg.
    Bernabé; 19, Pvt, Ragsdale's Batt'n of Tex Cav.
    Bernardo; 24, Pvt, C, 8th Tex Inf, disability discharge Sept 20, 1863.
    Braulio; Pvt, C, Ragsdale's Batt'n of Tex Cav.
    Carlos; 26, Pvt, D, 3d Tex Inf, b. Mier, Tamps, d Dec 20, 1861.
    Cesario; 35. Pvt, H, 33d Tex Cav; A, Benavides' Reg.
    Crecensio; Pvt, Skidmore's Co, 29th Brig, TM, Pct 1, San Patricio Cty.
    E; Pvt, C, 8th Tex Inf, d Dec 6, 1863 (Victoria).
    Emanuel; Pvt, D, 22d Tex Cav.
    Encarnación; 26, Pvt, H, 33 Tex Cav, killed (gunshot wound),
        March 10, 1862 (Nuevo Laredo, Tamps), b Laredo, Tex, laborer.
    Estevano; 26, Pvt, Thomas' Co of Partisan Rangers.
    Eugenio; 26. 4th Sgt, H, 33d Tex Cav; Sgt, A, Benavides' Reg.
    Feliciano; 29, Pvt, A, Ragsdale's Batt'n of Tex Cav, d Nov 25, 1862, rejoined.
    Fernando; 25, Pvt, I, 8th Tex Inf, d Feb 28, 1862 (Corpus Christi), b. Tex.
    Fernando; 45, Pvt, Tom's Co, TM, Atascosa Cty.
    Francisco; Pvt, C, Ragsdale's Batt'n of Tex Cav.
    Francisco; Pvt, Mann's Batt'n of Tex Cav.
    Geraldo; Pvt, B, 24th Brig, TM.
    Gerardo; Pvt, 14th Tex Field Battery.
    Gerónimo; Pvt, E, 3d Tex Inf.
    Gollo; 3d Sgt, I, Benavides' Reg.
    Guadalupe; 19, Pvt, D, 2d Tex Mounted Rifles; B, Baylor's Reg,
        Arizona Brigade.
    Guadalupe; 3d Sgt, Treviño's Co of Partisan Rangers.
    Guadalupe; 2d Cpl, Zapata's Co, TST, Pct 10 (San Diego), Nueces Cty.
    Hilario; Pvt, 8th Tex Field Battery.
    Ignacio; Pvt, Medina Guards, 40th Brig, TM, Bexar Cty.
    Ildefonso; 49, Pvt, Bustillo's Co, Bexar Cty; 5th Sgt, I, 33d Tex Cav.
    J; Pvt, B, 2d Tex Mounted Rifles.
    J; Pvt, C, 8th Tex Inf, d Dec 6, 1863 (Victoria).
    Jesús; Pvt, Gray's Co, 30th Brig, TM, Pct 5, Bexar Cty.
    Jesús; 22, Pvt, H, 8th Tex Inf; E, Benavides' Reg.
    Jesús; Pvt, A, 33d Tex Cav; A, Benavides' Reg.
    Jesús; Pvt, 27, Treviño's Co of Partisan Rangers.
    John; Pvt, Teel's Co, TST.
    Jorge; 1st Sgt, I, Benavides' Reg.
    Jose; Pvt, A, 3d Batt'n of Tex Cav.
    José María; Pvt, Lamar HG, 29th Brig, TM, Refugio Cty.
    José María; Pvt, Zapata's Co, TST, Pct 10 (San Diego), Nueces Cty.

GARCÍA [continued]
 José María; Pvt, Medina Guards, 40th Brig, TM, Bexar Cty.
 José María; 28, Pvt, Bustillo's Co, Bexar Cty.
 José María; 35. Jr 1st Lt, H, 33d Tex Cav; 1st Lt, A, Benavides' Reg.
 José María; 27, Pvt, Thomas' Co of Partisan Rangers.
 Juan; Pvt, C, 3d Tex Inf, d Feb 4, 1862.
 Juan; Pvt, Kemper City & Carlos Ranch Co, 24th Brig, TM, Victoria Cty.
 Juan; 50, Pvt, Bustillo's Co, Bexar Cty.
 Juan; Pvt, Medina Guards, 40th Brig, TM, Bexar Cty.
 Juan; 28, Pvt, Thomas' Co of Partisan Rangers.
 Julián; Pvt, F, 3d Tex Inf, d June 22, 1862.
 Justo; Pvt, Coast Guards, 32d Brig, TM, Cameron Cty.
 Leonardo; 38, Sgt, H, 33d Tex Cav; Sgt, A, Benavides' Reg.
 Leonicio; Pvt, Lamar HG, 29th Brig, TM, Refugio Cty.
 Librado; Pvt, D, Ragsdale's Batt'n of Tex Cav.
 Lino; 20, Pvt, I, 33d Tex Cav.
 Lucas; 1st Cpl, Zapata's Co, TST, Pct 10 (San Diego), Nueces Cty.
 Lucas; 40, Pvt, H, 33d Tex Cav.
 Luis; Cpl, H, 6th Tex Inf.
 Luis; 32, Cpl, H, 8th Tex Inf; Sgt, E, Benavides' Reg.
 M; Pvt, E, 8th Tex Inf, d Dec 6, 1863 (Victoria).
 M; Pvt, Treviño's Co of Partisan Rangers.
 Manuel; 19, Pvt, C, 8th Tex Inf, b. Mier, Tamps.
 Manuel; Pvt, D, 3d Tex Inf, d Dec 20, 1861.
 Marcello; 33, 2d Cpl, I, 33d Tex Cav; Cpl, B, Benavides' Reg.
 Mariano; 25, Pvt, Bustillo's Co, Bexar Cty.
 Mariano (1st); 42, Pvt, H, 8th Tex Inf, disability discharge (chronic rheumatism and general debility) April 30, 1863, b. Bexar Cty, farmer.
 Mariano (2d); Pvt, H, 8th Tex Inf.
 Mariano; Pvt, E, Benavides' Reg.
 Martín; 30, Pvt, Treviño's Co of Partisan Rangers.
 Melchor; Pvt, I, Benavides' Reg.
 Miguel; 28, Pvt, C, 8th Tex Inf, charged with embezzlement Jan 14, 1863.
 Nepomuceno; 25, 4th Sgt, 8th Tex Inf, d Dec 21, 1863 (Columbus).
 Nicanor; 40, Pvt, Mitchell's Co, 3d Frontier Dist, Bandera Cty.
 Pablo; 20, Pvt, D, 2d Tex Mounted Rifles.
 Paulino; Pvt, Lamar HG, 29th Brig, TM, Refugio Cty.
 Pedro; Pvt, Gray's Co, TM, Pct 5, Bexar Cty.
 Polinario; 20, Pvt, G, 8th Tex Inf.
 Práxides; Pvt, H, 8th Tex. Inf; E, Benavides' Reg.
 Presidio; 25, Pvt, H, 8th Tex Inf.
 Prudencio; Pvt, Engledow's Co, 29th Brig, TM, Nueces Cty.
 Rafael; Pvt, D, Benavides' Reg.
 Rafael; Pvt, 6th Tex Field Battery.
 Ramón; 20, Pvt, H, 33d Tex Cav; A, Benavides' Reg.
 Refugio; Pvt, Kemper City & Carlos Ranch Co, 24th Brig, TM, Victoria Cty.
 Roberto; Pvt, I, 25th Tex Cav.
 T; Pvt, 8th Tex Inf, d Dec 6, 1863 (Victoria).
 Telésforo; 27, Pvt, Treviño's Co of Partisan Rangers.
 Teodero; Pvt, Gray's Co, TM, Pct 5, Bexar Cty.

GARCÍA [continued]
    Teodoro; Pvt, Rhodes' Co, 3d Batt'n of Tex Cav.
    Teodoro; Pvt, 6th Tex Field Battery.
    Trinidad; Bugler, A, Ragsdale's Batt'n; Pvt & Bugler, D, Benavides' Reg.
    Valentín; 33, Pvt, C, 3d Tex Inf, b San Luis Potosí, SLP, d Nov 1, 1861.
    Vicente; 20, Pvt, C, 8th Tex Inf; C, Benavides' Reg. b Mex, laborer.
    Vicente; Pvt, Gray's Co, TM, Pct 5, Bexar Cty.
    Urban; Conscript.
    W (II); 29, Pvt, G, 8th Tex Inf.
    Ylario; 29, Pvt, C, 8th Tex Inf.
    Ynocencio; 28, Pvt, H, 8th Tex Inf.
GARIBAY
    F; Pvt, Treviño's Co of Partisan Rangers.
    Ysabel; Pvt, H, 8th Tex Inf.
GARZA
    Alejo; Pvt, Skidmore's Co, 29th Brig, TM, Pct 1, San Patricio Cty.
    Anacleto; Pvt, H, 33d Tex Cav.
    Andrés; 22, Pvt, Thomas' Co of Partisan Rangers.
    Candelario; 27, Pvt, H 33d Tex Cav; A, Benavides' Reg.
    Cirinco; Pvt, Gray's Co, TM, 30th Brig, Pct 5, Bexar Cty.
    David; Pvt, D, 17th Tex Inf.
    Estanislado; Pvt, H, 33d Tex Cav; A, Benavides' Reg.
    Esteban; 26, Pvt, B, 2d Tex Mounted Rifles; F, Benavides' Reg.
    Eugenio; 45, 3d Lt, I, 33d Tex Cav; 2d Lt, B, Benavides' Reg.
    Félix; 26, Pvt, Thomas' Co of Partisan Rangers.
    Francisco; Pvt, Lamar HG, 29th Brig, TM, Refugio Cty.
    Francisco; 22, Pvt, I, 8th Tex Inf; D, Benavides' Reg.
    Francisco; Pvt, Minute Men, TM, Starr Cty.
    Gerónimo; Pvt, A, Waul's Tex Legion.
    Ildefonso; 21, Pvt, H, 33d Tex Cav; Cpl, A, Benavides' Reg.
    J; Pvt, Treviño's Co of Partisan Rangers.
    Jesús; Duff's Co, Bexar Cty; Pvt, A, 33d Tex Cav.
    Jesús; Pvt, C, 3d Tex Inf, b Matamoros, Tamps, disability discharge
        Aug 12, 1862.
    Jesús; 31, Pvt, A, 3d Tex Inf, died, July 14, 1861, from a blow to the head
        by a musket.
    Jesús; 2d Lt, Bustillo's Co, Bexar Cty.
    Jesús; 45, Pvt, C, 3d Tex Inf, b Matamoros, NL.
    Jesús; 27, Pvt, B, 2d Tex Mounted Rifles.
    John; Pvt, Kemper City & Carlos Ranch Co, 24th Brig, TM, Victoria Cty.
    José; Pvt, E, 33d Tex Cav.
    José María; 31, Pvt, Thomas' Co of Partisan Rangers.
    José R; 1st Lt, K, 6th Tex Inf; H, 17th Cons Dismounted Cav.
    Juan; 28, Pvt, Bustillo's Co, Bexar Cty.
    Juan; Pvt, A, 11th Inf.
    Juan N; Pvt, Minute Men, TM, Starr Cty.
    Juan; Pvt, I, Benavides' Reg.
    Juan de Leon; Pvt, Lamar HG, 29th Brig, TM, Regufio Cty.
    Lázaro; 18, Mus & Pvt, C, 8th Tex Inf; C, Benavides' Reg,
        b San Antonio, Tex, laborer.

GARZA [continued]
   Leandro; 17, Pvt, E, 8th Tex Inf.
   Luciano; 24, 2d Lt, Thomas' Co of Partisan Rangers.
   Luis; 28, Pvt, C, 8th Tex Inf, d June 1863.
   Magdaleno; 24, Pvt, C, 3d Tex Inf, b Linares, Tamps, d Nov 61.
   Manuel; Pvt, F, 3d Tex Inf.
   Manuel; Pvt, 14th Tex Field Battery.
   Manuel; 24, Pvt, Gray's Co, 30th Brig, TM, Pct 5, Bexar Cty.
   Marcos; Pvt, F, 3d Tex Inf.
   Michael; Pvt, G, 2d Tex Mounted Rifles.
   Miguel; 26, Pvt, Bustillo's Co, Bexar Cty;
      Cpl, A, Ragsdale's Batt'n of Tex Cav, d Nov 22, 1862.
   N; Treviño's Co of Partisan Rangers.
   Nepomuceno; 25, Pvt, H, 33d Tex Cav; A, Benavides' Reg.
   Pablo; Pvt, D, Benavides' Reg.
   Pablo; 19, Sgt, A, Ragsdale's Batt'n of Tex Cav, d Jan 14, 1864.
   Perfecto; 23, Pvt, I, 33d Tex Cav.
   Protacio; 21, Pvt, I, 33d Tex Cav, killed in late 1862 or early 1863.
   R; Pvt, Treviño's Co of Partisan Rangers.
   Rafael; Pvt, F, 3d Tex Inf.
   Rafael; Pvt, A, 1st Tex Cav; 3d Batt'n of Tex Cav.
   Rafael B; 23, Pvt, I, 8th Tex Inf, d Feb 28, 1862 (Corpus Christi), b. Texas.
   Rafael; 27, Pvt, H, 33d Tex Cav; B, Benavides' Reg.
   Ramón; Pvt, Minute Men, TM, Starr Cty.
   Ramón; Pvt, B, 8th Tex Cav (Terry's Tex Rangers).
   Ricardo; 42, Pvt, Gray's Co, 30th Brig, TM, Pct 5, Bexar Cty.
   Santos; 32, Pvt, Bustillo's Co, Bexar Cty.
   Serapio; Capt, Minute Men, TM, Starr Cty.
   Severiano; 24, Pvt, I, 8th Tex Inf, disability discharge
      (chronic rheumatism) July 1, 1862, ranchero.
   Severiano; 24, Pvt, Neal's Co, b. Tex.
   Simón; 39, Pvt, K, 6th Tex Inf.
   Telésforo; Pvt, Treviño's Co of Partisan Rangers.
   Tomás; Pvt, I, Benavides' Reg.
   Vicente; 39, Pvt, I, 33d Tex Cav; Bugler, E, Benavides' Reg.
   Victoriano; 24, Pvt, D, 3d Tex Inf, b. Camargo, Tamps, d Jan 1, 1862.
   Wenceslao; Sgt, H, 36th Tex Cav.
   William; 30, Pvt, G, 8th Tex Inf, d June 1, 1863.
   Ynés; Pvt, Zapata's Co, Pct 10 (San Diego), Nueces Cty.
GIL
   Francisco; Pvt, H, Benavides' Reg.
   Luis; 30, Cpl, H, 33d Tex Cav; A, Benavides' Reg.
GODINES
   Jesús; 23, Pvt, C, 3d Tex Inf.
   Julián; Pvt, C, Ragsdale's Batt'n of Tex Cav.
GOLARI
   Manuel; 32, 3d Sgt, H, 8th Tex Inf.
GÓMEZ (Gomes)
   Atanacio; Pvt, F, 1st Tex Cav.
   Atanacio; Pvt, Skidmore's Co, 29th Brig, TM, Pct 1, San Patricio Cty.

GÓMEZ (Gomes) *[continued]*
    Calisto; Pvt, Coast Guards, 32d Brig, TM, Cameron Cty.
    F; Pvt, A, 1st Texas State Troops; Treviño's Co of Partisan Rangers.
    Feliciano; C, 2d Tex Mounted Rifles.
    Inocencio; 20, Pvt, C, 8th Tex Inf, b Mex, laborer.
    John; 26, Pvt, G, 8th Tex Inf.
    José María; 30, Pvt, 3d Tex Inf, b Chihuahua, Chi, d Dec 20, 1861.
    Juan José; 35, Pvt, H, 33d Tex Cav; A, Benavides' Reg.
    Julián; 20, Pvt, Jeff Davis HG, 29th Brig, TM, Refugio Cty.
    Julián; Pvt, B, 3d Reg, 29th Brig, TST.
    Luciano; Pvt, Gray's Co, TM, Pct 5, Bexar Cty.
    Luis; 22, Pvt, H, 8th Tex Inf, teamster.
    Mariano; 34, 2d Cpl, C, 3d Tex Inf, b Guanajuato, Gua, d March 3, 1862.
    Mauricio; 31, Pvt, E, 8th Tex Inf, d Dec 6, 1863 (Victoria).
    Salomé; 23, Pvt, Thomas' Co of Partisan Rangers.
    Silverio; Pvt, Gray's Co, TM, Pct 5, Bexar Cty.
    Tomás; 38, Pvt, Bustillo's Co, Bexar Cty.
GÓNGORA
    Agustín; Pvt, H. Baird's Reg of Tex Cav.
    E; Pvt, C, 8th Tex Inf, Dec 6, 1863 (Victoria).
GONI
    Santiago; 24, Pvt, H, 8th Tex Inf.
GONZÁLES
    A; Pvt, C, 3d Tex Inf, b. Victoria, Texas, d Dec 12, 1862.
    Andrés; 25, Pvt, C, 3d Tex Inf, b Matamoros, Tam, d Feb 17, 1862, apprehended June 25, 1862, CM for desertion, July 23, 1862, found guilty and sentenced to "hard labor" for the remainder of the war and to have an eighteen-pound ball and chain attached to his leg.
    Antonio; Pvt, G, 12th Tex Inf.
    Antonio; Pvt, Medina Guards, 40th Brig, TM, Bexar Cty.
    Antonio; 30, Pvt, Gray's Co, 30th Brig, TM, Pct 5, Bexar Co.
    Apolino; 31, Pvt, Bustillo's Co, Bexar Cty, H, 33d Tex Cav; A, Benavides' Reg.
    Atanacio; 26, Pvt, C, 8th Tex Inf, d Nov 1, 1862.
    B; Pvt, Treviño's Co of Partisan Rangers.
    Benito; Pvt, F, 3d Tex Inf, d Feb 23, 1862.
    Bonifacio; Pvt, 8th Tex Field Battery.
    Brígido; 30, Pvt, Tom's Co, 3d Frontier Dist, Atascosa Cty.
    Carlos; Pvt, C, 3d Tex Inf, d June 18, 1862.
    Cirilio; Pvt, Jeff Davis HG, 29th Brig, TM, Refugio Cty.
    Darío; 20, 2d Lt, H, 33d Tex Cav.
    Deciderio; 42, Pvt, C, 3d Tex Inf, b. Matamoros, Tamps, d Sept 15, 1862.
    Dimas; 42, Pvt & Bugler, H, 8th Tex Inf; E, Benavides' Reg.
    Domingo; Pvt, B, Ragsdale's Batt'n of Tex Cav.
    E; Pvt, Treviño's Co of Partisan Rangers.
    E; 36, Pvt, Gussett's Co, 3d Frontier Dist, TST, Live Oak Cty.
    Emanuel; Pvt, D, 25th Tex Cav.
    Eugenio; 4th Sgt, Minute Men, TM, Starr Cty.
    Eugenio; 2d Cpl, I, Benavides' Reg.
    Eulalio; Pvt, F, 3d Tex Inf, d April 29, 1862.

GONZÁLES [continued]
F; Pvt, Victoria Aids, Victoria Cty.
Felipe; Pvt, C, Benavides' Reg.
Fermín; 30, Pvt, C, 8th Tex Inf, d June 1863.
Francisco; 25, Pvt, C, 8th Tex Inf; H, Benavides' Reg.
Francisco; 44, C, Pvt, 3d Tex Inf, b Monterrey, NL.
G; Pvt, Johnson Station Rangers, 20th Brig, TM, Tarrant Cty.
Gomes; 36, Pvt, H, 8th Tex Inf.
Gregorio; Pvt, A, 3d Tex Inf.
Guadalupe; 24, Pvt, H, 8th Tex Inf.
Hilario; 23, Pvt, D, 2d Tex Mounted Rifles.
Irineo; 38, Pvt, Mitchell's Co, 3d Frontier Dist, TST, Bandera Cty.
J; Pvt, Lewis' Co, 24th Brig, TM, Calhoun Cty.
J; Pvt, B, 24th Brig, TM.
Jesús; Pvt, B, Ragsdale's Batt'n of Tex Cav.
Jesús; Pvt, H, 3d Tex Inf.
Jesús; Pvt, Medina Guards, 40th Brig, TM, Bexar Cty.
Jesús; Pvt, H, 8th Tex Inf.
Jesús; 20, Pvt, C, 3d Tex Inf, b. NL.
Jesús; 23, Pvt, I, 8th Tex Inf.
Jesús; Pvt, A, Benavides' Reg.
John; Pvt, D, 17th Tex Inf.
José M; Pvt, Zapata's Co, TST, Pct 10 (San Diego), Nueces Cty.
José María; Pvt, Zapata's Co, Pct 10, (San Diego), Nueces Cty.
Juan; Pvt, 8th Tex Field Battery.
Juan; 30, Pvt, D, 3d Tex Inf. b Matamoros, Tamps, d May 14, 1863.
Juan; Pvt, Zapata's Co, TST, Pct 10 (San Diego), Nueces Cty.
Juan; 24, Pvt, D, 3d Tex Inf, b. Matamoros, Tamps.
Juan B; Pvt, Zapata's Co, TST, Pct 10 (San Diego), Nueces Cty.
Julián; Pvt, C, Ragsdale's Batt'n of Tex Cav.
Librado; 20, Pvt, C, 8th Tex Inf, d Oct 24, 1862 (Victoria).
Lino; Pvt, Minute Men, TM, Starr Cty.
Luis; 18, Pvt, H, 33d Tex Cav; A, Benavides' Reg.
M; Pvt, C, 8th Tex Inf, d Dec 6, 1863 (Victoria).
Manuel; Pvt, D, 25th Tex Cav.
Manuel; 29, Pvt, Treviño's Co of Partisan Rangers.
Manuel; 20, Pvt, E, 8th Tex Inf, d Oct 16, 1862 (Corpus Christi).
Manuel; 50, 3d Cpl, C, 3d Tex Inf, b. Monterrey, NL,
    disability discharge Sept 20, 1861.
Martín; 2d Lt, H, 33d Tex Cav.
Miguel; 35. Cpl, Treviño's Co of Partisan Rangers.
Mónico; Pvt, H, 33d Tex Cav; A, Benavides' Reg.
P; 49, Pvt, A, 23d Brig, TST, Austin Cty.
Pascual; 25, Pvt, C, 8th Tex Inf, d Nov 1, 1862.
Polonio; 30, Pvt, H, 33d Tex Cav.
Rafael; Pvt, 3d Batt'n of Tex Cav.
Rafael; Pvt, Zapata's Co, Pct 10 (San Diego), Nueces Cty.
Rafael; Pvt, H, 24th Tex Cav.
Regufio; Pvt, A, 3rd (Yager's) Batt'n of Tex Cav.
Ricardo; 23, Pvt, I, 8th Tex Inf, b. Tex.

GONZÁLES [continued]
    Ricardo; Pvt, D, Ragsdale's Batt'n of Tex Cav.
    Ricardo; 26, Pvt, H, 33d Tex Cav; A, Benavides' Reg.
    Santos; 42, Pvt, Mitchell's Co, 3d Frontier Dist, Bandera Cty.
    Tomás; Capt, 9th Tex Inf & Hughes Co of Texas Light Artillery.
    Trinidad; Pvt, B, 33d Tex Cav.
    Valentín; Pvt, C, Ragsdale's Batt'n of Tex Cav.
    Ventura; 28, Pvt, Thomas' Co of Partisan Rangers.
    Ventura; 50, Pvt, H, 33d Tex Cav; A, Benavides' Reg.
    Vicente; 28, Pvt, H, 8th Tex Inf; E, Benavides' Reg.
    Yndalecio; 22, Pvt, Thomas' Co of Partisan Rangers.
GORTARI
    Blas; 18, Pvt, H, 8th Tex Inf; Sgt, E, Benavides' Reg.
    Félix C; 21, 1st Lt, C, 8th Tex Inf; C, Benavides' Reg.
    Manuel; Sgt, H, 8th Tex Inf; Pvt, E, Benavides' Reg.
    Nieves; 26, Pvt, H, 8th Tex Inf; E, Benavides' Reg.
GRIEGO
    Julio; Pvt, C, Ragsdale's Batt'n of Tex Cav.
    Lesario; Pvt, C, Ragsdale's Batt'n of Tex Cav.
    N; Pvt, Treviño's Co of Partisan Rangers.
GUADALUPE
    J; Pvt, Teel's Co, TST; B, 2d Tex Mounted Rifles.
GUAJARDO
    Aniceto; Pvt, A, Ragsdale's Batt'n of Tex Cav.
    Demetrio; 22, Pvt, G, 3d Tex Inf, d May 18, 1862.
    J; Pvt, Teel's Co, TST.
    Juan M; Pvt, B, Ragsdale's Batt'n of Tex Cav.
    Louis J; Pvt, B, Ragsdale's Batt'n of Tex Cav.
    M; Cpl, A, Ragsdale's Batt'n of Tex Cav.
    Mariano; Pvt, B, Ragsdale's Batt'n of Tex Cav.
GUANO
    Damacio; Pvt, I, 28th Tex Cav.
GUERRA
    Francisco; Pvt, Coast Guards, 32d Brig, TM, Cameron Cty.
    Jesús; Pvt, Gray's Co, TM, Pct 5, Bexar Cty.
    Manuel; 23, Pvt, Teel's Co, TST; B, 2d Tex Mounted Rifles.
    Martín; 35, Pvt, I, 8th Tex Inf.
    Silvestre; 24, Pvt, Thomas' Co of Partisan Rangers.
GUERRERO
    Ángel; 24, Musician, Treviño's Co of Partisan Rangers.
    Antonio; Pvt, A, Mann's Reg of Tex Cav.
    Concepción; 26, Pvt, I, 33d Tex Cav; B, Benavides' Reg.
    Felipe; 24, Pvt, Bustillo's Co, Bexar Cty.
    Felipe; 30, Pvt, B, 2d Tex Mounted Rifles.
    Librado; 27, Pvt, I, 33d Tex Cav; B, Benavides' Reg.
    Manuel; 23; Pvt, B, 2d Tex Mounted Rifles.
    Manuel; 28, Pvt, C, 8th Tex Inf, d June 1863.
    Martín; Pvt, C, 8th Tex Inf.
    Narciso; Pvt, I, Benavides' Reg.
    Tomás; Cpl, E, 10th Tex Inf.

GUTIÉRREZ
- Antonio; 19, Pvt, H, 8th Tex Inf; E, Benavides' Reg.
- Celso; Pvt, Zapata's Co, TST, Pct 10 (San Diego), Nueces Cty.
- Faustino; 30, Pvt, A, Ragsdale's Batt'n of Tex Cav.
- Juan; 36, Pvt, C, 3d Tex Inf, b. San Fernando, Tamps, d Sept 18, 1862.
- Juan; Pvt, B, Baylor's Reg (Arizona) of Tex Cav.
- Nepomuceno; 30, Pvt, C, 3d Tex Inf, d Sept 15, 1862.
- Onofre; Pvt, H, 33d Tex Cav.
- Pedro; 20, Pvt, H, 33d Tex Cav; A, Benavides' Reg.
- Quinino; 25, Pvt, H, 33d Tex Cav; A, Benavides' Reg.
- S; Pvt, Treviño's Co of Partisan Rangers.
- Sernano; Pvt, B, Benavides' Reg.
- Tomasino; 30, Pvt, C, 3d Tex Inf, b Matamoros, Tamps.

GUZMÁN
- Alejandro; 25, Pvt, I, 33d Tex Cav.
- Benigno; 25, Pvt, I, 33d Tex Cav.
- Eustacio; Pvt, Medina Guards, 40th Brig, TM, Bexar Cty.
- José M; Pvt, Zapata's Co, TST, Pct 10 (San Diego), Nueces Cty.
- José Maria Garcia; Pvt, Rhodes' Co, 3rd (Yager's) Tex Cav.
- Juan; 30, Pvt, I, 33d Tex Cav.
- Juan; 3rd Cpl, Zapata's Co, TST, Pct 10 (San Diego), Nueces Cty.
- Maximo; Yager's Batt'n, 3d Tex Cav.
- Santos; Pvt, Medina Guards, 40th Brig, TM, Bexar Cty.
- Victor; Pvt, Rhodes' Co, Yager's Batt'n, 3d Tex Cav.

H

HASSO; see Jasso

HERNÁNDEZ
- Alejos; 25, 3d Cpl, C, 8th Tex Inf, d June 1863.
- Ambrosio; Pvt, Medina Guards, 40th Brig, TM, Bexar Cty.
- Amos; Bugler, E, 6th Tex Cav.
- Anastacio; Pvt, Zapata's Co, TST, Pct 10 (San Diego), Nueces Cty.
- Andrés; Pvt, G, 3rd Tex Inf.
- Ángel; 25, Pvt, C, 8th Tex Inf, b Mex, laborer.
- Aniceto; Pvt, C, 3d Tex Inf.
- Antonio; 22, Pvt, H, 8th Tex Inf; E, Benavides' Reg.
- Antonio; 25, Pvt, Bustillo's Co, Bexar Cty.
- Bartolo; 32, Pvt, H, 8th Tex Inf.
- Benito; Pvt, B, 33d Tex Cav.
- Benito; 18, Pvt, E, 8th Tex Inf.
- Bruno; 27, Pvt, I, 33d Tex Cav; B, Benavides' Reg.
- Carlos; 24, Pvt, C, 3d Tex Inf, d Dec 1, 1861.
- Casimiro; Pvt, C, 3d Tex Inf, d June 21, 1862.
- Catarino; Pvt, Medina Guards, 40th Brig, TM, Bexar Cty.
- Crecencio; 35, Pvt, Gray's Co, 40th Brig, TM, Pct 5, Bexar Cty; 3d Cpl, B, Benavides' Reg.
- D; 1st Sgt, D, Benavides' Reg.
- Doroteo; 27, Pvt, A, Ragsdale's Batt'n of Tex Cav.
- E; Pvt, Treviño's Co of Partisan Rangers.

HERNÁNDEZ [continued]
　Eduardo; 28, Pvt, A, Ragsdale's Batt'n of Tex Cav; Cpl, B & D,
　　Benavides'Reg.
　Esteban; Pvt, I, Benavides' Reg.
　F; Pvt, G, 8th Tex Inf.
　Feliciano; 23, Pvt, A & D, 3d Tex Inf, d May 14, 1863.
　Felipe; 37, Pvt, G, 3d Tex Inf, d Oct 7, 1861.
　Fernando; 26, Pvt, Duran's Co & Tom's Co, FST, Atascosa Cty.
　Fernando; 20, Sgt, A, Ragsdale's Batt'n of Tex Cav;
　　1st Sgt, D, 33d Tex Cav; Sgt, Benavides' Reg.
　Fortunato; Sgt, A, Ragsdale's Batt'n of Tex Cav.
　Francisco; Pvt, F, 3d Tex Inf.
　Gerardo; 50, Pvt, Tom's Co, TM, Atascosa Cty.
　Gervacio; Pvt, D, Benavides' Reg.
　Ignacio; Pvt, F, 33d Tex Cav; B, Ragsdale's Batt'n of Tex Cav.
　J; Pvt, D, Benavides' Reg.
　Jesús; 43, Cpl, F, 3d Tex Inf, d April 28, 1865, rejoined (Hempstead).
　Jesús; 26, Pvt, E, 3d Tex Inf, d Dec 6, 1863 (Victoria).
　Jesús; Cpl, F, 3d Tex Inf.
　Jesús; Pvt, E, 8th Tex Inf.
　Jesús; Pvt, Medina Guards, 40th Brig, TM, Bexar Cty.
　Jorge; Musician, C, 6th Tex Inf.
　Jose; 17, Pvt, F, 3d Tex Inf, d Jan 2, 1862; F, Benavides' Reg.
　José M; 26, Pvt, C, 8th Tex Inf, discharged, August 1862.
　José M; 29, Pvt, C, 8th Tex Inf, disability discharge
　　(chronic rheumatism) June 12, 1863, b Bexar Cty, laborer.
　José María; Pvt, A, 3d Tex Inf.
　José María; Pvt, H, 8th Tex Inf.
　José María; 28, Pvt, B, 2d Tex Mounted Rifles.
　Juan; Pvt, Jeff Davis HG, 29th Brig, TM, Refugio Cty.
　Lanterio; Pvt, C, Ragsdale's Batt'n of Tex Cav.
　Marcos; Pvt, F, 3d Tex Inf.
　Mariano; 25, Pvt, Bustillo's Co, Bexar Cty.
　Mariano; Pvt, Treviño's Co of Partisan Rangers.
　Mariano; 25, Pvt, A & F, 3d Tex Inf.
　Mario; Pvt, F, 3d Tex Inf.
　Mauricio; 30, Pvt, Bustillo's Co, Bexar Cty.
　Mauricio; Pvt, A, F, 3d Tex Inf.
　Mauricio; 31, Pvt, B, 2d Tex Mounted Rifles.
　Meliton; 18, Pvt, C & F, 3d Tex Inf, b Salinas, NL, d April 19, 1862.
　Miguel; Pvt, B, Benavides' Reg.
　Muncio; Pvt, B, 2d Tex Mounted Rifles.
　Nicanor; 22, Mus, C, 8th Tex Inf, d, rejoined Dec 31, 1863;
　　1st Cpl, C, Benavides' Reg.
　Nicolás; 28, Pvt, C & I, 8th Tex Inf.
　Nicolás; 24, Pvt, C, 3d Tex Inf, d Dec 17, 1861.
　Pablo; 27, Pvt, A, Ragsdale's Batt'n of Tex Cav.
　Pedro; Pvt, Medina Guards, 40th Brig, TM, Bexar Cty.
　Pedro; Pvt, Jeff Davis HG, 29th Brig, TM, Refugio Cty.
　Pedro; 35, Pvt, C, 3d Tex Inf, b San Luis Potosí, SLP.

HERNÁNDEZ [continued]
- Polinario; Pvt, D, Ragsdale's Batt'n of Tex Cav.
- Rosario; Pvt, Kemper City & Davis Ranch Co, 24th Brig, TM, Victoria Cty.
- Silvestre; 20, Pvt, C, 3d Tex Inf, b Aguascalientes, Ags, d Oct 10, 1862.
- Sóstenes; 20, Pvt, H, 33d Tex Cav; A, Benavides' Reg.
- Teodoro; Pvt, Medina Guards, 40th Brig, TM, Bexar Cty.
- V; Pvt, F, 1st Tex Heavy Artillery.
- V; Pvt, A, Ragsdale's Batt'n of Tex Cav.
- Vicente; 19, Pvt, Teel's Co of TST; D, 2d Tex Mounted Rifles; C, Ragsdale's Batt'n of Tex Cav.
- Ynocencio; 27, Pvt, C, 3d Tex Inf, b San Luis Potosí, SLP, deserted, rejoined, d again May 12, 1862.

HERRERA
- Amado; Pvt, C, Benavides' Reg.
- Amado; Pvt, F, 3d Tex Inf, d May 20, 1862.
- Benili, Pvt, E, Benavides' Reg.
- Benito; Pvt, Medina Guards, 40th Brig, TM, Bexar Cty.
- Benito; 31, Pvt, H, 8th Tex Inf.
- Blas, Jr; 2d Cpl, Medina Guards, 40th Brig, TM, Bexar Cty.
- Bruno; Pvt, I, 33d Tex Cav.
- Elijio; 22, 3d Cpl, I, 33d Tex Cav; Sgt, B, Benavides' Reg.
- Esteban; Pvt, I, 33d Tex Cav; Sgt, B, Benavides' Reg.
- Francisco; 33, Pvt, B, 2d Tex Mounted Rifles, Medical Discharge.
- Jesús; 21, Pvt, H, 33d Tex Cav; A, Benavides' Reg.
- Jesús; 22, Pvt, I, 33d Tex Cav, B, Benavides' Reg.
- José María; Pvt, I, 2d Tex Mounted Rifles.
- Juan; Pvt, B, Ragsdale's Batt'n of Tex Cav.
- Juan José; Pvt, H, 8th Tex Inf, died of disease Nov 28, 1862.
- Juan José; Pvt, Medina Guards, 40th Brig, TM, Bexar Cty.
- M; Pvt, H, 2nd Tex Mounted Rifles.
- Manuel C; Capt, 30th Brig, TM, Pct. 5, Wilson Cty.
- Natividad; 24, Pvt, H, 33d Tex Cav; Sgt, A, Benavides' Reg.
- Pedro; 20, Pvt, I, 33d Tex Cav; Cpl, B, Benavides' Reg.
- Prudencio; 31, Pvt, H, 33d Tex Cav; Cpl, A, Benavides' Reg.

HIBARRA; see Ibarra

HIDALGO
- Juan; 30, Pvt, F, 3d Tex Inf.

HINOJOSA
- Cortinas; Pvt, Coast Guards, 32d Brig, TM, Cameron Cty.
- Jesús; 25, Pvt, I, 8th Tex Inf, disability discharge (catelepsy) Sept 11, 1863, b Tex, ranchero.
- José; Pvt, 17th Field Battery; Baylor's Reg, Arizona Brig.
- José M; 2d Sgt, Zapata's Co, TST, Pct 10 (San Diego), Nueces Cty.
- Juan; Pvt, Zapata's Co, TST, Pct 10 (San Diego), Nueces Cty.
- Juan José; 24, Pvt, I, 8th Tex Inf, b Tex.
- Julián; Pvt, Jeff Davis HG, 29th Brig, TM, Refugio Cty.
- Julio; Pvt, Minute Men, TM, Starr Cty.
- Lino; Pvt, Minute Men, TM, Starr Cty.
- Martín; 30, Pvt, I, 8th Tex Inf, b. Tex, teamster.
- Santiago; Pvt, F, 1st (Yager's) Tex Cav.

HINOJOSA [continued]
    Tomás; Pvt, Coast Guards, 32d Brig, TM, Cameron Cty.
    Tomás; 22, 1st Sgt, D, 2d Tex Mounted Rifles.
HOLGUÍN (Olguin)
    Andrew; 27, Pvt, E, 8th Tex Inf, d June 30, 1863.
    Esmalgildo; 21, Pvt, E, 8th Tex Inf; 4th Cpl, C, Benavides' Reg.
    José María; Mus, 2d Tex Mounted Rifles (Mesilla, NM).
    Pedro; 25, Pvt, C & E, 8th Tex Inf.
    Telésforo; 28, Pvt, E, 8th Tex Inf, d Dec 3, 1863 (Victoria).
HOROSCO
    Desiderio; Pvt, Medina Guards, 40th Brig, TM, Bexar Cty.
HOSEA
    Arthur B; Sgt, B, 16th Tex Inf.
    GW; 2d Lt, A, 35th Tex Cav.
    María Telles; Pvt, E, 24th Tex Cav.
    Matthew; Pvt, E & G, Waul's Tex Legion.
    TJ; Pvt, E, 5th Tex Cav.
    WH; Pvt, E, 5th Tex Cav.
HOWARD
    Juan; 19, Pvt, Bustillo's Co, Bexar Cty.
HOYOS
    Francisco; 1st Cpl, Medina Guards, 40th Brig, TM, Bexar Cty.
    T; Pvt, G, 12th Tex Inf.
HUERTA
    Victoriano; 26, Pvt, C, 3d Tex Inf, d Dec 14, 1861.
HUIZAR
    Juan; Pvt, B, Ragsdale's Batt'n of Tex Cav.
    Vicente; Pvt, B, Ragsdale's Batt'n of Tex Cav.

I

IBAÑEZ: See YBAÑES
IBARRA
    JM; Pvt, Treviño's Co of Partisan Rangers.
    Leonardo; Pvt, Zapata's Co, TST, Pct 10 (San Diego), Nueces Cty.
    Matías; Pvt, B, Ragsdale's Batt'n of Tex Cav.
IGLESIAS
    Antonio; 21, Pvt, Bustillo's Co, Bexar Cty; A, 3d Tex Inf, d 21 June 1862.
INDO
    Miguel; Pvt, Gray's Co, TM, Pct 5, Bexar Cty.
INFANTE
    J; Pvt, C, Cater's Batt'n of Tex Cav.
    T; Pvt, G, 8th Tex Inf.
ITURBIDE
    Francisco; Pvt, Teel's Co, TST; C, Ragsdale's Batt'n of Tex Cav.

J

JAIMES [Jaime]
    José; 38, Pvt, H, 8th Tex Inf; E, Benavides' Reg.
JASSO
    Casamiro; Pvt, Zapata's Co, TST, Pct 10 (San Diego) Nueces Cty.

JIMÉNEZ
    Ángel; Pvt, I, 33d Tex Cav; Cpl, B, Benavides' Reg.
    Antonio; 46, Pvt, Gray's Co, TM, 30th Brig, Pct 5, Bexar Cty.
    Benito; 18, Pvt, C, 8th Tex Inf, d Aug 1862.
    Bensealado; Pvt, F, 3d Tex Inf, d Nov 8, 1862, apprehended.
    Esteban; 35, Pvt, Gray's Co, 30th Brig, TM, Pct 5, Bexar Cty.
    Francisco; Capt, 30th Brig, TM, Pct 3 & 4, Wilson Cty.
    Francisco; 36, Pvt, Gray's Co, 30th Brig, TM, Pct 5, Bexar Cty.
    J; Pvt, Treviño's Co of Partisan Rangers.
    Jesús; Pvt, Gray's Co, TM, Pct 5, Bexar Cty; F, 3d Tex Inf.
    Mariano; Pvt, D, Ragsdale's Batt'n of Tex Cav.
    Mónico; 21, Pvt, F, 3d Tex Inf, d 23 Sept 1862.
    Rafael; Pvt, Rhodes' Co, 3d Batt'n of Tex Cav.
    Veusilado; 4th Cpl, Bustillo's Co, Bexar Cty.
    Wenceslao; Cpl F, 3d Tex Inf.
JUÀREZ
    Antonio; Pvt, I, 33d Tex Cav; B, Benavides' Reg.
    C; Pvt, Teel's Co, TST; B, 2d Tex Mounted Rifles.
    Ignacio; 28, Pvt, Bustillo's Co, Bexar Cty.
    Ildefonso; 22, 5th Sgt, 33d Tex Cav; B, Benavides' Reg.
    Juan; Pvt, 8th Tex Field Batt.
    Lorenzo; 46, Pvt, Bustillo's Co, Bexar Cty.
    Toribio; 26, Pvt, I, 33d Tex Cav; B, Benavides' Reg.

L

LAFUENTE
    Juan; 40, Pvt, Gray's Co, TM, 30th Brig, Pct 5, Bexar Cty.
LAMBARAS
    Elocor; Pvt, Lamar HG, 29th Brig, TM Refugio Cty.
LANDA
    Alejandro; Pvt, F, 3d Tex Inf, d May 15, 1863.
    Edward; 13, Pvt & Musician, C, 8th Tex Inf, d Dec 21, 1863 (Columbus).
LANDÍN
    Felipe; Pvt, I, Benavides' Reg.
LARA
    Juan; 25, Pvt, G, 3d Tex Inf, d May 15, 1863, CM June 29, 1862, found guilty
        of disposing of one blanket and sentenced to hard labor for two months.
LEAL
    A; Pvt, Treviño's Co of PR; 14th Tex Field Battery.
    Agapito; Pvt, Gray's Co, TM, Pct 5, Bexar Cty.
    Alfonso; 30, Pvt, 2d Tex Mounted Rifles.
    Ciriaco; 18, Pvt, C, 3d Tex Inf, d Dec 9, 1861.
    Cristóbal; 30, Pvt, Thomas' Co of Partisan Rangers.
    Esteban; Pvt, Gray's Co, TM, Pct 5, Bexar Cty.
    F; Pvt, Teel's Co, TST; B, 2d Tex Mounted Rifles.
    Fernando; Pvt, F, 1st Tex Cav.
    Francisco; Pvt, Gray's Co, TM, Pct 5, Bexar Cty; Sgt, F, 3d Tex Inf.
    Ildefonso; Pvt, B, 2d Tex Mounted Rifles.
    Ildefonso; 33, Sgt, H, 8th Tex Inf.
    J; Pvt, A, Border's Reg of Tex Cav.

LEAL [continued]
   J Pedro; Pvt, F, 1st Tex Cav.
   Joaquín; Pvt, Skidmore's Co, 29th Brig, TM, Pct 1, San Patricio Cty.
   José; 2d Lt, 30th Brig, TM, Pct 11, Bexar Cty.
   Juan; Pvt, Gray's Co, TM, Pct 5, Bexar Cty.
   Macario; 35, Pvt, H, 33d Tex Cav; A, Benavides' Reg.
   Manuel; Pvt, Gray's Co, TM, Pct 5, Bexar Cty.
   Melesio; 30, Pvt, H, 8th Tex Inf.
   Narciso; Pvt, H, 33d Tex Cav.
   Pedro; Pvt, Engledow's Co, 29th Brig, TM, Nueces Cty.
   Pilar; Pvt, Gray's Co, TM, Pct 5, Bexar Cty.
   Rafael; 24th Tex Cav [no other data].
   Tiburcio; Sgt, F, 3d Tex Inf, Shreveport, La, hospital with syphilis, Aug 1864.
LEANDRO
   Antonio; 29, Pvt, E, 8th Tex Inf.
LECHUGA
   F; Pvt, Teel's Co, TST.
   Librado; Pvt, C, Ragsdale's Batt'n of Tex Cav.
   Luis; Pvt, C, Ragsdale's Batt'n of Tex Cav.
LEDESMA
   Juan Antonio; Pvt, Lamar HG, 29th Brig, TM, Refugio Cty.
   Manuel; Pvt, Lamar HG, 29th Brig, TM, Refugio Cty.
LEIJA
   Clemente; Pvt, I, 33d Tex Cav.
LEÓN
   B; C, 16th Tex Inf.
   Bernardino; Pvt, I, Benavides' Reg.
   Juan de Dios; Cpl, C, Benavides' Reg.
   L; Pvt, G, 11th (Spraight's) Batt'n of Vols.
   Luis; Pvt, I, 33d Tex Cav.
   Martín; 25, Pvt, C, 3d Tex Inf, b Monerrey, NL, d May 2, 1862.
   Pablo; 37, Pvt, C & F, 3d Tex Inf, b Monterrey, NL.
   Rafael; 29, Pvt, C, 3d Tex Inf, b Cadereyta, NL, d Oct 23, 1861.
LERMA
   R; Pvt, Treviño's Co of Partisan Rangers.
LEYBA (Leyva)
   Lázaro; 30, Pvt, C, 8th Tex Inf.
LICÓN
   Pedro; 22, Pvt, C, 8th Tex Inf, disability discharge (chronic syphilitic rheumatism) Dec 31, 1863, b Mex, laborer.
LIMA
   Tomás; Pvt, B, Ragsdale's Batt'n of Tex Cav.
LOA
   Antonio; 19, Pvt, C, 8th Tex Inf, d Nov 16, 1862, rejoined Nov 21, 1862.
LONGORIA
   Cedro; Pvt, K, 24th Tex Cav.
   Ciprio; Pvt, F, 2d Tex Mounted Rifles.
   Eulogio; Pvt, I, Benavides' Reg.
   Fontorio; Pvt, I, Benavides' Reg.
   Francisco; Pvt, D, 1st Tex Cav.

LONGORIA [continued]
    Francisco; Pvt, D, Ragsdale's Batt'n of Tex Cav.
    Francisco; Pvt, C, 5th Tex Cav.
    Juan; Pvt, Minute Men, TM, Starr Cty.
    Nasario; 38, Pvt, Thomas' Co of Partisan Rangers.
    Pedro; 28, Pvt, Treviño's Co of Partisan Rangers.
    Policarpio; 22, C, 5th Tex Cav.
    Senabio; Pvt, Minute Men, TM, Starr Cty.
LÓPEZ (Lopes)
    A; Pvt, F, 12th Tex Cav.
    Agapito; Pvt, Minute Men, TM, Starr Cty.
    Andreas; Pvt, F, 3d Tex Inf, d May 6, 1862.
    Andrés; Pvt, H, 3d Tex Inf.
    Andrew; 19, Pvt, H, 3d Tex Inf.
    Antonio; 4th Cpl, Treviño's Co of Partisan Rangers.
    Antonio; Pvt, B, 6th Tex Cav.
    Ben; Pvt, H, 7th Tex Cav.
    Brígido; 24, Pvt, A, Ragsdale's Batt'n of Tex Cav.
    Catarino; Pvt, B, Ragsdale's Batt'n of Tex Cav.
    Donacio; 28, Pvt, D, 3d Tex Inf, b. Mier, Tamps.
    Félix; Pvt, D, 2nd Tex Mounted Rifles.
    Félix; A, 35th Tex Cav.
    Félix; Pvt, D, 3d Tex Inf.
    Fernando; 2d Sgt, Engledow's Co, 29th Brig, TM, Nueces Cty.
    Francisco; 23, Pvt, D, 3d Tex Inf, b. Camargo, Tamps.
    Gerardo; 30, Sgt, Thomas' Co of Partisan Rangers.
    Gregory; Pvt, A, 11th Tex Inf.
    Isaac; Pvt, E, 6th Tex Inf.
    J; Pvt, Weisiger's Co, Giddings' Batt'n of Tex Cav.
    Jacinto; Pvt, Minute Men, TM, Starr Cty.
    Joel; Pvt, H, 12th Tex Inf.
    Juan; Pvt, 8th Tex Field Battery.
    Juan Manuel; 21, Pvt, Bustillo's Co, Bexar Cty; A, 3d Tex Inf, d Sept 26, 1861.
    Julián; Pvt, Zapata's Co, Pct 10 (San Diego), Nueces Cty.
    Julián; Cpl, C, Ragsdale's Batt'n of Tex Cav.
    Lázaro; 4th Sgt, Minute Men, TM, Starr Cty.
    Lázaro; Pvt, G, 2d Tex Mounted Rifles.
    Leonardo; 40, Pvt, Bustillo's Co, Bexar Cty.
    Leonito; Pvt, B, 2d Tex Mounted Rifles.
    M; G, Timmons' Reg of Tex Inf; Waul's Tex Legion.
    Manuel; 16, Pvt, H, 3d Tex Inf.
    Manuel; 23, Pvt, E & H, 8th Tex Inf; E, Benavides' Reg.
    Mariano; 17, Pvt, Tom's Co, 3d Frontier Dist, Atascosa Cty.
    Michael; Pvt, C & G, 9th Tex Inf.
    Miguel; Pvt, A, Timmons' Reg of Tex Inf; Waul's Tex Legion.
    Pedro; Pvt, Zapata's Co, Pct 10 (San Diego), Nueces Cty.
    Pedro; Pvt, B, Ragsdale's Batt'n of Tex Cav.
    Peter; Pvt, G, 12th Tex Inf.
    Prudencio; 30, Pvt, H, 8th Tex Inf.

LÓPEZ (Lopes) [continued]
 Rafael; Pvt, Minute Men, TM, Starr Cty.
 Rafael; Pvt, Engledow's Co, 29th Brig, TM, Nueces Cty.
 Santiago; Pvt, F, Waul's Tex Legion.
 Savior; Pvt, G, 12th Inf.
 Seferino; Pvt, Minute Men, TM, Starr Cty.
 Viviano; 24, Pvt, I, 33d Tex Cav; B, Benavides' Reg.
 Xavier; Pvt, G, 12th Tex Inf.
LORENZO
 Nicolás; Pvt, H, Benavides' Reg.
LOSAYO
 León; 29, Pvt, A, 33d Tex Cav, disability discharge May 7, 1862.
LOZA
 Blas; 33, Pvt, Mitchell's Co, 3d Frontier Dist, Bandera Cty.
LOZANO (Losano)
 B; Pvt, C, 4th Tex Cav.
 Cristóforo; 24, 2d Lt, Jeff Davis HG, 29th Brig, TM, Refugio Cty;
  Pvt, E. 8th Tex Inf, d July 15, 1863.
 Elías; Pvt, Jeff Davis HG, 29th Brig, TM, Refugio Cty.
 Elías; 19, Pvt, C, 4th Tex Cav.
 Nasario; 27, Pvt, A, Ragsdale's Batt'n of Tex Cav.
 Pedro; 30, Pvt, A, Ragsdale's Batt'n of Tex Cav; D, Benavides' Reg.
 Salvador; Pvt, Jeff Davis HG, 29th Brig, TM, Refugio Cty.
 Tomás; 23, Pvt, H, 8th Tex Inf; E, Benavides' Reg.
LUCERO
 FM; Pvt, D, Benavides' Reg.
 Florencio; 2d Sgt, Treviño's Co of Partisan Rangers.
 Francisco; Pvt, F, 3d Tex Inf.
 S; Pvt, Treviño's Co of Partisan Rangers.
LUNA
 Guadalupe; Pvt, D, Benavides' Reg.
 James; Pvt, D, 25th Tex Cav.
 Jesús; Pvt, H, 24th Tex Cav.
 José; Pvt, I, Benavides' Reg.
 José Ángel; 30, Pvt, Bustillo's Co, Bexar Cty.
 Matías; Pvt, Coast Guards, 32d Brig, TM, Cameron Cty.

M

MACHADO
 Ynés; 25, Pvt, I, 8th Tex Inf, d Feb 28, 1862, b. Mex.
MACHILDO
 T; Pvt, B, 2d Tex Mounted Rifles.
MACIEL
 Vicente; Pvt, B, 33d Tex Cav.
MACÍAS
 José; 25, Pvt, G, 3d Tex Inf, CM for theft.
 Pablo; 34, Pvt, F, 3d Tex Inf, d Nov 7, 1862.
 Salomé; Pvt, F, 3d Tex Inf, d May 15, 1863.
MADRIGAL
 Máximo; Pvt, B, Ragsdale's Batt'n of Tex Cav.

MADRIGALES
    F; 37, Pvt, G, 8th Tex Inf.
MALDONADO
    Claudio; Pvt, Zapata's Co, TST, Pct 10 (San Diego), Nueces Cty.
MANCHA
    Jesús; Pvt, C, 8th Tex Inf, b. Mex, laborer.
MANSOLA
    Antonio; Pvt, G, 12th Tex Inf.
    Lorenzo; Pvt, A, 17th Tex Cav.
    Mariano; Pvt, B, Ragsdale's Batt'n of Tex Cav.
MARCOS
    Claro; Pvt, B, Ragsdale's Batt'n of Tex Cav.
    Juan M; Pvt, B, Ragsdale's Batt'n of Tex Cav.
MARIANO
    Joseph C; Cpl, K, 16th Tex Cav.
    Macedonia; 39, Pvt, C, 3d Tex Inf, b San Luis Potosí, SLP, d Nov 1, 1861.
    Viviano; Pvt, Medina Guards, 40th Brig, TM, Bexar Cty.
MARINO
    Roberto; Pvt, Gray's Co, TM, Pct 5, Bexar Cty.
MÁRQUEZ
    Antonio; 30, Pvt, C & F, 3d Tex Inf, b Tampico, Tamps.
MARTIN
    Ignacio; Sgt, C, Ragsdale's Batt'n of Tex Cav.
    Leonidas M; 1st Lt, K, 6th Tex Cav.
    Orlando; 2nd Lt, B, 1st (Yager's) Tex Cav.
    Sebastián; Pvt, A, 6th Tex Inf.
MARTÍNEZ
    Adrián; 23, Cpl, C, 3d Tex Inf, accidentally shot and killed, June 4, 1862.
    Anselmo; 45, Pvt, F, 3d Tex Inf.
    Antonio; Pvt, Rhodes' Co, 3d Batt'n of Tex Cav.
    Antonio; Pvt & Musician, F, 3d Tex Inf.
    Antonio; 21, Pvt, G, 3d Tex Inf.
    Antonio; 24, Pvt, C, 8th Tex Inf, disability discharge
        (pulmonary rheumatism) March 7, 1862, b Mex, laborer.
    Benito; 17, Pvt, E, 8th Tex Inf, d Dec 3, 1863 (Victoria).
    Carlos; Cpl, C, Ragsdale's Batt'n of Tex Cav; Benavides' Reg.
    Carlos; Pvt, H, Baird's Reg, Arizona Brig.
    Casimiro; E, Madison's Reg of Tex Cav; Pvt, B, Ragsdale's Batt'n of Tex Cav.
    Ercinio; 27, Pvt, D, 3d Tex Inf, b. Vera Cruz, VC.
    Erimes; Pvt, D, 3d Tex Inf.
    Esperidión; 21, Pvt, A, Ragsdale's Batt'n of Tex Cav.
    Eugenio; 27, Pvt, E, 8th Tex Inf, d Oct 16, 1862 (Corpus Christi).
    Fermín; 1st Sgt, Bustillo's Co, Bexar Cty.
    Fermín; Cpl, H, 36th Tex Cav.
    Fernando; 25, D, Pvt, 3d Tex Inf, b. Vera Cruz, VC, d Sept 19, 1862.
    Francisco; 19, Pvt, C, 8th Tex Inf; D, Benavides' Reg.
    Francisco; 19, Pvt, A, Ragsdale's Batt'n of Tex Cav.
    Francisco; Pvt, H, 33d Tex Cav; A, Benavides' Reg.
    Gabriel; Jr 2d Lt, 30th Brig, TM, Pct 11, Bexar Cty.
    Irineo; 27, Pvt, D, 3d Tex Inf, b Vera Cruz, VC, d Dec 24, 1861.

MARTÍNEZ [continued]
    J; Pvt, Treviño's Co of Partisan Rangers.
    Jesús; 28, Pvt, 2d Tex Mounted Rifles, POW, paroled at Albuquerque, NM May 26,1862.
    José; Pvt, D, Benavides' Reg.
    José A; Pvt, 8th Tex Frontier Batt'n.
    José M; Pvt, B, Ragsdale's Batt'n of Tex Cav.
    José María; 37, Pvt, Bustillo's Co, Bexar Cty.
    José María; 28, Pvt, A, 3d Tex Inf, discharged June 23, 1862, b San Antonio, Tex.
    Josiah; 24, Pvt, E & F, 8th Tex Inf, d Dec 3, 1863 (Victoria).
    Juan; Pvt, Medina Guards, 40th Brig, TM, Bexar Cty.
    Juan; 24, Pvt, I, 33d Tex Cav; C, Benavides' Reg.
    Juan; Pvt, Engledow's Co, 29th Brig, TM, Nueces Cty.
    Lauriano; Pvt, C, Ragsdale's Batt'n of Tex Cav.
    Manuel; 31, Pvt, H, 33d Tex Cav.
    Marcos; Pvt, I, Benavides' Reg.
    Maximiano; 3d Sgt, Bustillo's Co, Bexar Cty.
    Moisés; Pvt, D, Benavides' Reg.
    O; Pvt, Duff's Co, Bexar Cty.
    Pedro; Pvt, I, Benavides' Reg.
    Prudencio; Pvt, K, 24th Tex Cav.
    R; 1st Lt, Cater's Batt'n of Tex Cav.
    Rafael; Pvt, H, 8th Tex Inf.
    Sinfriano; Pvt, A, Benavides' Reg.
    Sixto; 19, Pvt, H, 33d Tex Cav; A, Benavides' Reg.
    Susino; Pvt, I, Benavides' Reg.
    Teodoro; Pvt, Rhodes' Co, 3d Batt'n of Tex Cav.
    Valentín; 19, Pvt, I, 33d Tex Cav; B, Benavides' Reg.
    Vicente; Pvt, H, 8th Tex Inf; 1st Lt, A, Ragsdale's Batt'n of Tex Cav.
    Vicente; 23, 1st Lt, D, Benavides' Reg, d Nov 1862, rejoined.
    William; Pvt, Mounted Militia Co, Pct 3 & 4, Nueces Cty.
    Ygnacio; Pct, C, Ragsdale's Batt'n of Tex Cav.
MARUGO
    Damacio; 28, Pvt, C, 8th Tex Inf.
MASCÁ
    Secundio; Pvt, C, Benavides' Reg.
MASCORO
    Rafael; Pvt, Coast Guards, 32d Brig, TM, Cameron Cty.
MATA
    Deciderio; Pvt, A, Benavides' Reg.
    Gregorio; 46, Pvt, Gray's Co, TM, 30th Brig, Pct 5, Bexar Cty.
    Luerino; 46, Pvt, Gray's Co, TM, 30th Brig, Pct 5, Bexar Cty.
    Pedro; 20, Pvt, 3d Tex Inf, b Matamoros, Tamps.
MATERO
    Alafito; Pvt, I, Benavides' Reg.
MECINDO
    Lancedo; 2d Sgt, C, Benavides' Reg.
MEDINA
    Lucio; Pvt, A, Benavides' Reg.

MEDINA [continued]
   Manuel; Pvt, Gray's Co, TM, 30th Brig, Pct 5, Bexar Cty.
MEDRANO
   Antonio; 42, Pvt, Thomas' Co of Partisan Rangers.
   Bartolo; 35, Pvt, 3d Tex Inf, b San Fernando, Tamps, d Sept 1, 1862.
   Juan; 49. Pvt, Treviño's Co of Partisan Rangers.
   Macedonio; 39, Pvt, 3d Tex Inf, b. San Luis Potosí, SLP.
MEJÍA
   Simón; 28, Pvt, C, 8th Tex Inf.
MELGAREJO
   Cristóbal; 24, 2d Sgt, C, 3d Tex Inf, b Jalapa, VC, d April 23, 1862.
MENCHACA
   B; Pvt, Treviño's Co of Partisan Rangers.
   Bernardo; 25, Pvt, B, 2d Tex Mounted Rifles.
   Fabian; 20, Pvt, G, 3d Tex Inf.
   Fernando; conscript [no other data].
   Francisco; 27, Pvt, H, 8th Tex Inf.
   Javián; 16, Pvt, Bustillo's Co, Bexar Cty.
   Jesús; Pvt, C, 8th Tex Inf.
   John; 24, Pvt, D, 2d Tex Mounted Rifles.
   José A; Pvt, H, 4th Tex Cav.
   José M; Capt, 6th Tex Cav.
   Manuel; Pvt, B, 33d Tex Cav.
   Martín; Pvt, A, Ragsdale's Batt'n of Tex Cav.
MÉNDEZ (Mendes)
   Antonio; D, 1st Tex Heavy Artillery & 15th Texas Field Battery.
   Antonio; 26, Pvt, C, 8th Tex Inf, d June 1863, charges preferred, July 12, 1863, drunkeness in the streets of San Antonio and striking a guard; C, Benavides' Reg.
   Antonio; Pvt, C, Baird's Reg of Tex Cav.
   Doroteo; 20, Pvt, D, 2d Tex Mountd Rifles.
   Jesús; 49, Pvt, Gray's Co, 30th Brig, TM, Pct 5, Bexar Cty.
   Juan; Pvt, I, 33d Tex Cav.
   Manuel; 36, Pvt, Bustillo's Co, Bexar Cty.
MENDIOLA
   Aniseto; Pvt, I, 33d Tex Cav.
   Antonio; Pvt, C, Baird's Reg, Arizona Brig.
   Juan; Pvt, I, 33d Tex Cav.
   Julián; 21, Pvt, H, 33d Tex Cav; A, Benavides' Reg.
   Pilar; 25, Pvt, H, 33d Tex Cav.
   Ramón; Pvt, I, Benavides' Reg.
   Santiago; 21, Pvt, H, 33d Tex Cav.
   Valentín; 19, Pvt, I, 33d Tex Cav.
MENDOZA
   Cristóbal; 48, Pvt, Gray's Co, 30th Brig, TM, Pct 5, Bexar Cty.
   Florencio; Pvt, D, Ragsdale's Batt'n of Tex Cav; A, Benavides' Reg.
   Freeman; Pvt, E, 24th Tex Cav.
   Hosea; Pvt, B, Waul's Tex Legion.
   Juan; Pvt, C, 2d Texas Troops.
   Manuel; 36, Pvt, G, 3d Tex Inf, d May 16, 1863.

MENDOZA [continued]
  Matilda; 24, Pvt, A, 3d Tex Inf, d Sept 23, 1862.
  Silvestre; 21, Pvt, D, 2d Tex Mounted Rifles.
MERCADO
  Juan; Cpl, H, 33d Tex Cav.
  Juan; 27, Pvt, Thomas' Co of Partisan Rangers.
  Juan Jr; 2d Lt, Medina Guards, 40th Brig, TM, Bexar Cty.
MESA
  José María; Pct, C, Ragsdale's Batt'n of Tex Cav; D, Benavides' Reg.
MESTAS
  Manuel; 22, Pvt, D, 2d Tex Mounted Rifles.
MESTES (Mestez)
  Lázaro; Pvt, K, 2d Tex Mounted Rifles;I, 33d Tex Cav.
MESTIAS
  Lázaro; Pvt, I, 33d Tex Cav.
MISELUS
  Pedro; Pt, I, Benavides' Reg.
MITCHELL
  Poncho; Pvt, E, 3d Tex Inf.
MOLANO
  José María; 32, Pvt, Thomas' Co of Partisan Rangers.
  Juan; 28, Cpl, Thomas' Co of Partisan Rangers.
MOLINA
  Antonio; 22, Pvt, I, 33d Tex Cav; B, Benavides' Reg.
  Antonio; Pvt, C, Ragsdale's Batt'n of Tex Cav.
  Cayetano; 30, Pvt, I, 8th Tex Inf, d March 7, 1863 (Corpus Christi).
  Eutimio; 23, Pvt, I, 33d Tex Cav.
  F; Pvt, Treviño's Co of Partisan Rangers.
  Juan G; 3d Cpl, I, Benavides' Reg.
  Juan R; 48, Pvt, Tom's Co, TM, Atascosa Cty.
  Luis; Pvt, Coast Guards, 32d Brig, TM, Cameron Cty.
  Regino; Pvt, Duran's Co, FST, Atascosa Cty.
MOLLA
  Félix; Pvt, Jeff Davis HG, 29th Brig, TM, Refugio Cty.
MONDRAGÓN
  E; Pvt, Mitchell's Minute Men, TM, Bexar Cty.
  Francisco; 20, Pvt, H, 8th Tex Inf; 2d Lt, B, Benavides' Reg.
  Francisco; 18, Pvt, 3d Tex Inf.
  Franco; 2d Lt, H, Baird's Reg, Arizona Brig.
MONJARAS
  Benito; 20, Pvt, H, 8th Tex Inf.
MONTALVO
  Antonio; 25, Pvt, H, 8th Tex Inf.
  Blas; 20, Pvt, H, 8th Tex Inf.
  Cresencio; Pvt, H, 8th Tex Inf.
  Eliseo; Pvt, C, Ragsdale's Batt'n of Tex Cav.
MONTATTO
  José; Pvt, C, Ragsdale's Batt'n of Tex Cav.
MONTES
  Alejo; Pvt, Mitchell's Minute Men, TM, Bexar Cty.

MONTES [continued]
    Anastasio; 22, Pvt, 2d Tex Mounted Rifles.
    Cresencio; 18, Pvt, H, 8th Tex Inf.
    Felipe; Pvt, B, Ragsdale's Batt'n of Tex Cav.
    JM; Pvt, F, Benavides' Reg.
    José M; Pvt, A, 17th Tex Cav.
    Joseph; Pvt, B, 2d Tex Mounted Rifles.
    Juan; 20, Pvt, H, 8th Tex Inf; Cpl, E, Benavides' Reg.
    Nicacio; 23, Pvt, H, 8th Tex Inf, disability discharge (chronic syphilitic rheumatism) Dec 31, 1862, b San Antonio, Tex, farmer.
    Pablo; 26, Cpl, C, 8th Tex Inf; C, Benavides' Reg.
    Pedro; Pvt, I, Benavides' Reg.
MONTOYA
    Anastacio; 25, Pvt, G, 3d Tex Inf.
    Antonio; 33, Pvt, A, 3d Tex Inf, d May 27, 1861.
    M; Pvt, Treviño's Co of Partisan Rangers.
MORA
    A Robert; Pvt, A, 11th Inf.
    Emilio; Pvt, A, 11th Tex Inf.
    José; Pvt, G, 17th Consolidated Tex Dismounted Cav.
    José M; Pvt, A, 11th Tex If.
    Juan; Pvt, C, Ragsdale's Batt'n of Tex Cav.
    Juan; Pvt, H, Baird's Reg of Tex Cav.
    Luis; Pvt, E, 19th Tex Inf.
    Roberto; Pvt, A, 1st Tex Inf & 11 Tex Inf.
MORAL
    José; 20, Pvt, I, 33d Tex Cav.
    Victor; 24, Pvt, I, 33d Tex Cav.
MORALES
    Antonio; Pvt, A, 3d Tex Inf.
    Francisco; 35, Pvt, C, 8th Tex Inf, cobbler.
    Olivario; Pvt, 8th Tex Field Battery.
    Polinario; 23, Pvt, Bustillo's Co, Bexar Cty.
    Ventura; Pvt, Jeff Davis HG, 29th Brig, TM, Refugio Cty.
MORENO
    Antonio; 30, Pvt, Bustillo's Co, Bexar Cty,; H, 3d Tex Inf, disability discharge April 22, 1863 (wounded in the arm).
    Bartolo; 29, 3d Sgt, H, 33d Tex Cav; Sgt, B, Benavides' Reg.
    Carlos; Pvt, 4th Tex Field Battery.
    Damasio; Pvt, I, 33d Tex Cav; B, Benavides' Reg.
    José María; 28, 1st Sgt, H, 33d Tex Cav.
    Manuel; 18, Pvt, C, 3d Tex Inf, b Matamoros, Tamps, d Nov 1, 1861.
    N; 17, Pvt, G, 8th Tex Inf.
    Rafael; 18, Pvt, C, 3d Tex Inf, b Matamoros, Tamps.
    Segundo; 20, Pvt, I, 33d Tex Cav; B, Benavides' Reg.
    Ylario; 19, Pvt, I, 33d Tex Cav; B, Benavides' Reg.
MOYA
    Blas; 17, Pvt, H, 8th Tex Inf.
MUGUERZA
    Pedro; 33, Pvt, A, Benavides' Reg, quartermaster's clerk.

MUNGUÍA
    Anastacio; 26, Pvt, E, 1st Tex Cav, GCM, San Antonio, Sept 29, 1862, sleeping while on guard, found guilty and sentenced to 30 days at hard labor, d Dec 8, 1863 (Victoria).
    Anastacio; Pvt, C, 8th Tex Inf.
    Epifanio; 36, Pvt, Thomas' Co of Partisan Rangers.
    Francisco; 45, Pvt, Thomas' Co of Partisan Rangers.
    Jacinto; 24, Pvt, Thomas' Co of Partisan Rangers.
    Jesús; 28, Pvt, Thomas' Co of Partisan Rangers.
    Nepomuceno; 26, Pvt, Thomas' Co of Partisan Rangers.
    Pedro; 20, Pvt, Thomas' Co of Partisan Rangers.
    Ramón; 34, Pvt, Thomas' Co of Partisan Rangers.

MUÑOZ (Munos)
    Florencio; 22, Pvt, F, 3d Tex Inf, b Brownsville, Tex, d Feb 18, 1862.
    Isidro; Pvt, Medina Guards, 40th Brig, TM, Bexar Cty.
    José María; 35, Pvt, C, 8th Tex Inf.
    José María; 19, Pvt, H, 3d Tex Inf.
    Juan; Pvt, F, 3d Tex Inf, d Jan 2, 1862.
    Luis; McNeel's Coast Guards, TST,
    Pifano; 27, Pvt, C, 8th Tex Inf.

MURILLO
    Alejandro; Pvt, Jeff Davis HG, 29 Brig, TM, Refugio Cty.
    S; Pvt, Teel's Co, TST.

MÚSQUIZ
    Segundo; 35, Pvt, C, 8th Tex Inf; 3d Sgt, C, Benavides' Reg.

N

NAVARRO
    Alejandro; 23, Pvt, H, 33d Tex Cav, teamster.
    Ángel; 34, Capt, H, 8th Tex Inf.
    Celso C; 32, Sgt, H, 8th Tex Inf; Sgt, E, Benavides' Reg.
    Cresencio; Pvt, H, 36th Tex Cav.
    E; Pvt, Duff's Co, Bexar Cty.
    Encarnación; Pvt, D, 35th Tex Cav.
    Eugene; 1st Lt, K, 6th Tex Inf & 15th Tex Vols (inf & cav).
    José Antonio G; 1st Lt, Mitchell's Minute Men, TM, Bexar Cty.
    Juan; Jr 2d Lt, Mission Guards, 30th Brig, TM, Bexar Cty.
    Juan; Pvt, I, 33d Tex Cav.
    Lino; Pvt, Jeff Davis HG, 29th Brig, TM, Refugio Cty.
    Mauricio; Pvt, C, Benavides' Reg.
    Sixto; 28, Pvt, 2d Tex Mounted Rifles.
    Sixto E.; 29, Capt, H, 8th Tex Inf; Capt, E, Benavides' Reg.
    Valentín; 25, 3d Cpl, G, 8th Tex Inf; C, Benavides' Reg, d, rejoined Dec 31, 1863.
    Valentín; 24, Pvt, G, 3d Tex Inf, d Oct 6, 1861.

NIETO
    Andrés; 40, Pvt, A, 3d Tex Inf, b Texas, discharged July 12, 1862.
    Hilario; Pvt, D, 35th Tex Cav.

NOESSEL
>Félix; Pvt, Graham's Mounted Coast Guards, TST; Sgt, F, 1st Tex Cav; Jr 2d Lt, C, 8th Tex Inf; Benavides' Reg.

NUÑEZ
>Cleofas; 19, Pvt, H, 3d Tex Inf.
>José María; 40, 1st Cpl, I, 33d Tex Cav.
>Leandro; Pvt, F, 3d Tex Inf, d Nov 20, 1862.
>M; Pvt, Treviño's Partisan Rangers.

O

OCHOA
>Cornelio; 29, Pvt, Thomas' Co of Partisan Rangers.
>Eucancio; Pvt, I, Benavides' Reg.
>Francisco; 32, Pvt, H, 33d Tex Cav; A, Benavides' Reg.
>Jacinto; Pvt, I, Benavides' Reg.
>Nator; 29, Pvt, Thomas' Co of Partisan Rangers.
>Nicolás; 37, Pvt, Thomas' Co of Partisan Rangers.
>Pacífico; 57, Pvt, Thomas' Co of Partisan Rangers.

OLGUÍN; see Holguin

OLIVA
>Antonio; 58, Pvt, H, 3d Tex Inf, b Monterrey, NL, disability discharge April 6, 1863.

OLIVARES
>Agapito; 44, Pvt, Thomas' Co of Partisan Rangers.
>Leonardo; Pvt, Minute Men, TM, Starr Cty.
>Matías; Pvt, Medina Guards, 40th Brig, TM, Bexar Cty.
>Narcisco; Pvt, Zapata's Co, TST, Pct 10 (San Diego), Nueces Cty.
>Pablo; Pvt, B, 2d Tex Mounted Rifles.
>Polinario; Pvt, Zapata's Co, TST, Pct 10 (San Diego), Nueces Cty.
>Rafael; 30, Bugler, H, 33d Tex Cav; A, Benavides' Reg.

OLIVERA
>Nieves; 30, Pvt, F, 3d Tex Inf, d Sept 19, 1862.

OLMOS
>Vicente; 26, Pvt, I, 2d Tex Mounted Rifles.

OLVERA (Olbera)
>Antonio; 30, Pvt, I, 33d Tex Cav; B, Benavides' Reg.
>José María; 25, Pvt, I, 33d Tex Cav.
>Lorenzo; Pvt, Zapata's Co, Pct 10 (San Diego), Nueces Cty.

ORIANGO
>Bruno; Pvt, B, Ragsdale's Batt'n of Tex Cav.
>Juan; Pvt, B, Ragsdale's Batt'n of Tex Cav.

OROSCO
>S; Pvt, Treviño's Co of Partisan Rangers.
>Y; Pvt, Treviño's Co of Partisan Rangers.

ORTEGA
>Narciso; Pvt, I, Benavides' Reg.

ORTEGÓN
>Eduardo; 35, Pvt, Bustillo's Co, Bexar Cty.
>José; 21, Pvt, D, 2d Tex Mounted Rifles.

ORTIZ
- Antonio; Pvt, B, Waul's Tex Legion.
- Antonio; 20, Pvt, I, 8th Tex Inf, d March 7, 1863 (Corpus Christi).
- B; Pvt, Treviño's Co of Partisan Rangers.
- Celso; Pvt, A, Mann's Reg of Tex Cav.
- Esmerigildo; Cpl, Rhodes' Co, 3d Batt'n of Tex Cav.
- Estanislado; Pvt, A, 3d Tex Inf, d March 17, 1862; Ragsdale's Batt'n of Tex Cav.
- Jesús; 23, Pvt, A, Ragsdale's Batt'n of Tex Cav; D & I, Benavides' Reg.
- Juan; Pct, C, Ragsdale's Batt'n of Tex Cav.
- Juan Antonio; 24, Pvt, I, 8th Tex Inf, d August 11, 1862 (Corpus Christi).
- Juan José; Pvt, I, 33d Tex Cav; B, B, Benavides' Reg.
- Luján; Pvt, Victoria Aids, Victoria Cty.
- Luz; 32, Pvt, Pvt, A, Ragsdale's Batt'n of Tex Cav; D, Benavides' Reg.
- Martín; Pvt, C, Benavides' Reg.
- Miguel; Pvt, F, 16th Tex Inf.
- Mónico; 34, Sgt, A, Ragsdale's Batt'n of Tex Cav; D, Benavides' Reg.
- P; Pvt, Victoria Aids, Victoria Cty.
- Pedro; 22, Pvt, A, Ragsdale's Batt'n of Tex Cav; D, Benavides' Reg.
- R; Pvt, Victoria Aids, Victoria Cty.
- Rafael; 28, Pvt, Bustillo's Co, Bexar Cty; C, Ragsdale's Batt'n of Tex Cav.
- S; Pvt, Victoria Aids, Victoria Cty.
- Selso; A, Mann's Reg, Tex Cav.
- Serpano; Pvt, D, 3d Tex Inf, b, Jalapa, VC, d Sept 15, 1862.
- Víctor; Cpl, Rhodes' Co, 3d Batt'n of Tex Cav.

OSUÑA
- Guadalupe; 25, Pvt, D, 2d Tex Mounted Rifles; Cpl, E, Ragsdale's Batt'n of Tex Cav.
- Hilario; 2d Cpl, Bustillo's Co, Bexar Cty; Sgt, F, 3d Tex Inf.
- Victor; Cpl, Rhodes' Co, 3rd (Yager's) Tex Cav.
- Viviano; 25, Pvt, Bustillo's Co, Bexar Cty.

OZOS
- Simón; 20, Pvt, A, Ragsdale's Batt'n of Tex Cav.

P

PACHECO
- Albino; Ragsdale's Batt'n of Tex Cav.
- Fabián; Pvt, Gray's Co, TM, Pct 5, Bexar Cty; H, 8th Tex Inf.
- Felipe; Pvt, Rhodes' Co, 3d Batt'n of Tex Cav.
- Francisco; Pvt, Gray's Co, TM, Pct 5, Bexar Cty.
- Francisco; Pvt, B, Ragsdale's Batt'n of Tex Cav.
- Luciano; Pvt, F, 3d Tex Inf, d Sept 20, 1862.
- Martín; Musician, F, 20th Tex Inf.

PADILLA
- José; Pvt, Medina Guards, 40th Brig, TM, Bexar Cty.

PADRÓN
- David; Pvt, B, 17th Tex Inf.

PALACIO
- Anaceto; Pvt, 8th Tex Field Batt'n.
- Francisco; Pvt, G, 16th Tex Inf.

PALACIO[continued]
  Leandro; 18, Pvt, Littleton's Co, Ford's Reg.
PALUCO
  Juan; Pvt, 24, Gray Co, 30th Brig, TM, Pct 5, Bexar Cty.
PAREDES
  Jesús; Pvt, H, 33d Tex Cav; F, Benavides' Reg.
  Manuel; 23, Pvt, H, 33d Tex Cav; A, Benavides' Reg.
PATILLO
  Daniel A; Pvt, F, Ragsdale's Batt'n of Tex Cav.
PEDRAZO
  Faustino; 30, Pvt, C, 8th Tex Inf.
PELLOQUÍN
  César; 17, Pvt, A, Ragsdale's Batt'n of Tex Cav.
PEMÉREZ
  Nicolás; Pvt, E, 8th Tex Inf.
PEÑA
  Cenobio; 35, Pvt, H, 33d Tex Cav; A, Benavides' Reg.
  Liberto; Pvt, Gray's Co, TM, Pct 5, Bexar Cty.
  Luis; 25, Pvt, A, 3d Tex Inf, d Sept 23, 1862.
  Manuel; Pvt, Zapata's Co, TST, Pct 10 (San Diego), Nueces Cty.
  Modesto; Pvt, I, 2d Tex Inf.
  Ramón; Pvt, D, Benavides' Reg.
PEÑAL
  Joseph; Pvt, K, 9th Tex Cav.
PEÑALOZA
  Joseph M; 28, 2d Lt, 30th Brig, TM, Pct 1, Bexar Cty;
    Capt, C & E, 8th Tex. Inf; Capt, C, Benavides' Reg.
PERALES
  JF; Pvt, F, 3d Tex Inf.
PEREA
  Herbacio; Pvt, B, Ragsdale's Batt'n of Tex Cav.
PEREIRA
  Madero; Pvt, B, Ragsdale's Batt'n of Tex Cav.
PÉREZ (Peres)
  A; Pvt, E, 33d Tex Cav, d & arrested April 30, 1864.
  A; Pvt, Teel's Co, TST.
  Alejos; Pvt, C, 2d Tex Cav, 8th Tex. Inf, d Dec 6, 1863 (Victoria).
  Alejos; 26, 4th Cpl, B, 2d Tex. Mounted Rifles
  Alejos; 1st Sgt, Zapata's Co, TST, Pct 10 (San Diego), Nueces Cty.
  Anastacio; 25, Pvt, Zapata's Co, TST,
    Pct 10 (San Diego), Nueces Cty; I, 8th Tex Inf.
  Ángel; 40, Pvt, Tom's Co, TM, Atascosaa Cty.
  Antonio; Pvt, B, 2d Tex Mounted Rifles.
  Antonio; 19, Cpl, H, 3d Tex Inf.
  B; Pvt, Teel's Co, TST; B, 2d Tex Mounted Rifles.
  Benito; 36, 1st Sgt, C & F, 3d Tex Inf, b. Mexico City, Mex, d May 12, 1863.
  Damacio; Pvt, C, Benavides' Reg.
  Desiderio; 23, Pvt, 2d Tex Mounted Rifles, POW.
  Eugenio; 19, Pvt, C, 3d Tex Inf.
  Eusebio; 24, Pvt, H, 8th Tex Inf; D, Benavides' Reg.

PÉREZ (Peres) [continued]
    Eusebio; Pvt, Medina Guards, 40th Brig, TM, Bexar Cty.
    Francisco; Mus, 2d Tex Mounted Rifles (Mesilla, NM).
    Francisco; Pvt, 2d Tex Field Battery.
    Ignacio; 23, Pvt, A, Ragsdale's Batt'n of Tex Cav; D, Benavides' Reg.
    JM; Pvt, Treviño's Co of Partisan Rangers.
    Jamas; Pvt, E, Benavides' Reg.
    Jesús; 23, Pvt, Thomas' Co of Partisan Rangers.
    Jesús; Pvt, Treviño's Co of Partisan Rangers.
    Jesús; Pvt, Medina Guards, 40th Brig, TM, Bexar Cty.
    José Antonio; Pvt, Duran's Co, FST, Atascosa Cty.
    José María; 29, Pvt, H, 8th Tex Inf.
    Juan; 3d Sgt, Treviño's Co of Partisan Rangers.
    Magdaleno; 30, Pvt, E, 8th Tex Inf, d Dec 3, 1863 (Victoria).
    Narciso; Pvt, Zapata's Co, TST, Pct 10 (San Diego), Nueces Cty.
    Norberto; 29, Pvt, C, 8th Tex Inf; C, Benavides' Reg.
    Pablo; Pvt, Zapata's Co, TST, Pct 10 (San Diego), Nueces Cty.
    Roberto; Pvt, C, Benavides' Reg.
    Rosario; 28, Pvt, Bustillo's Co, Bexar Cty.
    Teodoro; 22, Pvt, Bustillo's Co, Bexar Cty; A, 3d Tex Inf.
    Tomás; 20, Pvt, H, 8th Tex Inf.
    Tomás; 2d Lt, Duran's Co, FST, Atascosa Cty.
    Valente; Pvt, Zapata's Co, TST, Pct 10 (San Diego), Nueces Cty.
    Viviano; 30, Pvt, Littleton's Co, Ford's Reg.
    Ygnacio; Pvt, A, Ragsdale's Batt'n of Tex Cav.
    Ygnacio; 19, Cpl, H, 3d Tex Inf.
PERIDO
    Clovin; Pvpt, C, Benavides' Reg.
PINTO
    Cristóbal; 30, Pvt, C, 3d Tex Inf, b San Luis Potosí, SLP, d Feb 4, 1862.
PLAZA
    Edward; Pvt, G, 3d Tex Inf, d May 30, 1862.
    Vicente; 35, Pvt, H, 33d Tex Cav; A, Benavides' Reg, blacksmith & farrier.
POLANCO
    Manuel; 28, Pvt, H, 8th Tex Inf.
POLINARES
    Victor; 18, Pvt, C, 8th Tex Inf.
PONCÉ
    Nicolás; Sgt, A, 12th Tex Cav.
PORRAS
    Jesús; 37, Cpl, Treviño's Co of Partisan Rangers.
POSTELLO
    C; 18, Pvt,
POSTILLO
    Eduardo; 27, Pvt, D, 3d Tex Inf, b. Zacatecas, Zac.
    Leonardo; 29, Pvt, D, 3d Tex Inf, b. Zacatecas, Zac, d Dec 25, 1861.
PROTIM
    Manuel Alfaro; 2d Lt, Gray's Co, TM, Pct 5, Bexar Cty.
PRADO
    Locario; Pvt, A, 11th Tex Inf.

PRUNEDA
    Casildo; Pvt, Minute Men, TM, Starr Cty.
PULIDO
    Canuto; Pvt, F, 3d Tex Inf, d Jan 2, 1862.
    Ylario; Pvt, I, Benavides' Reg.

Q

QUIÑONES
    Candelario; 22, Pvt, Bustillo's Co, Bexar Cty.
QUINTERO
    Fernández; 28, Pvt, G, 3d Tex Inf, d Nov 8, 1862.
    Francisco; Pvt, A, Ragsdale's Batt'n of Tex Cav;
        3d Cpl, D, Benavides' Reg.
    Gabriel; 21, Pvt, C, 3d Tex Inf, b Victoria, Tamps, d April 29, 1862.
    Jesús; 30, Pvt, Gray's Co, 30th Brig, TM, Pct 5, Bexar Cty.
    Jesús; Pvt, A, Ragsdale's Batt'n of Tex Cav.
    John A; 23, Cpl, A, 3d Tex Inf, d March 17, 1862.
    Manuel; Pvt, Medina Guards, 40th Brig, TM, Bexar Cty.
    Tomás; 25, 3d Sgt, A, Ragsdale's Batt'n of Tex Cav; 2d Sgt, D,
        Benavides' Reg.
    Vidal; Pvt, Gray's Co, TM, Pct 5, Bexar Cty.
QUINTO
    Agustín; Pvt, B, Ragsdale's Batt'n of Tex Cav.
QUIROGA
    Juan; 23, Pvt, G, 3d Tex Inf, d Oct 8, 1861.

R

RAMÍREZ (Ramires)
    Antonio; 24, Pvt, C & H, 8th Tex Inf.
    Antonio; 40, Pvt, H, 3d Tex Inf, d May 18, 1863.
    Enemicio; Pvt, Lamar HG, 29th Brig, TM, Refugio Cty.
    Epifanio; 46, Pvt, Gray's Co, TM, Pct 5, Bexar Cty.
    Eulogio; 18, Cpl, C, 3d Tex Inf, b Matamoros, Tamps, d June 18, 1862.
    Genaro; 24, Pvt, I, 33d Tex Cav; B, Benavides' Reg.
    Heraldo; Mus, Pvt, C, 8th Tex Inf.
    Juan; 24, Pvt, E, 8th Tex Inf, d Dec 3, 1863 (Victoria).
    Juan; Pvt, Coast Guards, 32d Brig, TM, Cameron Cty.
    Juan; 19, Pvt, Thomas' Co of Partisan Rangers.
    Juan; Pvt, Zapata's Co, TST, Pct 10 (San Diego), Nueces Cty.
    Julián; Pvt, Zapata's Co, TST, Pct 10 (San Diego), Nueces Cty.
    Leonidas; 17, Pvt, C, 8th Tex Inf, charges preferred,
        neglect of duty, February 13, 1863.
    Nicolás; 19, Pvt, E, 8th Tex Inf.
    Pedro; Pvt, Gray's Co, TM, Pct 5, Bexar Cty.
    Pedro; 23, Pvt, D, 2d Tex Mounted Rifles.
    Roberto; 43, Pvt, G, 3d Tex Inf.
    Ynosente; Pvt, Minute Men, TM, Starr Cty.
RAMÓN
    A; Pvt, Teel's Co, TST.
    Genza; Pvt, I, Benavides' Reg.

RAMÓN [continued]
    Geraldo; 18, Mus & Pvt, C, 8th Tex Inf, d Dec 21, 1863 (Columbus); C, Benavides' Reg.
    Martín; 27, 4th Sgt, I, 33d Tex Cav.
    Seferino; Pvt, F, 3d Tex Inf, d Feb 25, 1862.

RAMOS
    A; Pvt, A, 15th Tex Field Battery.
    Ángel; Pvt, B, Ragsdale's Batt'n of Tex Cav.
    Antonio; Mus & Pvt, F, 8th Tex Inf.
    H; Pvt, Crump's Reg of Tex Cav.
    Juan; 35, Pvt, C, 8th Tex Inf; D, Benavides' Reg.
    Juan; Pvt, C, Benavides' Reg.
    Julián; Pvt, Zapata's Co, Pct 10 (San Diego), Nueces Cty.
    Luciano; Pvt, 4th Tex Field Battery
    Manuel; Pvt, 8th Tex Inf.
    Manuel; Pvt, F, 3d Tex Inf, disability discharge Aug 31, 1864.
    Pascual; 31, Pvt, Bustillo's Co, Bexar Cty; C 8th Tex Inf, disability discharge (fistula in the perineum and scrotum) April 24, 1863, b Mex, laborer.
    Pedro; 25, Pvt, Bustillo's Co, Bexar Cty; Pvt, I, 33d Tex Cav.
    Tomás; Pvt, B, Ragsdale's Batt'n of Tex Cav.

RANGEL
    Antonio; Pvt, Zapata's Co, TST, Pct 10 (San Diego), Nueces Cty.
    Francisco; 40, Pvt, Bustillo's Co, Bexar Cty; G, 3d Tex Inf.
    Gabriel; Pvt, Zapata's Co, TST, Pct 10 (San Diego), Nueces Cty.
    H; Pvt, Crump's Reg of Tex Cav.
    Jesús; Pvt, Zapata's Co, TST, Pct 10 (San Diego), Nueces Cty.
    Luciano; Pvt, 4th Tex Field Battery.
    Macedonia; Pvt, Zapata's Co, TST, Pct 10 (San Diego), Nueces Cty.
    Manuel; Pvt, F, 3d Tex Inf.
    Narciso; Pvt, B, Ragsdale's Batt'n of Tex Cav.
    Natividad; 28, Pvt, F, 3d Tex Inf, d Sept 23, 1862.
    Pascual; Pvt, C, 8th Tex Inf.
    Rosales; Pvt, Engledow's Co, 29th Brig, TM, Nueces Cty.
    Tomás; Pvt, B, Ragsdale's Batt'n of Tex Cav.
    Ursino; Pvt, Zapata's Co, TST, Pct 10 (San Diego), Nueces Cty.

REGALADO
    Francisco; Pvt, D, Ragsdale's Batt'n of Tex Cav.

RENDÓN
    Dionisio; Pvt, H, 33d Tex Cav; A, Benavides' Reg.
    Ignacio; Pvt, A, 3d Batt'n of Tex Cav.
    Teófilo; 26, Musician, I, 8th Tex Inf, d June 13, 1863 (Corpus Christi), b Mex.

RESÉNDEZ
    G; Pvt, C, 8th Tex Inf, d Dec 6, 1863 (Victoria).
    Guadalupe; Pvt, Zapata's Co, TST, Pct 10 (San Diego), Nueces Cty.
    Severo; Pvt, A, 3d Batt'n of Tex Cav.

REYES
    Andrés; Pvt, B, Benavides' Reg.
    Balvino; 36, Pvt, Bustillo's Co, Bexar Cty.

REYES [continued]
    Catarino; Pvt, Medina Guards, 40th Brig, TM, Bexar Cty.
    Francisco; 40, Pvt, C, 8th Tex Inf; C, Benavides' Reg.
    Juan; Pvt, Medina Guards, 40th Brig, TM, Bexar Cty.
    Juan; Pvt, Teel's Co, TST; B, 2d Tex Mounted Rifles.
    Juardelos; Pvt, E, Benavides' Reg.
    Luis; 30, Pvt, Treviño's Co of Partisan Rangers.
    Manuel; Pvt, Medina Guards, 40th Brig, TM, Bexar Cty.
    Manuel; Pvt, 8th Tex Field Battery.
    Matilde; Pvt, Jeff Davis HG, 29th Brig, TM, Refugio Cty.
    Pedro; 38, Pvt, G, 8th Tex Inf, AWOL, June 1863.
    Peter; Pvt, I, 2d Tex Mounted Rifles.
    Polinario; 19, Pvt, C, 8th Tex Inf, d Sept 13, 1862.
    Práxides; Pvt, F, Hardeman's Reg, Arizona Brig.
    Práxides; 19, Pvt, A, Ragsdale's Batt'n of Tex Cav.
    Refugio; 30, Pvt, C, 8th Tex Inf; C, Benavides' Reg.
    Víctor; Pvt, 8th Tex Field Battery.
RIBERO
    D; Pvt, C, 8th Tex Inf, d Dec 6, 1863 (Victoria).
RINCÓN
    José; 19, Pvt, A, Ragsdale's Batt'n of Tex Cav.
RIOJAS
    Jesús; Pvt, I, Benavides' Reg.
RÍOS
    C; Pvt, C, 4th Tex Cav.
    Cayetano; Pvt, Zapata's Co, TST, Pct 10 (San Diego), Nueces Cty.
    Dimas; Pvt, F, 3d Tex Inf.
    Fermín; 28, Pvt, H, 3d Tex Inf.
    Manuel; 30, Pvt, Watkins' Co, 3d Frontier Dist, Uvalde Cty.
    Nabor; Pvt, Zapata's Co, TST, Pct 10 (San Diego), Nueces Cty.
    Rafael; Pvt, Minute Men, TM, Starr Cty.
RIVAS
    Agustín; 23, Pvt, A, 2d Tex Inf, d June 21, 1862.
    Andrés; Pvt, B, 2nd Tex Mounted Rifles.
    Eduardo; 24, Pvt, H, 8th Tex Inf; E, Benavides' Reg.
    Federico; 25, Pvt, B, 2d Tex Mounted Rifles.
    Indalecio; 28, Pvt, B, 2d Tex Mounted Rifles; F, Benavides' Reg.
    José; 3d Cpl, C, Ragsdale's Batt'n of Tex Cav.
    Juan; Pvt, A, Ragsdale's Batt'n of Tex Cav.
    Juan Manuel; 22, Pvt, A, 3d Tex Inf.
    Mauricio; Pvt, A, Ragsdale's Batt'n of Tex Cav.
RIVERA
    Diego; Pvt, Zapata's Co, TST, Pct 10 (San Diego), Nueces Cty.
    Elijio; 26, Pvt, Bustillo's Co, Bexar Cty.
    Eugenio; Pvt, Zapata's Co, TST, Pct 10 (San Diego), Nueces Cty.
    Francisco; 26, Pvt, Bustillo's Co, Bexar Cty.
    M; San Elizario Spy Co, 2d Tex Mounted Rifles.
    Rodrigo; 30, Pvt, I, 8th Tex Inf, d Feb 28, 1862 (Corpus Christi), b Mex.
    Tito P; Pvt, B, 1st Tex Cav; Sgt, E, 33d Tex Cav.

ROBLEDO
  Frausto; Pvt, I, Benavides' Reg.
ROBLES
  Dolores; 23, Pvt, A, Ragsdale's Batt'n of Tex Cav.
  Juan; 23, Pvt, I, 33d Tex Cav; B, Benavides' Reg.
  Panciano; 25, Pvt, A, Ragsdale's Batt'n of Tex Cav.
ROCHA
  Julián; 35, Pvt, I, 33d Tex Cav.
RODRÍGUEZ (Rodrigues)
  AB; Pvt, 15th Tex Field Battery.
  Alcario; 18, Pvt, C, 8th Tex Inf, d, rejoined Dec 31, 1863.
  Agustín; 28, Pvt, Bustillo's Co, Bexar Cty.
  Anastacio; 31, Pvt, C, 8th Tex Inf, d June 1863.
  Andrés; 28, Pvt, C, 8th Tex Inf, b Mexico, laborer.
  Antonio; 43, Pvt, Gray's Co, TM, Pct 5, Bexar Cty.
  Antonio; 40, C, 3d Tex Inf, b. Guadalajara, Jal.
  Benito; Pvt, Minute Men, TM, Starr Cty.
  Benito; Pvt, 8th Tex Field Battery.
  Cayetano; 18, Pvt, C, 3d Tex Inf, b. Marina, Tamps, d March 13, 1862.
  Celso; 24, Pvt, Gray's Co, 30th Brig, TM, Pct 5, Bexar Cty.
  Cesario; 30, Pvt, I, 33d Tex Cav; Cpl, B, Benavides' Reg.
  Damacio; Pvt, B, Ragsdale's Batt'n of Tex Cav.
  Doroteo; Pvt, Jeff Davis HG, 29th Brig, TM, Refugio Cty.
  Enemecio; Pvt, Lamar HG, 29th Brig, Refugio Cty.
  Espinosa; Pvt, C, Benavides' Reg.
  Espiridión; 29, Pvt, C, 8th Tex Inf, b Mexico, laborer & teamster.
  Evaristo; 19, Pvt, I, 33d Tex Cav; G, Benavides' Reg.
  Francisco; Pvt, Medina Guards, 40th Brig, TM, Bexar Cty.
  Francisco; Pvt, B, Ragsdale's Batt'n of Tex Cav.
  Francisco; Pvt & Bugler, A, 26th Tex Cav.
  Francisco; 24, Pvt, G, 3d Tex Inf, disability discharge October 1861.
  Frank; Pvt & Bugler, A, 26th Tex Cav.
  Frank; Pvt, E, 1st Tex Heavy Art.
  Gervacio; Pvt, B, 2d Tex Mounted Rifles.
  Guadalupe; 18, Pvt, C, 3d Tex Inf, b Monterrey, NL, d Dec 15, 1861.
  Gumecindo; 22, Cpl, H, 8th Tex Inf.
  Hilario; 22, Tom's Co, TST, Atascosa Cty.
  Isabel; 31, Pvt, H, 8th Tex Inf.
  Isidro; 24, Pvt, F, 3d Tex Inf, disability discharge July 25, 1863.
  J; Pvt, Treviño's Co of Partisan Rangers
  JP; 34, Pvt, Mitchell's Co, 3d Frontier Dist, Bandera Cty.
  Jesús; 23, Pvt, H, 3d Tex Inf.
  Jesús; 2d Sgt, Bustillo's Co, Bexar Cty.
  Jesús; 25, 4th Cpl, C, 8th Tex Inf.
  Jesús; 27, Pvt, I, 33d Tex Cav; C, Benavides' Reg.
  Jesús; 18, Pvt & Mus, A & F, 3d Tex Inf, b Monterrey, NL, d Dec 18, 1861.
  Jesús; 21, Pvt, Bustillo's Co, Bexar Cty.
  Jesús; 1st Sgt, Treviño's Co of Partisan Rangers.
  Jesús; Pvt, Treviño's Co of Partisan Rangers.
  Jesús Manuel; Pvt, Gray's Co, 30th Brig, TM, Bexar Cty.

RODRÍGUEZ (Rodrigues) [continued]
    José; Pvt, Jeff Davis HG, 29th Brig, TM, Refugio Cty.
    José; 32, Pvt, B, 2d Tex Mounted Rifles.
    José; Pvt, Oury's Co, Herbert's Batt'n of Arizona Cav.
    José M; Pvt, D, 16th Tex Cav.
    José María; 28, Cpl, C, 8th Tex Inf; E, Benavides' Reg,
        b San Antonio, Tex, laborer.
    José María; 47, 1st Sgt, F, 3d Tex Inf, b. Coah, disability
        discharge Sept 20, 1862.
    José María; 25, Pvt, H, 8th Tex Inf.
    José María; Pvt, Jeff Davis HG, 29th Brig, TM, Refugio Cty.
    José María; 28, Pvt, Bustillo's Co, Bexar Cty.
    Juan; 21, Recruit, C, 3d Tex Inf.
    Juan; Sgt, Rhodes' Co, 3d Batt'n of Tex Cav.
    Juan; 29, Pvt, C, 8th Tex Inf, d Dec 21, 1863 (Columbus); C, Benavides' Reg.
    Juan; Pvt, Gray's Co, TM, Pct 5, Bexar Cty.
    Juan José; Pvt, Medina Guards, 40th Brig, TM, Bexar Cty.
    Juan M; 1st Lt, Gray Town Pioneers, Pct 5, 30th Brig, TM, Bexar Cty.
    Lapinesion; 2d Lt, Gray Town Pioneers, 30th Brig, TM, Bexar Cty.
    Manuel; 18, Pvt, C, 8th Tex Inf, d Aug 1862.
    Manuel; 27, Pvt, Bustillo's Co, Bexar Cty.
    Manuel; 42, Pvt, Tom's Co, TST, Atascosa Co.
    Marcelo; Pvt, Medina Guards, 40th Brig, TM, Bexar Cty.
    Marcelino; 35, Pvt, Gray's Co, TM, 30th Brig, Pct 5, Bexar Cty.
    Mariano; 22, Pvt, H, 8th Tex Inf; Sgt, E, Benavides' Reg.
    Maximiliano; 2d Lt, Gray's Co, TM, 30th Brig, Pct, 5, Bexar Cty.
    Martiniano; 21, Pvt, Bustillo's Co, Bexar Cty; F, 3d Tex Inf.
    Miguel; 23, Pvt, B, 2d Tex Mounted Rifles.
    Miguel; Pvt, A, 3d Tex Batt'n of Tex Cav.
    N; Pvt, B, Chisum's Reg of Tex Cav.
    Narciso; Pvt, Waxahachie Co, 19, Brig, TM, Ellis Cty.
    Narciso; Cpl, H, 18th Tex Cav.
    Navaira; Sgt, F, Benavides' Reg.
    Nepomuceno; 2d Lt, Gray's Co, TM, Pct 5, Bexar Cty.
    P; Pvt, Treviño's Co of Partisan Rangers.
    Pedro; Pvt, Duran's Co, FST, Atascosa Cty.
    Pedro; 30, Pvt, C, 3d Tex Inf, b Soto, NL, d Dec 5, 1861.
    Prudencio; Pvt, Gray's Co, 30th Brig, TM, Pct 5, Bexar Cty.
    Rafael; Pvt, Medina Guards, 40th Brig, TM, Bexar Cty.
    Rafael; 27, Pvt, D, 3d Tex Inf, b NL, d Dec 1, 1861.
    Rafael; 30, Pvt, H, 33d Tex Cav; A, Benavides' Reg.
    Rafael; Pvt, Kemper City & Carlos Ranch Co, 24th Brig, TM, Victoria Cty.
    Ricardo; 23, Pvt, E, 8th Tex Inf, d Oct 16, 1862 (Corpus Christi).
    Rivera; Pvt, I, 8th Tex Inf.
    Roque; 24, Pvt, I, 33d Tex Cav.
    S; Pvt, Teel's Co, TST.
    S; Pvt, Treviño's Co of Partisan Rangers.
    Salvador; 23, Pvt, Gray's Co, 30th Brig, TM, Pct 5, Bexar Cty;
        C, 8th Tex Inf, d Dec 21, 1863 (Columbus).
    Serapio; 38, Pvt, Gray's Co, 30th Brig, TM, Pct 5, Bexar Cty.

RODRÍGUEZ (Rodrigues) *[continued]*
    Simón; Pvt, 26, Tom's Co, TST, Atascosa Cty.
    Simón (2d); Pvt, 30, Tom's Co, TST, Atascosa Cty.
    T; Pvt, B, 2d Tex Mounted Rifles.
    Timoteo; Pvt, H, 8th Tex Inf; B, Benavides' Reg.
    Tomás; Pvt, D, Benavides' Reg.
    Tomás A; 23, 2d Lt, H, 8th Tex Inf; Lt, Ragsdale's Batt'n of
        Tex Cav; Capt & Adj, Benavides' Reg.
    Trinidad; Pvt, I, Benavides' Reg.
    Ventura; Pvt, B, Ragsdale's Batt'n of Tex Cav.
    Ysidro; 23, Pvt, Bustillo's Co, Bexar Cty.
ROMÁN
    Francisco; 19, Bugler, I, 33d Tex Cav.
    José María; 19, Pvt, E, 8th Tex Inf.
ROMERO
    Eutimio; 35, Pvt, D, 2d Tex Mounted Rifles.
    Felipe; 34, Pvt, Gray's Co, 30th Brig, TM,
        Pct 5, Bexar Cty; B, Ragsdale's Batt'n of Tex Cav.
    Francisco; Pvt, B, Ragsdale's Batt'n of Tex Cav.
    Luis; Pvt, A, Grandbury's Consolidated Tex Brig; H, 6th Tex Inf.
    Presentario; Pvt, I, Benavides' Reg.
ROMO
    Nicolás; Pvt, C, 3rd (Yager's) Batt'n of Tex Cav.
ROSALES
    Ándres; 23, Pvt, I, 8th Tex Inf, b Tex, d Feb 28, 1862 (Corpus Christi).
    Pedro; 30, Pvt, C, 8th Tex Inf, discharged Aug 1862.
    R; Pvt, E, Border's Reg of Tex Cav.
    Vidal; Pvt, C, Ragsdale's Batt'n of Tex Cav.
    Vidal; Pvt, E, Madison's Reg, Arizona Brig.
ROYO[?]
    José María; Pvt, Treviño's Co of Partisan Rangers.
RUBALCABA
    Antonio; 22, Pvt, A, 3d Tex Inf, d Dec 19, 1861.
RUBIO
    Adriano; 25, Pvt, C, 8th Tex Inf; C, Benavides' Reg.
    Francisco; Pvt, B, 2d Tex Mounted Rifles; F, Benavides' Reg.
    Juan; 25, Pvt, E, 8th Tex Inf.
    Salomé; 25, Pvt, H, 33d Tex Cav.
RUELAS
    Claudio; 29, Pvt, C, 3d Tex Inf, b Tampico, Tamps, d Sept 8, 1862.
RUIS; see Ruiz
RUIZ
    Alex M; Capt, A, 3d Tex Inf.
    Alejo; Pvt, H, 8th Tex Inf, disability discharge Sept 1, 1862.
    Brade; 21, Pvt, D, 2d Tex Mounted Rifles.
    Carpio; 26, Pvt, C, 3d Tex Inf, b Matamoros, Tamps, d Sept 7, 1862.
    Eugene; 3rd Sgt, Medina Guards, 40th Brig, TM, Bexar Cty.
    Eugene; Pvt, B, 2d Tex Mounted Rifles.
    Eugenio; Pvt, F, Benavides' Reg.
    Francisco; Cpl, Rhodes' Co, 3d Batt'n of Tex Cav.

RUIZ [continued]
   Gabriel; Pvt, Medina Guards, 40th Brig, TM, Bexar Cty;
      B, Ragsdale's Batt'n of Tex Cav.
   Jesús; Pvt, F, 2d Tex Mounted Rifles.
   José; Pvt, Treviño's Co of Partisan Rangers.
   José Antonio; 41, Pvt, Duran's Co & Tom's Co, FST, Atascosa Cty.
   José María; 23, Pvt, Gray's Co, TM, Pct 5, Bexar Cty;
      A, 3d Tex Inf, d April 19, 1862.
   Marcelino; 25, Pvt, C, 8th Tex Inf, d Nov 15, 1862,
      rejoined from desertion, Nov 19, 1862.
   Matías; 25, Pvt, D, 2d Tex Mounted Rifles.
   Pedro; 4th Cpl, Medina Guards, 40th Brig, TM, Bexar Cty.
   Pedro; 22, Pvt, D, 3d Tex Inf, d Feb 16, 1862.

S

SABADO
   Rafael; enrolled & furloughed, Victoria Cty.
SAIS
   Albino; 28, Pvt, Thomas' Co of Partisan Rangers.
   Basilio; Pvt, Medina Guards, 40th Brig, TM, Bexar Cty.
   Colpia; Pvt, Skidmore's Co, 29th Brig, TM, Pct 1, San Patricio Cty.
   Guadalupe; 20, Pvt, C, 3d Tex Inf, b Matamoros, Tamps.
   José; 23, Pvt, I, 8th Tex Inf, b. Tex.
   Manuel; 19, Pvt, I, 8th Tex Inf.
   Martín; Pvt, A, Yaeger's Batt'n of Tex Cav.
   Sixto; Pvt, Coast Guards, 32d Brig, TM, Cameron Cty.
   Ylanio; Pvt, I, Benavides' Reg.
SAIZ; see Sais
SAENZ
   Juan; Pvt, Zapata's Co, TST, Pct 10 (San Diego), Nueces Cty.
SALAS
   José M; Pvt, Zapata's Co, TST, Pct 10 (San Diego), Nueces Cty.
SALADO
   Marcello; Pvt, Medina Guards, 40th Brig, TM, Bexar Cty.
SALAZAR
   Candelario; Pvt, Kemper City & Carlos Ranch Co, 24th Brig, TM,
      Victoria Cty.
   Casimiro; Mus, 2d Tex Mounted Rifles (Mesilla NM).
   Crecencio; 28, Pvt, C, 3d Tex Inf, b Reynosa, Tamps, d Dec 14, 1861.
   Fernando; Pvt, Rhodes' Co, 3d Batt'n Tex Cav.
   Francisco; Pvt, D, Benavides' Reg.
   Griserto; Pvt, Rhodes' Co, 3d Batt'n Tex Cav.
   José; Pvt, C, Ragsdale's Batt'n of Tex Cav.
   Juan; Pvt, C, Ragsdale's Batt'n of Tex Cav.
   Margarito; Pvt, F, 1st Tex Cav.
   Natividad; Pvt, F, 3d Tex Inf, d April 29, 1862.
   Narciso; Pvt, A, Ragsdale's Batt'n of Tex Cav; D, Benavides' Reg.
   Patricio; 22, Pvt, E, 8th Tex Inf, d Oct 16, 1862 (Corpus Christi).
   Santiago; 18, Pvt, E, 8th Tex Inf.
   T; Pvt, D, 5th Tex Cav.

SALAZAR [continued]
    Tomás; Pvt, C, 36th Tex Cav.
    Vicente; 18, Pvt, I, 8th Tex Inf.
SALCEDO
    Mariano; Pvt, E, Madison's Reg of Tex Cav.
SALINAS
    Andrés; 27, 1st Sgt, Thomas' Co of Partisan Rangers.
    Agustín; Pvt, Minute Men, TM, Starr Cty.
    Calestino; 20, Pvt, C, 3d Tex Inf, b Soto la Marina, Tamps.
    Carlos M; 28, 4th Cpl, I, 33d Tex Cav; B, Benavides' Reg.
    Damacio; Pvt, Zapata's Co, TST, Pct 10 (San Diego), Nueces Cty.
    Desiderio; Pvt, Zapata's Co, TST, Pct 10 (San Diego) Nueces Cty.
    Francisco; 22, Pvt, Thomas' Co of Partisan Rangers.
    Jacobo; 23, 2d Lt, I, 33d Tex Cav.
    Jesús; Pvt, Gray's Co, TM, Pct 5, Bexar Cty.
    José; Pvt, B, Baylor's Reg, Arizona Brig; 17th Tex Field Battery.
    José; 22, Pvt, D, 2d Tex Mounted Rifles.
    José M; Pvt, Zapata's Co, TST, Pct 10 (San Diego), Nueces Cty.
    Juan; 3d Sgt, Minute Men, TM, Starr Cty.
    Manuel; Pvt, C, Ragsdale's Batt'n of Tex Cav; B, Benavides' Reg.
    Martín; 25, Pvt, C, 3d Tex Inf, b Agualeguas, NL, d Dec 11, 1861.
    Mauricio; Pvt, Zapata's Co, TST, Pct 10 (San Diego), Nueces Cty.
    Mónico; 30, Pvt, H, 33d Tex Cav.
    Pablo; Pvt, 2d Tex Field Battery.
    Rafael; Pvt, D, Ragsdale's Batt'n of Tex Cav; D, Benavides' Reg.
    Ramón; 37, Cpl, Thomas' Co of Partisan Rangers.
    Refugio; Pvt, Engledow's Co, 29th Brig, TM, Nueces Cty.
    Vicente; 40, Cpl, F, 3d Tex Inf.
    Ynés; Pvt, C, Ragsdale's Batt'n of Tex Cav.
SALÍVAR
    Vicente; Pvt, I, 8th Tex Inf.
SALTILLO
    Manuel; Pvt, 8th Tex Field Battery.
SALOMÉ
    Bacilio; 25, Pvt, H, 33d Tex Cav.
SAMBRANO
    José; Pvt, Gray's Co, TM Pct 5, Bexar Cty.
SAMORA
    Gregorio; Pvt, C, 8th Tex Inf.
SANCEDO
    Albio; Pvt, G, 3d Tex Inf.
    Juan; 2d Lt, C, 8th Tex Inf.
    Mecindo; Sgt, C, 8th Tex Inf.
    Severiano; 16, Pvt, H, 8th Tex Inf, disability discharged (chronic cystitis) May 26, 1863, b Mexico, farmer.
    Umecindo; 26, 3d Sgt, H, 8th Tex Inf, absent in confinement by civil authorities (San Antonio) March 1863, rejoined Dec 1863, b Mex, laborer.
SANCHES; see Sánchez

SÁNCHEZ
    Agapito; 20, Pvt, D, 2d Tex Mounted Rifles.
    Anselmo; 25, Pvt, Bustillo's Co, Bexar Cty.
    Antonio; 25, Pvt, H, 33d Tex Cav.
    Antonio; Pvt, D, 6th Batt'n of Tex Cav.
    Antonio; Pvt, 6th Tex Field Battery.
    Brígido; Pvt, I, Benavides' Reg.
    Cecilio; 28, Pvt, Gray's Co, TM, 30th Brig, Pct, 5, Bexar Cty.
    Clemente; 21, Pvt, H, 33d Tex Cav.
    D; Pvt, Teel's Co, TST; B, 2d Tex Mounted Rifles.
    Demetrius; 29, Pvt, Treviño's Co of Partisan Rangers.
    Desiderio; 24, Pvt, I, 8th Tex Inf, b. Tex.
    Epifanio; 18, Pbt, Bustillo's Co, Bexar Cty.
    Eugenio; 23, Pvt, H, 33d Tex Cav.
    Félix; 37, Pvt, Treviño's Co of Partisan Rangers.
    Francisco; 30, Pvt, C, 3d Tex Inf, b Tamps, d Jan 21, 1862.
    Francisco; 18, Pvt, H, 33d Tex Cav; A, Benavides' Reg.
    Ignacio; Pvt, A, Benavides' Reg. k, Las Rucias, Tex, June 25, 1864.
    Jesús; 20, Pvt, A, 3d Tex Inf, d Mar 17, 1862.
    Jesús; Pvt, Engledow's Co, 29th Brig, TM, Nueces Cty.
    José; Pvt, K, 2d Tex Inf.
    Juan; Pvt, G, 2d Tex Inf.
    Juan; 24, Pvt, Tom's Co, TM, Atascosa Cty; G, 3d Tex Inf, d May 2, 1862.
    Juan Esteban; Pvt, F, 3d Tex Inf, d Jan 30, 1862.
    Julián; 26, Pvt, H, 8th Tex Inf, disability discharge (concussis corcri)
        March 1863, b Mex, merchant.
    Justo; Pvt, C, Ragsdale's Batt'n of Tex Cav.
    León; 25, Pvt, H, 33d Tex Cav.
    M; Pvt, Whitehead's Co, 1st Tex Inf.
    Manuel; Pvt, Medina Guards, 40th Brig, TM, Bexar Cty.
    Manuel; Pvt, H, 4th Tex Cav.
    Manuel; Pvt, Duran's Co, FST, Atascosa Cty.
    Marcelino; Pvt, H, 17th Tex Cav.
    Mariano; 28, Pvt, C, 3d Tex Inf, b Reynosa, Tamps, d Sept 18, 1862.
    Mario; Pvt, C, 3d Tex Inf.
    Mario; Pvt, H. 6th Tex Inf.
    Miguel; Pvt, Medina Guards, 40th Brig, TM, Bexar Cty.
    Néstor; 22, Pvt, C, 8th Tex Inf, CM, b Mex, laborer.
    Pedro; 35, Pvt, Littleton's Co, Ford's Reg.
    Pedro; Pvt, F, 1st Tex Cav.
    Plácides; Pvt, G & H, 2d Tex Inf.
    Rufino; 18, Pvt, H, 8th Tex Inf.
    Simón; 24, Pvt, I, 8th Tex Inf.
    Stephen; Pvt, H, 17th Tex Cav.
    Tomás; Pvt, B, Ragadale's Batt'n of Tex Cav.
    Wash [UH?]; Pvt, Stockton Cavalry, Johnson Cty.
    Yginio; Pvt, H, 33d Tex Cav.
SANDOVAL
    Benigno; 26, Pvt, G, 3d Tex Inf, CM for theft Oct 4, 1862.
    Carlos; 1st Cpl, Treviño's Co of Partisan Rangers.

SANDOVAL [continued]
    Crisanto; 35, Pvt, Bustillo's Co, Bexar Cty.
    Fernando; 42, 1st Sgt, Durand's Co and Tom's Co, FST, Atascosa Cty.
    Gregorio; 22, Pvt, C, 3d Tex Inf, Monterrey, NL, d Feb 13, 1862.
    Ignacio; Pvt, F, 3d Tex Inf.
    Jesús; Sgt, C, Ragsdale's Batt'n of Tex Cav; Pvt, C, Benavides' Reg.
    Pilar; Pvt, A, Ragsdale's Batt'n of Tex Cav.
    Tomás; 50, Pvt, Treviño's Co of Partisan Rangers.
    Vemgio; 28, Pvt, Bustillo's Co, Bexar Cty.
    Ygnacio; 5th Sgt, Bustillo's Co, Bexar Cty.

SAN MIGUEL
    Alejandro; 35, Pvt, I, 33d Tex Cav; B, Benavides' Reg.
    Andrew; Pvt, K, 6th Tex Inf.
    Blas; Pvt, D, Benavides' Reg.
    D; Pvt, Treviño's Co of Partisan Rangers.
    Domingo; 27, Pvt, H, 33d Tex Cav; A, Benavides' Reg.
    Felipe; 35, Pvt, Medina Guards, 40th Brig, TM, Bexar Cty; H, 33d Tex Cav.
    George; Pvt, A, 3d Tex Inf.
    Jacinto; Pvt, 17th Tex Field Batt.
    Nabor; 35. Pvt, H, 33d Tex Cav; A, Benavides' Reg.
    Rafael; Pvt, A Ragsdale's Batt'n of Tex Cav; A, Benavides' Reg.

SANTANA
    Juan; Pvt, B, 33d Tex Cav.
    Santiago; 25, Pvt, D, 2d Tex Mounted Rifles.

SANTA ANNA
    Benito; 41, Pvt, Treviño's Co of Partisan Rangers.
    Francisco; 45, Pvt, Treviño's Co of Partisan Rangers.

SANTIAGO
    Cocoy; Pvt, B, 2d Tex Mounted Rifles.

SANTOS
    José M; Pvt, I, Benavides' Reg.
    Nataniel; Pvt, H, Baird's Reg, Arizona Brig.
    Seferino; 25, Pvt, C, 3d Tex Inf, b Monterrey, NL, d Oct 23, 1861.
    Tijerina; 26, Pvt, C, 3d Tex Inf, b Monterrey, NL.

SAUCEDA
    Albino; 18, Pvt, G, 3d Tex Inf.
    Juan; 33, 2d Lt, C, 8th Tex Inf.

SAYAVEDRA
    Manuel; Pvt, H, 8th Tex Inf.

SEGUÍN
    J Antonio; 39, Pvt, Gray's Co, TM, Pct 5, Bexar Cty.

SEGURA
    Juan; 25, Pvt, C, 8th Tex Inf.
    Teodoro; Pvt, Rhodes' Co, 3d Batt'n of Tex Cav.
    Tomás; 23, Pvt, Bustillo's Co, Bexar Cty.
    Tomás; 26, Pvt, A, 3d Tex Inf, d Dec 17, 1861.

SEIZ
    Antonio; Pvt, B, Ragsdale's Batt'n of Tex Cav.
    Basilio; Pvt, B, Ragsdale's Batt'n of Tex Cav.

SEPÚLVEDA
    Antonio; 19, Pvt, C, 3d Tex Inf, b San Luis Potosí, SLP.
SERDA; see Cerda
SERNA
    Antonio; Pvt, Rhodes' Co, 3rd (Yager's) Tex Cav.
    Blas; Pvt, B, 33d Tex Cav.
    Ignacio F; Pvt, B, 1st Tex Cav; Pvt, A, 33d Tex Cav.
SIERRA
    Antonio; 1st Lt, Bustillo's Co, Bexar Cty.
    Antonio; Capt, 30th Brig, TM, Pct 11, Bexar Cty.
    Juan; 30, Pvt, B, 2d Tex Mounted Rifles.
    Juan; H, 8th Tex Inf; Pvt, E, Benavides' Reg.
    Norberto; 1st Lt; Mission Guards, 30th Brig, TM, Bexar Cty.
    Vicente; Pvt, B, Baylor's Reg, Arizona Brig.
SIFUENTES
    Bartolo; 32, Pvt, Bustillo's Co, Bexar Cty.
SOLÍS
    Antonio; Pvt, Minute Men, TM, Starr Cty.
    Eugenio; 26, Pvt, H, 33d Tex Cav.
    Jesús; Pvt, Zapata's Co, TST, Pct 10 (San Diego), Nueces Cty.
    Jesús; 55, 2d Sgt, Treviño's Co of Partisan Rangers.
    José M; 37, Pvt, Treviño's Co of Partisan Rangers.
    Juan; 23, Pvt, I, 33d Tex Cav.
    Santiago; 32, Pvt, Treviño's Co of Partisan Rangers.
    Seferino; 28, Pvt, A, Benavides' Reg.
    Ygnacio; Pvt, C, 8th Tex Inf.
    Ysidro; 23, Pvt, Treviño's Co of Partisan Rangers.
SOLIZ; see Solís
SOSA
    F; Pvt, Teel's Co, TST.
    Guillermo; Pvt, A, Ragsdale's Batt'n of Tex Cav; 1st Cpl, D, Benavides' Reg.
    John D; 2d Cpl, C, Benavides' Reg.
    Juan de Dios; Pvt, A, Ragsdale's Batt'n of Tex Cav.
    Raúl; Pvt, Ferguson's Co, Victoria Cav, Victoria Cty.
    Vicente; 30, Pvt, Gray's Co, TM, 30th Brig, Pct 5, Bexar Cty.
SOTELLO
    Antonio; 30, Pvt, H, 33d Tex Cav.
    Ignacio; 43, Pvt, Tom's Co, 3d Frontier Dist, Atascosa Cty.
SOTO
    Antonio; Pvt, H, 33d Tex Cav; 2d Cpl, C, Benavides' Reg.
    Antonio; Pvt, 2d Tex Field Battery.
    Agustín; 23, Pvt, C, 3d Tex Inf, b Puebla, Pue, d Oct 20, 1861.
    Juan J; Pvt, B, Ragsdale's Batt'n of Tex Cav.
    Juan Manuel; 28, Pvt, C, 8th Tex Inf, d Nov 15, 1862, rejoined
        Nov 19, 1862, CM; C, Benavides' Reg.
    Lino; 23, Pvt & Musician, C, 3d Tex Inf, b Mex, Mex, d Nov 18, 1861
        apprehended Dec 2, 1861.
    Martín; 18, Pvt, C, 8th Tex Inf; C, Benavides' Reg.
    Vicente; 26, Pvt, G, 3d Tex Inf.
    Ysciendro; Pvt, C, Benavides' Reg.

SOTO [continued]
 Ysidro; 25, Pvt, C, 8th Tex Inf, b Mex, laborer.
SUÁREZ
 Ysabel; 35, Pvt, C, 8th Tex Inf; C, Benavides' Reg.

T

TABOR
 Calixto; Pvt, Medina Guards, 40th Brig, TM, Bexar Cty.
 D; Pvt, C, Benavides' Reg.
 Darío; Pvt, Medina Guards, 40th Brig, TM, Bexar Cty.
 Enríquez; Pvt, A, Ragsdale's Batt'n of Tex Cav; D, Benavides' Reg.
 Lobos; 28, Pvt, C, 3d Tex Inf, b, Camargo Tamps.
 Sabas; 28, Pvt, C, 3d Tex Inf, b Camargo, Tamps, d June 1862.
TAFOLLA
 James; Pvt & Musician, B, 33d Tex Cav.
TALAMANTES
 Eulajio; Pvt, C, Ragsdale's Batt'n of Tex Cav.
 José María; Pvt, F, 3d Tex Inf; F, 8th Tex Inf.
 Mariano; 45, Pvt, Gray's Co, TM, 30th Brig, Pct 5, Bexar Cty.
 Toribio; Cpl A, Ragsdale's Batt'n of Tex Cav.
TAPIA
 Antonio; Pvt, I, Benavides Reg.
 León, 19, Cpl, Thomas' Co of Partisan Rangers.
 P; Pvt, G, 8th Tex Inf.
TAPIANO
 Joseph; 2d Cpl, Duran's Co, FST, Atascosa Cty.
TARANGO
 Julio; Pvt, C, Benavides' Reg.
TEJADA
 Emeterio; Pvt, F, 3d Tex Inf, d May 15, 1863.
 Francisco; Pvt, H, 8th Tex Inf.
 Gregorio; Pvt, H, 8th Tex Inf.
 Ignacio; 28, Pvt, B, 33d Tex Cav, disability discharge (chronic rheumatism) June 19, 1863.
 Jesús; Pvt, H, 8th Tex Inf.
 Rafael; Pvt, Treviño's Co of Partisan Rangers.
 Severiano; Pvt, Treviño's Co of Partisan Rangers.
TELLES
 H; 19, Pvt, B, 3d Tex Inf, d June 1, 1863.
 José María; Pvt, E, 24th Tex Inf.
 Luis; 19, Pvt, Medina Guards, 40th Brig, TM, Bexar Cty; I, 33d Tex Cav.
TIJERINA
 Francisco; 23, Pvt, H, 8th Tex Inf.
 Gregorio; 22, Pvt, H, 8th Tex Inf.
 Juan; St, Thomas' Co of Partisan Rangers.
TOLEDO
 Pablo; Pvt, C, Ragsdale's Batt'n of Tex Cav.
TOPIANO
 Joseph; 48, Pvt, Tom's Co, TM, Atascosa Cty.

TORRES
>[no first name given]; Pvt, G, Mann's Reg of Tex Cav.
>Ángel C; Pvt, D, 1st Tex Cav, farrier.
>Antonio; Pvt, C, Benavides' Reg.
>Cesario; 1st Lt, 30th Brig, TM, Pct 11, Bexar Cty.
>Enríquez; Pvt, Medina Guards, 40th Brig, TM, Bexar Cty.
>Epemenio; 23, Pvt, C, 3d Tex Inf, b Matamoros, Tamps, d March 13, 1862.
>Francisco; 29, Pvt, C, 3d Tex Inf, d May 15, 1863.
>Jacinto; 29, Sgt, C, 3d Tex Inf, d Feb 4, 1862.
>Mañana[?]; Pvt, I, Benavides' Reg.
>Modesto; Pvt, B, 33d Tex Cav.
>Secundino; 35, Pvt, Gray's Co, 30th Brig, TM, Pct 5, Bexar Cty.
>Severiano; Pvt, E, Madison's Reg, Arizona Brig.
>Severo; Pvt, C, Ragsdale's Batt'n of Tex Cav.
>Trinidad; 30, Pvt, I, 33d Tex Cav.
>Trinidad; Pvt, 8th Tex Field Battery.

TRECHO
>Cazalario; 29, E, 8th Tex Inf, d Aug 17, 1862.

TREJO
>Catarino; Pvt, C, Ragsdale's Batt'n of Tex Cav.
>Cristóbal; 20, Pvt, C, 3d Tex Inf, b Camargo, Tamps, d Oct 10, 1861.
>Tirso; Pvt, C, Ragsdale's Batt'n of Tex Cav.

TREVIÑO
>Anastacio; 24, Pvt, Thomas' Co of Partisan Rangers.
>Andreas; 27, Pvt, C, 3d Tex Inf, b. Los Animas, Tex, d Dec 1, 1861.
>Bonifacio; Pvt, Rhodes' Co of Partisan Rangers.
>Carlos; 28, Pvt, I, 8th Tex Inf, d Feb 28, 1862 (Corpus Christi), b. Tex.
>Cazalario; Pvt, E, 8th Tex Inf.
>Cesario; Pvt, H, 33d Tex Cav; A, Benavides' Reg.
>Clemente; 30, Pvt, E, 8th Tex Inf, d Dec 3, 1863 (Victoria).
>Damasio; 23, Pvt, C, 3d Tex Inf, d Feb 12, 1862.
>Eugenio; 40, Pvt, H, 33d Tex Cav; A, Benavides' Reg.
>Francisco; 22, Pvt, G, 3d Tex Inf, d May 16, 1863.
>J; Capt, Cater's Batt'n of Texas Cav.
>Jesús; Pvt, E & H, 36th Tex Cav.
>Jesús; 30, Pvt, H, 8th Tex Inf.
>John; 27, Pvt, G, 8th Tex Inf, AWOL June 1863.
>Jorge; 1st Lt, Minute Men, TM, Starr Cty.
>José; 55, Pvt, Treviño's Co of Partisan Rangers.
>José; 20, Pvt, H, 33d Tex Cav; A, Benavides' Reg.
>Julián; Pvt, Minue Men, TM, Starr Cty.
>Justo; 37, Capt, Treviño's Co of Partisan Rangers.
>L; Capt, Cater's Batt'n of Tex Cav.
>Lesario; Pvt, A, Ragsdale's Batt'n of Tex Cav.
>Longino; 20, Pvt, I, 33d Tex Cav; B, Benavides' Reg.
>Lorenzo; 33, 3d Sgt, B, 2d Tex. Mounted Rifles.
>Lorenzo; Capt, Treviño's Co of Partisan Rangers.
>Manuel; 30, Pvt, H, 33d Tex Cav; A, Benavides' Reg.
>Manuel; Pvt, Coast Guards, 32d Brig, TM, Cameron Cty.
>Martín; 26, Pvt, Treviño's Co of Partisan Raners.

TREVIÑO [continued]
- Oliverio; 24, l, 8th Tex Inf, d Feb 28, 1862 (Corpus Christi), b. Tex.
- Pedro; 40, Pvt, Gray's Co, TM, 30th Brig, Pct 5, Bexar Cty.
- Pedro; 27, 2d Lt, I, 33d Tex Cav.
- Polinario; 20, Pvt, H, 33d Tex Cav.
- Rafael; 28, Pvt, G, 3d Tex Inf, CM July 24, 1862 for selling a $5.25 blanket, found guilty, sentenced to two months at hard labor with an eighteen-pound ball and chain attached to his leg.
- Tomás; 22, Pvt, I, 8th Tex Inf, d Feb 28, 1862 (Corpus Christi), b Tex.
- Ygnacio; 64, Pvt, Treviño's Co of Partisan Rangers.
- Yndalecio; 2d Lt, Rhodes' Co, 3d Batt'n of Tex Cav.

TRUJILLO
- Jesús; 26, Pvt, A, 3d Tex Inf, d July 11, 1861.

U

ULIBARRÍ
- Pablo; 24, Duran's Co, FST, Atascosa Cty; Pvt, 2d Tex Mounted Rifles; 4th Cpl, H, 8th Tex Inf; Cpl, I, 33d Tex Cav.
- Trinidad; 26, Pvt, H, 8th Tex Inf.

URBAN
- Michael; 32, Pvt, K, 3d Tex Inf, discharged Aug 19, 1862.

URESTI
- Julián; Pvt, E, 8th Tex Inf.

URISTA
- Julián; 19, Pvt, E, 8th Tex Inf, d Aug 17, 1862.
- Manuel; Pvt, C, 16th Tex Inf.

URSUELOS
- Sóstenes; 24, Pvt, D, 2d Tex Mounted Rifles.

V

VACA; see Baca

VALADEZ
- Juan Amio; Pvt, Treviño's Co of Partisan Rangers.

VALDEZ
- Ambrosio; Pvt, D, 1st Tex Cav.
- Antonio; 30, Pvt, Treviño's Co of Partisan Rangers.
- D; Pvt, Teel's Co, TST; B, 2d Tex Mounted Rifles.
- Emeterio; Pvt, I, Benavides' Reg, k Las Rucias, Tex, June 25, 1864.
- Eulogio; Pvt, I, Benavides' Reg.
- Eugenio; 28, Pvt, C, 8th Tex Inf.
- Eugenio; 27, Pvt, G, 3d Tex Inf, d Oct 8, 1861.
- Francisco; Pvt, C, Benavides' Reg.
- Francisco; Pvt, Treviño's Co of Partisan Rangers.
- Ignacio; 38, Pvt, C, 8th Tex Inf, b Mex, hatmaker.
- Inis [Jenis]; Pvt, C, 8th Tex Inf.
- José M; 2d Cpl, Treviño's Co of Partisan Rangers.
- José M; Pvt, F, 2d Tex Mounted Rifles.
- José María; Pvt, D, 1st Tex Inf; H, 8th Tex Inf.
- José María; 25, Pvt, F, 3d Tex Inf, d Sept 6, 1862.
- Juan; 22, Pvt, E, 8th Tex Inf.

VALDEZ [continued]
    Manuel; 32, Pvt, Bustillo's Co, Bexar Cty; H, 33d Tex Cav; A,
        Benavides' Reg.
    Nicanor; Pvt, B, 33d Tex Cav.
    Santos; 20, Pvt, E, 8th Tex Inf.
VALENZUELA
    Incarnación; 32, Pvt, G, 3d Tex Inf.
VALENCIANO
    Florencio; Pvt, Arizona Rangers, 2nd Tex Mounted Rifles.
VALLE
    Alejos; Pvt, Zapata's Co, TST, Pct 10 (San Diego), Nueces Cty.
    Silvestre; Pvt, Rhodes' Co, 3d Batt'n of Tex Cav.
VALLEJO
    Trinidad; 46, Pvt, Bustillo's Co, Bexar Cty.
VALLES
    Locario; 29, Pvt, H, 33d Tex Cav; A, Benavides' Reg.
VALVERDE
    Francisco; 33, Pvt, I, 33d Tex Cav.
    Francisco; Pvt, K, 2d Tex Mounted Rifles.
    John; Pvt, E, 1st Tex Cav; C, 8th Batt'n of Tex Cav.
VARA
    Santos Y.; Pvt, Minute Men, TM, Starr Cty.
VARGAS
    Alejandro; Pvt, I, 3d Tex Inf.
    Alex; Pvt, 8th Tex Field Battery.
    Antonio; Pvt, Medina Guards, 40th Brig, TM, Bexar Cty.
    Antonio; 24, Pvt, I, 33d Tex Cav.
    Benito; Pvt, Medina Guards, 40th Brig, TM, Bexar Cty;
        Cpl, A, Ragsdale's Batt'n of Tex Cav.
    Claudio; 30, Pvt, C, 8th Tex Inf; Benavides' Reg, b Mex, laborer.
    Cristóbal; Pvt, H, 8th Tex Inf.
    Felipe; 28, Sgt, C, 8th Tex Inf, d Dec 21, 1863 (Columbus);
        Sgt, C, Benavides' Reg.
    Florencio; Pvt, A, Ragsdale's Batt'n of Tex Cav.
    Gerónimo; Pvt, B, Ragsdale's Batt'n of Tex Cav.
    John; 29, Pvt, H, 3d Tex Inf.
    José María; 30, Pvt, C, 3d Tex Inf, d Jan 10, 1862, rejoined, d May 15,
        1863, b Matamoros, Tamps.
    Joseph; Sgt, 8th Tex Field Battery.
    Juan; Pvt, D, Ragsdale's Batt'n of Tex Cav.
    Polonio; 25, Pvt, I, 33d Tex Cav.
VARRNEA
    Victoriano; Pvt, A, Ragsdale's Batt'n of Tex Cav.
VÁSQUEZ (Vasques)
    Celso; Pvt, Duran's Co, FST, Atascosa Cty.
    Cristóbal; 28, Pvt, H, 8th Tex Inf.
    Francisco; Pvt, Zapata's Co, TST, Pct 10 (San Diego), Nueces Cty.
    José; 20 Pvt, C, 8th Tex Inf; B, Benavides' Reg.
    José; Pvt, I, Benavides' Reg.
    Juan; Pvt, Duran's Co, FST, Atascosa Cty.

VÁSQUEZ (Vasques) [continued]
    Juan; 28, Pvt, C, 3d Tex Inf, b San Fernando, Tamps.
    Juan; Pvt, F, 3d Tex Inf.
    Juan; Pvt, C, 3d Tex Inf.
    Pánfilo; 38, Pvt, F, 3d Tex Inf, b Coahuila, disability discharge Feb 16, 1863.
    Policarpio; 19, Pvt, F, 3d Tex Inf, d Sept 6, 1862.
    Serrano; Pvt, A, 3d (Yager's) Tex Cav.
    Saturnino; 35, Pvt, H, 33d Tex Cav.
    Tomás; 26, Pvt, D, 3d Tex Inf, b. Reynosa, Tamps, d April 1, 1862.
    Zacarías; Pvt, F, 3d Tex Inf, D 6 May 1862, d May 6, 1862.

VELA
    Calistro; Pvt, Zapata's Co,
    Cecilio; 2d Sgt, Minute Men, TM, Starr Cty.
    Domingo; 32, Pvt, H, 33d Tex Cav.
    E; Pvt, A, Ragsdale's Batt'n of Tex Cav.
    Ermenencio; Pvt, D, Benavides' Reg.
    Jesús; 24, Pvt, H, 33d Tex Cav; A, Benavides' Reg.
    Juan; Pvt, A, 3d Batt'n of Tex Cav.
    Leocardio; 25, Pvt, D, 3d Tex Inf, b. Matamoros, Tamps, d March 16, 1862.
    Nuncio; Cpl, D, Ragsdale's Batt'n of Tex Cav.
    Paulino; Pvt, B, 2d Tex Mounted Rifles.
    Santos; Pvt, Minute Men, TM, Starr Cty.
    Severo; Pvt, G, Benavides' Reg.
    Víctor; 3d Cpl, Lone Star Rifles, Victoria, Victoria Cty.
    Víctor; Pvt, Medina Guards, 40th Brig, TM, Bexar Cty.
    Victoriano; 18, Pvt, H, 33d Tex Cav.

VELÁSQUEZ
    Antonio; Pvt, F, 3d Tex Inf.
    José María; 40, Pvt, C & G, 3d Tex Inf, b Puebla, Pue,
        disability discharge July 12, 1864.
    Juan; 60, Pvt, C, 3d Tex Inf, b. Puebla, Pue.

VERA
    Ángelo; Pvt, H, 16th Tex Inf.
    Eugenio; 20, Thomas' Co of Partisan Rangers.
    Juan; Pvt, Coast Cuards, 32d Brig, TM, Cameron Cty.

VERAS
    Felipe; Pvt, 4th Tex Field Battery.

VIAL
    Francisco; Pvt, Medina Guards, 40th Brig, TM, Bexar Cty.

VIDAL
    Adrián J; 1st Lt, A, 33d Tex Cav, d Oct 28, 1863.

VIDAURRI
    Atanacio; Jr. 2d Lt, I, Benavides' Reg.
    Villegas; 22, Pvt, 3d Tex Inf b NL.

VILLANUEVA
    Anastacio; 36, Pvt, Bustillo's Co, Bexar Cty.
    Andrés; Pvt, Treviño's Co of Partisan Rangers.
    Candelario; Pvt, F, 3d Tex Inf.
    Félix; Pvt, Skidmore's Co, 29th Brig, TM, Pct 1, San Patricio Cty.
    Santiago; Pvt, F, 3d Tex Inf; D, Benavides' Reg.

VILLASANA
    Refugio; 26, Cpl, F, 3d Tex Inf, b Matamoros, Tamps,
        disability discharge June 14, 1864.
VILLAREAL; see Villarreal
VILLARREAL
    Andrés; 28, Pvt, Treviño's Co of Partisan Rangers.
    Antonio; Pvt, Minute Men, TM, Starr Cty.
    Antonio; 23, Pvt, C, 8th Tex Inf, b Mex, laborer
    Antonio; 35, Pvt, F, 3d Tex Inf, d 4 May 1862.
    Cecilio; 22, 4th Cpl, H, 33d Tex Cav; A, Benavides' Reg.
    Cleofas; 23, Pvt, Bustillo's Co, Bexar Cty; C, 8th Tex Inf.
    Cleofas; Pvt, C, Benavides' Reg.
    Clemente; 26, Pvt, E, 8th Tex Inf, d Dec 5, 1864 (Goliad) ("vamosed"
        in CMSR).
    Crecencio; 27, Pvt, Bustillo's Co, Bexar Cty.
    Ecleto; 23, Pvt, E, 8th Tex Inf, d June 1863.
    Feliciano; 5th Sgt, I, Benavides' Reg.
    Gregorio; Pvt, Minute Men, TM, Starr Cty.
    Indalecio; 24, Pvt, H, 33d Tex Cav.
    J; Pvt, A, Ragsdale's Batt'n of Partisan Rangers.
    Manuel; Pvt, Coast Guards, 32d Brig, TM, Cameron Cty.
    Martín; 22, Pvt, F, 3d Tex Inf, d 14 Feb 1862
    Onésimo; 24, Pvt, I, 8th Tex Inf, d Feb 28, 1862 (Corpus Christi), b Tex.
    Vicente; 25, Pvt, I, 8th Tex Inf, b Tex.
    Ventura; 24, Pvt, Bustillo's Co, Bexar Cty; A, 3d Tex Inf.
VILLALOBOS
    Julio; Pvt, Zapata's Co, TST, Pct 10 (San Diego), Nueces Cty.
VILLASANA
    Refugio; 26, Cpl, F, 3d Tex Inf.
VILLASTRIGO
    Tomás; 25, Pvt, H, 33d Tex Cav.
VILLEGAS
    R; Pvt, A, Ragsdale's Batt'n of Tex Cav.

W

WEBB
    Juan; 23, Pvt, C, 3d Tex Inf, b Matamoros, Tamps, d June 18, 1862.

X

XIMENEZ; see Jiménez

Y

YAGUINA
    José; Pvt, I, Benavides' Reg.
YBARBO
    José; Pvt, A, 11th Tex Inf.
    José; Pvt, 4th Tex Field Battery.
    León; 30, Sgt; E, 8th Tex Inf.
    Navele [?]; Pvt, A, 11th Tex Inf.
    Patricio; Pvt, A, 11th Tex Inf.

YBARBO [continued]
    Richardo; Pvt, A, 11th Tex Inf.
    Vetal; Pvt, A, 11th Tex Inf.
YBÁÑES
    José María; Pvt, Zapata's Co, TST, Pct 10 (San Diego), Nueces Cty;
        Pvt, Treviño's Partisan Rangers.
YERTO
    Jesús; 20, Sgt, C, 3d Tex Inf, b. Reynosa, Tamps.
YGLESIAS; see Iglesias.
YNOJOSA; see Hinojosa.
YTURRIA
    Manuel, II; Cpl, K, 6th Tex Inf; Capt, F, 3d Tex Inf.

Z

ZAMORA
    Altamirano; Pvt, Rhodes' Co, 3d Batt'n of Tex Cav.
    Antonio; Pvt, F, 3d Tex Inf, d May 14, 1863.
    Antonio; Pvt, K, 6th Tex Inf.
    Decidorio; 25, Pvt, G, 3d Tex Inf, d Oct 6, 1861.
    Francisco; Pvt, D, Griffin's Batt'n of Tex Inf.
    Gregorio; 19, Pvt, C, 8th Tex Inf.
    Joaquín; Pvt, Coast Guards, 32d Brig, TM, Cameron Cty.
ZAPATA
    Clemente; Capt, 29th Brig, Pct 10 (San Diego), Nueces Cty.
    Jesús; 46, Pvt, Gray's Co, TM, 30th Brig, Pct 5, Bexar Cty.
ZÁRATE
    Vicente; 22, Pvt, F, 3d Tex Inf; b Coah, disability discharge March 21, 1863.
ZAVALA (De Zavalla)
    Ricardo; Pvt, K, 26th Tex Cav.
ZEPEDA (Sepeda)
    Antonio; Pvt, C, Ragsdale's Batt'n of Tex Cav.
    Gabino; Pvt, Gray's Co, TM, Pct 5, Bexar Cty.
    Manuel; Pvt, Gray's Co, TM, Pct 5, Bexar Cty.
    Remigio; Pvt, B, Benavides' Reg.
    Romelo; 3d St, C, Ragsdale's Batt'n of Tex Cav.
    Teodoro; 45, Pvt, F, 3d Tex Inf.
ZERNA; see Serna.
ZERTUCHE
    Hernando; Pvt, K, 12th Tex Inf.
ZOTELLO; see Sotello
ZÚÑIGA
    Alejandro; 21m Pvt, H, 33d Tex Cav; A, Benavides' Reg.
    Santiago; 25, Pvt, C, 3d Tex Inf, b Tampico, Tamps, d 18 Sept 1862.

Appendix B
FEDERALS

Records relating to the *Tejanos* and *Mexicanos* who served in the Union 1st and 2d Texas Cavalry are found at both the National Archives in Washington, D.C., and at the Texas State Archives in Austin. They are far more complete than records of the *Tejanos* and *Mexicanos* who were in the Confederate Army. Many of the records have been condensed into "Compiled Service Records of Volunteer Union Soldiers who Served in Organizations from the State of Texas" and contained on thirteen rolls of microfilm (National Archives). Much of the information in these records is taken from company, detachment, and regimental muster rolls, as well as muster-out rolls completed at San Antonio in September 1865. Medical and hospital records in the "Compiled Service Records" also provide insight into the lives of the men in the Texas Union Army, as do prisoner-of-war and court-martial records. The latter two, although more complete than similar Confederate records, are often brief and frequently incomplete. Union records, unlike Confederate records, contain enlistment papers that give the recruit's age and in some instances, if known, the soldier's place of birth and occupation. All of these records are part of Record Group 94, Records of the Adjutant General's Office, at the National Archives.

The Texas State Archives has several muster rolls of the 1st and 2d Regiments. These were published in the *Adjutant General's Report, 1873* (Austin: Adjutant General's Office, 1875). In some instances these muster rolls show promotions and desertions not listed in the "Compiled Service Records." The State Archives also has a Regimental Order Book of the 2d Texas which contains important entries and data. As is the case with the Confederate records of *Tejanos* and *Mexicanos,* similar Union Army data are complicated by the fact that enrolling officers and adjutants were inept at spelling Hispanic names. Moreover, to complicate accuracy, many of the recruits were illiterate.

In the compiled list that follows, soldiers are listed alphabetically, followed by a brief service record that includes rank, age of the recruit upon enlistment, and the company the soldier served in. The first letter (A,B,C,D) indicates a company in the 2d Texas while the second (I,K,L,M) is the company in which the soldier served in the 1st Texas. If the soldier deserted, the place of desertion, if known, is given, as well as any court-martial charges. If the soldier received a disability discharge, the place of discharge, frequently a particular hospital, is listed with the medical reason for the discharge.

A few of the *Tejanos* and *Mexicanos* who served in the Union Army are listed on the 1890 Special Census Schedules of Union Civil War veterans or their widows. This information, if the veteran can be identified, is also specified in the list that follows. Several Union veterans are enumerated on the 1890 Special Census at San Elizario and Ysleta in El Paso County, at Pecos City in what was then Pecos County, as well as Old Tascosa in Oldham County. These individuals probably served with the Union Army in New Mexico, especially the California Column that occupied the territory beginning in 1862, or more likely with Gen. Henry H. Sibley's Confederate Army of New Mexico, or even other Confederate armies, and were misidentified (as was the situation in many counties throughout Texas). Regardless, they cannot be identified as members of the 1st or 2d Texas Union Cavalry.

The compilation of *Tejanos* and *Mexicanos* who served in the Civil War that follows is revised from a similar list that was originally published in *Mexican Texans in the Union Army* (El Paso: Texas Western Press, 1986).

ADDITIONAL ABBREVIATIONS USED:

IPR	Vidal's Independent Partisan Rangers
GCM	general court-martial
MIA	missing in action
POW	prisoner of war
QM	quartermaster
UVC	Union Veteran's Census (1890)

A

ABREGO
    Basilio; 23, Pvt, D & M, d March 11, 1864 (Brownsville).
    Joaquín J; 26, QM Sgt, A, B & K, herdsman.
    Priciliano; 23, Pvt, D, herdsman, b Reynosa, Tamps, d March 11, 1864.
    Nicolás; 23, Pvt, D, ranchero, b Matamoros, Tamps, d June 12, 1864.

AGAPITO
    R; Pvt, M [servant to Lt. Eugenio Guzmán].

AGUILAR
    Antonio; 38, Pvt, A & I, d Feb 2, 1864 (Santa Rosa).
    Cruz; 18, Pvt, F, d May 14, 1864 (Brownsville).
    José María; 21, Pvt, C & L, laborer.
    Marcelino; 25, Pvt, [Cook], D & M.

AGUIRRE
    Ambrosio; 26, Pvt, C & L, ranchero, d June 8. 1864 (Brownsville).
    José María; 26, Cpl, C & L, laborer.
    Manuel; 25, Pvt, IPR, soldier, d [date unknown].
    Pedro; 30, Pvt, IPR, tailor, d July 15, 1864 (from scout).

ALANÍS
    Francisco; 30, Pvt, A, d Feb 7, 1864 (Brownsville).

ALBARÁS
    Alejo; 21, Pvt, E, b San Carlos, Tamps.

ALEMÁN
    Antonio; 38, Sgt, D, d April 1864, rejoined April 25, 1864.
    Manuel; 22, Pvt, A & I, laborer, b Reynosa, Tamps.

ALMENDARES
    Francisco; 20, IPR, baker, d Jan 3, 1864 (Brownsville).

ALMENDÁREZ
    Feliciano; 21, Pvt, E & H.

ALMERÁS
    Ramón; 22, Pvt, IPR, farmer, d Feb 26, 1864.

ALOIS
    Iltis; 23, Pvt, H.

ALVARADO
    José María; Pvt, B & K, laborer; died at his home in Brownsville of smallpox, Dec 21, 1863.

ÁLVAREZ
    Manuel; 23, Pvt, C & L, laborer.
    Vidal; 22, Pvt, IPR, teamster, d July 28, 1864 (march from Brownsville to Brazos Santiago).

ANDARCIO
    Antonio; 27, Pvt, D, blacksmith, d March 1864 (Brownsville).
    Facundo; 27, Pvt, D & M, d [date unknown].

ANGUINANO
    Sabas; 23, Cpl, IPR, tailer, d July 26, 1864 (Brownsville).

ANTONIO
    Francisco; 32, Pvt, C & L, substitute.

ARÁMBULA
    Faustino; 28, Cpl, A & I, laborer, b Mier, Tamps.

ARÁMBULA [continued]
 Marcos; 32, Sgt, B & K, laborer, b. Embudo, Mex; died May 6, 1865 at Baton Rouge.
ARMARO
 Leonardo; Cpl, F, d Feb 15, 1864 (Brownsville).
ARREDONDO
 Cantú; 23, Pvt, B & K, herdsman, d Feb 7, 1864 (Santa Rosa).
 Juan; 31, Sgt, A & I, laborer, b Mier, Tamps.
AUGIANO
 Antonio; 27, Cpl, B & K.
AVILÉS
 Antonio; 24, Cpl, C & L, laborer.
 Francisco; 20, Cpl, C & L, laborer.
 Miguel Trinidad; 26, Pvt, C & L, laborer.

B

BALDERAS
 Antonio; 28, Cpl, B & K, herdsman.
 Ramón; 21, Cpl, C & L, laborer, d March 9, 1864 (Brownsville).
BALTINATO
 Martín; 21, Pvt, G, teamster, b Chihuahua, Chih.
BANDA
 Reymundo; 25, Pvt, C, herdsman, b La Villa de León, Tamps, d Feb 14, 1864 (Brownsville).
BANGAR
 Andrés; Pvt, IPR, d [date unknown].
BANTA
 Jesse; Pvt, A, d Aug 4, 1864 (White's Ranch).
BARRA
 Emmanuel; Pvt, G, d June 12, 1864 (Brownsville).
BARRERA
 Eligio; 21, Sgt, D & M, herdsman, b Linares, NL.
 Feliciano; 25, Pvt, A & I, b Monterrey, NL, d Aug 14, 1865 (Houston).
 Leandro; 32, Pvt, B, laborer, b Mier, Tamps, d June 12, 1864 (Brownsville).
 Pablo; 25, Pvt, B & K, laborer, d April 24, 1864 (Santa Rosa).
 Remigio; Pvt, H, d October 23, 1864 (Brazos Santiago).
BARRIENTOS
 Antonio; 29, Pvt, H & I, laborer, d [date unknown].
 Leandro; 25, Cpl, A & I, laborer, b Agualeguas, NL, d August 14, 1864 (Houston).
 Sebastiano; 25, bugler, A & I.
BARRIO
 Leonardo del; 21, Pvt, A & I, laborer, b Reynosa, Tamps.
 Pedro del; 26, Pvt, C & L, herdsman, d Jan 20, 1864 (Brownsville).
BASALDÓN
 Felipe; 30, Pvt, C & L.
BASALDÚAR
 Leandro; 21, Pvt, A & I, laborer, b Reynosa, Tamps.
BASSIA
 Antonio; 22, Pvt, E.

BAUTISTA
 Florencio; Pvt, G.
BAVIOS [Barrios?]
 Margarito; 26, Pvt, F, applied for pension, Feb 28, 1917.
BAYER
 Casimiro; 25, Pvt, H.
BEGACO [Villegas]
 Cruz; 22, Pvt, E, farmer, d April 8, 1864 (Laredo Expedition).
BENAVIDES
 Juan Francisco; 23, Pvt, B & K, laborer.
 Nicolás; 21, Pvt, C & L.
 Pedro; 22, Pvt, C & L, laborer, d Feb 5, 1864 (Brownsville).
 Trinidad; 30, Pvt, IPR, farmer, Brownsville, Texas, d July 28, 1864 (Brownsville to Brazos Santiago).
BENEDICT
 Andrés; 44, Pvt, C & H.
BENITES
 Dolores; 25, Pvt, C & L, herdsman, b Goliad Cty, Tex.
BENTONAS
 Anastasio; 41, Pvt, G, miner, b Los Esteros, Mex; confined at Houston, August 25, 1865; discharged March 2, 1867.
BERDÍN [Ferdin]
 Sóstenes; 23, Pvt, C & L, laborer, d Feb 4, 1864 (Brownsville).
BERNAL
 Dioncio; 21, Pvt, C & L, laborer.
 Guadalupe; 35, Pvt, H.
BESNA
 Ambrosio; Cpl, G.
BESSIA
 Antonio; 18, Pvt, E & G, farmer.
 Leonicio; 22, Pvt, E, d April 13, 1864 (Brownsville).
BLANCO
 Francisco; 20, Pvt, D & M, laborer, b Jalapa, VC.
BOCA
 Jesús Negro; 40, Pvt, A & I, laborer, b San Fernando, Tamps; disability discharge, June 17, 1865 (Baton Rouge Post Hospital).
BORREGO
 Ignacio; 24, Pvt, B & K, laborer.
 John; 30, Pvt, G.
BOSQUE
 Diacador; 22, Pvt, G.
BRICEÑO
 Jesús; 22, Pvt, E & H.
BRIONES
 Antonio; 22, Pvt, D & M, herdsman, b Ciudad Victoria, Tamps.
BUITRÓN
 Luis; Pvt, K.
BUENTELLO
 Cecilio; 27, Pvt, C, D & M, herdsman, b Matamoros, Tamps.

BURNES
    Juan; Pvt, A & I, d 8 Aug 1865 (Beaumont), accidentally wounded by Pvt Rafael Treviño, June 23, 1864.

C

CABALLERO
    José María; 23, Pvt, IPR, teamster, d Feb 1, 1864.
CABRERA
    Eleuterio; 21, Pvt, B, laborer.
    Juan; 21, Cpl, C & K.
CADENA
    Casimiro; 23, Cpl, G & H.
    Juan B; 28, Pvt, C, d April 10, 1864 (Brownsville).
    Santos; 30, 2d Lt, B & K, b Starr Cty, Tex, d June 7, 1864 (Brownsville).
CAFADRY
    José; Pvt, IPR.
CAMACHO
    Crispín; 33, Pvt, B & K, herdsman.
CAMPOS
    Antonio; 21, Pvt, C & L, laborer, d March 9, 1864 (Brownsville).
    Gorgonio; 24, Pvt, IPR, teamster, d May 5, 1864 (Santa Rosa).
    Juan; 30, Sgt, C & L.
CANO
    Gregorio; 36, Pvt, B & K, laborer.
CANTÚ
    Eugenio; 30, Pvt, C & L, laborer.
    Hilario; 18, Pvt, A, laborer; killed in action while skirmishing on Atchalafaya Bayou, La, July 18, 1864.
    Juan; 32, Cpl, A & I.
    Manuel; 26, Pvt, E & H, laborer, b Camargo, Tamps.
CÁRDENAS
    Evaristo; 29, Sgt, H, d Oct 23, 1864 (Brazos Santiago).
    Jesús; 19, Pvt, E, clarín, b Monterrey, NL, d May 22, 1864 (Brownsville).
CARMEN
    Mauricio del; 30, Pvt, (cook), E & H, laborer.
CARRERA
    Refugio; 23, Pvt, C & L.
CARRILLO
    Julián; 22, Pvt, D, herdsman, b San Antonio, Tex, d April 10, 1864 (Brownsville).
    Victor; 36, Pvt, (cook), C & L, herdsman.
CASANOVA
    Ventura; 26, Comm Sgt, C, laborer, b Bexar Cty, Tex, d April 10, 1864 (Brownsville).
CÁSARES
    Telésforo; Pvt, E.
CASTILLO
    Anastacio; 26, Pvt, D & M, vaquero; disability discharge, June 17, 1865 (Baton Rouge).
    Pedro de; 40, Sgt, D & M.

CASTILLO*[continued]*
 Víctor; 23, Pvt, A & I, laborer, b Ciudad Victoria, Tamps.
CASTRO
 Juan; 33, Cpl, B, & K, herdsman, d 5 May 1864 (Brownsville).
 Victoriano; 25, Pvt, C & L, d April 10, 1864 (Brownsville).
CEJAS
 Francisco; 37, Pvt, IPR, farmer, d July 28, 1864 (march from Brownsville to Brazos Santiago).
CASAS
 Celestino; 41, Pvt, B & K.
CEPEDA
 José; 22, Pvt, C & L, laborer.
CERVANTES
 Francisco; 35, Pvt, IPR, farmer, d July 28, 1864 (Brownsville).
 Francisco; 20, Pvt, IPR, farmer, d Feb 16, 1864.
CHARLES
 Eusebio; 22, Pvt, A & I, herdsman.
 Francisco; 25, Pvt, D.
 Vicente; 42, Pvt, A & I, herdsman.
CHAPA
 Antonio; 54, Pvt, C & L, laborer, b Chihuahua, Chi.
CHAVARÍA
 Antonio; 21, Pvt, H, d Oct 23, 1864 (Brazos Santiago).
CHÁVES
 Francisco; 25, Pvt, B & N, cartman, b Linares, NL.
 Hilario; Pvt, G, d Feb 15, 1864 (Brownsville).
CHRISTELLES
 Joseph; 25, Sgt, G.
CÍCERO
 Luis; 21, Pvt, F, d June 19, 1864 (Brownsville).
CIPRIANO
 Santiago; 26, Cpl, D & N, herdsman, b Laredo, Tex, d May 19, 1864 (Brownsville).
CISNEROS
 Ildefonso; 32, Pvt, D & N, laborer, d Jan 17, 1864 (Brownsville).
COBOS
 Froilán; 24, Pvt, IPR, farmer, d Jan 16, 1864 (Brownsville).
CONDE
 Alcario; 27, Sgt, IPR, farmer, b Galveston, Tex, d July 28, 1864 (march from Brownsville to Brazos Santiago).
CONTRERAS
 José; 21, Pvt, H, stockraiser, b Travis Cty, Tex.
CORDERO
 Antonio; 21, Pvt, C & L, herdsman.
CORTEZ
 Edward; 17, Pvt, G.
 Ella; Pvt, E, died of disease, June 16, 1864 (Brownsville).
 Fernando; 38, Pvt, IPR, teamster, d May 28, 1864.
 Julián; 21, Pvt, A & I, d Feb 18, 1864 (Santa Rosa); retaken from desertion, June 16, 1864.

CORTEZ [continued]
 Ricardo; 28, Pvt, IPR, blacksmith, d May 28, 1864.
CORTINAS
 Anacleto; 21, 1st Sgt, D & M, b Goliad, Tex.
COY
 Juan; 22, Bugler, C & L, stockraiser, b San Antonio, Tex.
CREADO
 Jesús; 25, Pvt, B & K.
CRUZ
 Francisco; Pvt, G, d Jan 15, 1864 (Port Isabel).
 José María; 30, Pvt, B & K, laborer, b Mier Tamps, died of
  disease, Nov 7, 1864 (Reg. Hospital, Morganza, La).
 Marcelino; 30, Pvt, C & I, laborer, Lampazos, NL,
  d August 14, 1865 (Houston).
 Margarito; 27, Pvt, IPR, teamster, b Mexico City, Mex, d July 15, 1864.
 Mariano; 22, Pvt, E & H, b Sabinas, NL.
 Silvestre; 29, Pvt, IPR, teamster, d July 28, 1864 (march from
  Brownsville to Brazos Santiago).
CUÉLLAR
 John C; 23, 1st Lt, A & I.
 Marcelino; 25, Cpl, A & I, herdsman.
 Rafael; Pvt, G, d. Feb 12, 1864 (Brownsville).
CURBIER
 Juan; 22, Cpl, C & L, laborer, b Bexar Cty, Tex.

D

DeÁBILO
 Martín; 21, Pvt, A, D & I, laborer, b San Fernando, Tamps;
  arrested and confined at Houston, Aug 24, 1865.
DeÁBREGO
 Mónico; 42, Capt, D & M, AWOL, April 12, 1864; dishonorably
  dismissed, July 12, 1864.
DEJADA
 Joseph; 45, Cpl, G.
DE LA ROSA
 Juan; Pvt, M.
DELCORTA
 Santiago; 26, Cpl, E, farmer.
DeJESÚS
 Bernardo; 27, Pvt, IPR, farmer, d March 21, 1864 (Brownsville).
DeLEÓN
 Eulalio; 27, Sgt, E, ranchero, d May 31, 1864 (Edinburg).
 Isidro; 25, Pvt, B & K, herdsman.
 Jesús; 26, Pvt, IPR, farmer, d May 28, 1864 (Edinburg).
 Juan; 50, Pvt, E & H, laborer; died from accidental gunshot,
  May 18, 1864 (Baton Rouge).
 Martin; Pvt, F, d January 1, 1864 (Brownsville).
 Pedro; 25, Sgt, B & K, herdsman.
 Reyes; 30, Pvt, A, laborer, d Feb 18, 1864 (Brownsville).
 Toribio; 25, Pvt, D & M, vaquero.

DELGADO
    Edobegen; 27, 1st Sgt, B & K, 27, herdsman.
    Trineo; 37, Pvt, A & I, laborer, d Feb 2, 1864 (Santa Rosa).
DEL NORTE
    Santiago; Cpl, E.
DePADRÓN
    Jesús; 20, Pvt, IPR, farmer, d Jan 25, 1864.
DÍAS
    Antonio Abad; 46, 2d Lt, C & E, stockholder, b Santa Clara, Tex;
        found guilty on various charges, dishonorably discharged,
        July 12, 1864 (Morganza, La).
DÍAZ
    Antulba; 45, Pvt, C.
    Inés; 30, Pvt, A & I, laborer; died of dysentery, July 6, 1864 (on
        steamer *Laurel Hill* (New Orleans).
    Jesús; 40, Pvt, A & I, herdsman.
    Selísforo; 23, Pvt, IPR, teamster, d July 15, 1864.
DURÁN
    Jesús; 22, Pvt, C, laborer, d March 31, 1864 (Brownsville).

E

ECHAVARRÍA
    Casimiro; 30, Cpl, IPR, farmer, d July 28, 1864 (march from
        Brownsville to Brazos Santiago).
ESCALANTE
    Ambrosio; 27, Pvt, G, farmer, b San Miguel, Gto.
ESCAMILLA
    Ángel; 26, Pvt, D & M.
    Durán; 26, Pvt, D, herdsman, b Laredo, Tex.
ESCOBAR
    Julio; 25, Pvt, D & M, laborer, d June 21, 1864 (Brownsville).
ESCOBEDO
    Justo; 38, Sgt, B & K, herdsman.
ESPARZA
    Bernardo; 22, Pvt, G.
ESPINOSA
    Julio; 24, Pvt, D & M, ranchero, b Matamoros, Tamps,
        d March 7, 1864 (Santa Rosa).
    Teófilo; 21, Pvt, H & L, laborer, b San Antonio, Tex.
    Victoriano; 22, Pvt, IPR, soldier, d March 26, 1864 (Brownsville).
ESQUIVEL
    Teodoro; 26, Pvt, C & L, laborer.

F

FALCÓN
    Cesario; 30, Capt, C, b Nueces Cty, Tex; resigned, March 10, 1865.
    José; 22, Pvt, A & I.
    Ramón García; 1st Lt, C & L, b Wilson Cty, Tex; died of disease,
        Jan 30, 1865 (Reg Hospital, Baton Rouge).

FERDINAND
: Joseph; 35, Pvt, D & M, d April 11, 1864 (Brownsville).

FERNÁNDEZ
: Diego; 23, QM Sgt, C & L, laborer, b Spain.
Indalecio; 23, Pvt, E & H, laborer, b Mier, Tamps.
J; Pvt, A, d Aug 21, 1863 (New Orleans).
James; 21, Pvt, D, laborer, b Piedras Negras, Coah, d April 22, 1864 (Brownsville).

FIGUEROA
: Eusebio; 23, Pvt, B & K, laborer, d May 21, 1864 (Santa Rosa).

FLORENCIA
: G; Pvt (company saddler), I.

FLORES
: Andrés; 21, Cpl, C, E & H, laborer, d June 1864, 21, (Brownsville).
Antonio; 22, Pvt, A & I, laborer, b Camargo, Tamps, d August 8, 1865 (Beaumont).
Dionicio; 22, Pvt, A & I, herdsman, d June 16, 1864 (Brownsville).
Eduardo; 21, C, L & H, laborer, d June 21, 1864 (Brownsville); 1890 UVC, Fairview, Wilson Cty.
Francisco; 25, Cpl, C, herdsman, d April 9, 1864 (Brownsville).
John; 25, Pvt, B, stockraiser, b Santa Rosa, Coah; disability discharge, June 17, 1865 (Gen Hospital, Baton Rouge).
José M; 20, Pvt, A, farmer, b San Antonio, Tex, d Sept 9, 1864 (White's Ranch).
Juan; 23, Pvt, IPR, saddler, d Jan 14, 1864.
Juan M; 22, Pvt, C & L, herdsman.
Librado; 21, Pvt, C & L, laborer, d Jan 24, 1864 (Brownsville).
Manuel; 30, Pvt, b Matamoros, Tamps, d June 21, 1864 (Brownsville).
Paulino; 21, Pvt, G, d June 18, 1864 (Brownsville); rejoined June 20, 1864.
Pedro; 30, Cpl, C, H & L, farmer, b. San Antonio, Tex, courtmartialed, Nov 18, 1864 (Brazos Santiago), sentenced to seven days' hard labor.
Rafael; 32, Sgt, B & K.
Refugio; trumpeter, G, d Feb 12, 1864 (Brownsville).
Tomás; 22, Pvt, B & K, laborer, d May 28, 1864 (Santa Rosa).

FONSECA
: Francisco; Pvt, L.

FUENTES
: Calixto; 18, Cpl, E.
Florencio; 23, Pvt, G, carpenter, b Matamoros, Tamps.
Luis; 25, Pvt, E, cigar maker, d Sept 30, 1864 (Hospital, Greenville, La); substitute for G.W. Breckenridge.
Marciano; 23, Pvt, A & I, laborer, d Feb 7, 1864 (Santa Rosa).
Sabas; 48, Pvt, B & I, herdsman.
Valentín; 23, Sgt, B & K, herdsman, d Feb 18, 1864 (Santa Rosa); retaken March 29, 1864.

G

GALINDO
: Idovijon [?]; 44, Pvt (cook), H, b El Paso, NM [Chih?]; died of disease, Jan 1, 1865 (Hospital, Brazos Santiago).

GALLARDO
    Francisco; 36, Cpl, D & M.
GALVÁN
    Antonio; 22, bugler, B & K, laborer, b Santa Rosa, Tex; CM April 22, 1865; sentenced to forfeit one month's pay.
    Daniel; 28, Pvt, B, laborer, d June 8, 1863 (Annunciation Square, New Orleans).
    Darío; 32, Pvt (company tailor), D & M, ranchero.
    Februcio; 30, Pvt, IPR, farmer.
GÁMEZ
    James; 30, Pvt, died April 16, 1864 (Post Hospital, Brownsville).
    Mauricio; 32, Pvt, A, laborer, b Agualeguas, NL.
GARABAI
    Hilario; 33, Pvt, B & K, laborer, d April 24, 1864 (Santa Rosa).
GARCÍA
    Abrám; 26, Pvt, A, d Feb 18, 1864 (Santa Rosa).
    Abrán; 39, Pvt, IPR, teamster.
    Agapito; Sgt, M.
    Agustín; 33, Cpl, D & M, b Saltillo, Coah.
    Alejandro; 19, Pvt, A & I.
    Antonio; 24, Pvt, G.
    Asencio; 44, Pvt, B & K, laborer.
    Augustín; 38, Pvt, A & M, laborer, b Matamoros, Tamps.
    Augustino; 28, Pvt, A & I.
    Diego; 22, Pvt, E & H, laborer, b Linares, NL, d Aug 14, 1865 (Camp Hamilton, Houston).
    Eduardo; 24, Pvt, D & M, d March 5, 1865 (Reg Hospital, Baton Rouge).
    Encarnación; 46, Sgt, C, laborer, b Bexar Cty, Tex.
    Encarnación; 45, Sgt L, ranchero, b Matamoros, Tamps, disability discharge, June 24, 1865 (Baton Rouge).
    Eulogio; 38, Pvt (hospital cook), B & I, laborer.
    Facundo; 27, Pvt, D & M, ranchero, b San Patricio, Tex, d 26 June 1864 (Brownsville).
    Froilán [?]; 27, Pvt, IPR, carpenter, d May 24, 1864 (Edinburg).
    Francisco; 29, Pvt, C & L, d April 28, 1864 (Brownsville).
    Francisco; 22, Pvt, D & M, herdsman; b Eagle Pass, Tex.
    Gabino; 28, Pvt, A & I, herdsman, d Feb 12, 1864 (Santa Rosa).
    Gregorio; 25, Pvt, D & K, d March 5, 1864 (Santa Rosa).
    Guadalupe; 38, Sgt, E & H, b Sabinas, NL.
    Ignacio; 45, Pvt, I, d Feb 10, 1864.
    James; 23, Pvt, I, d Feb 10, 1864.
    Jesús Eusebio; 35, A & E, stockraiser, b NL.
    Jesús; 31, Pvt, D & M, vaquero, GCM, May 1865.
    Jesús María; 20, Pvt, A & I, laborer, b Ciudad Victoria, Tamps, d July 1, 1865 (Natchez, Miss).
    Jesús María; 18, Pvt, D & M, ranchero, b Matamoros, Tamps, d June 21, 1864 (Brownsville).
    Juan; 33, Pvt, E, farmer, d May 12, 1864 (Brownsville).
    Juan; 34, Pvt, B & K, laborer, b Sabinas, NL, GCM, June 17, 1865; dishonorable discharge (Baton Rouge).

GARCÍA [continued]
- Juan Adolfo; 29, Pvt, A & I, herdsman.
- Julián; 28, Pvt, D & M, vaquero.
- Leandro; 20, Pvt, IPR, farmer.
- Leandro; 26, Pvt, E & H, b Ciénagas, Coah, d May 2, 1864 (Brownsville).
- Luis; 47, Pvt; B & K, laborer-herdsman; died of disease, Oct 30, 1864 (Reg Hospital, Morganza, La).
- Manuel; 24, Pvt, E, shoemaker; substitute for F. Van Benthursen.
- Máximo; 23, Sgt, D & M, herdsman.
- Miguel; 22, Pvt, A & I, laborer, b Monterrey, NL.
- Miguel; 23, Pvt, I, laborer, b San Miguel, Gto.
- Miguel; 20, Pvt, IPR, farmer, d Feb 8, 1864 (Brownsville).
- Pascual; Pvt, IPR, E, d Aug 3, 1865 (Neches River).
- Pedro; 25, Cpl, C & L, laborer, d March 9, 1864 (Brownsville).
- Pedro; 20, Pvt, IPR, farmer, d June 11, 1864.
- Pedro; 25, Pvt, E, farmer, d May 26, 1864 (Edinburg); GCM, executed, June 27, 1864 (Brownsville).
- Pilar; 25, Pvt, B & K, bricklayer, b El Paso, NM [Chih?].
- Polinario; 26, Sgt, C, b Kinney Cty, Tex; died April 4, 1864 of consumption (hospital, Baton Rouge).
- Reyes; 25, Pvt, E, carpenter, d April 15, 1864 (Brownsville).
- Sacrain; Pvt, K.
- Santos; 45, Cpl, B & K, blacksmith.
- Urbano; 21, Pvt, C & L, laborer.
- Vicente; 24, Pvt, H, d March 18, 1864 (Brownsville).
- Víctor; 18, Pvt, B & K, laborer, b Valle del Maiz, SLP.
- Victoriano; 26, Pvt, B & K, laborer, b El Carmen, SLP.

GARIBAY
- Julián; 25, Pvt, D & M, ranchero.

GARZA
- Agapito; 21, Sgt, D, laborer, d June 19, 1864 (Brownsville).
- Alejandro; 25, Pvt, A, laborer, d Feb 17, 1864 (Brownsville).
- Antonio; 21, Pvt, A & I, d. Feb 7, 1864 (Santa Rosa).
- Cayetano; 19, Cpl, B & K, wheelwright, b Monterrey, NL.
- Dionicio; 30, Pvt, C & L, laborer.
- Florencio; 26, Pvt (company saddler), A & I, laborer, b Ventura, Coah.
- Francisco; 27, Cpl, E, herdsman, b. Camargo, Tamps, d May 31, 1864 (Brownsville).
- George; 21, Cpl, D & M, laborer.
- Julián; 30, Pvt, A & I, herdsman, d Feb 10, 1864 (Santa Rosa); POW.
- Julián; 20, Pvt, D & M, ranchero.
- Julio; 23, Comm Sgt, A & I, laborer; b Matamoros, Tamps.
- Leandro; 22, Cpl, A & I, laborer, b Agualeguas, NL; d 15 May 1865 (Post Hospital, Baton Rouge).
- Liverando; Pvt, E, d May 2, 1864 (Brownsville).
- Luis; 28, Pvt, D & M, vaquero.
- Manuel; 23, Pvt, C & L, laborer; disability discharge, April 5, 1865 for secondary syphilis (New Orleans).
- Nabor; 30, bugler, A & I, laborer, d May 24, 1864 (Brownsville).

GARZA [continued]
    Pedro; 32, Pvt, C, laborer, b Monterrey, NL; GCM, May 25, 1864,
        Morganza, La; admitted to St. Louis Hospital, Morganza,
        Aug 3, 1864; died of disease, Aug 30, 1864 (Morganza, La).
    Prágedes; 43, 1st Sgt, D & M, laborer.
    Rafael; 30, Pvt, A & I, d May 24, 1864 (Edinburg).
    Ramón; 22, Pvt, A & I, d May 24, 1864 (Edinburg).
    Santiago; 23, Pvt (company cook), A & I, laborer, b Cadereyta, NL.
    Santos; 36, Sgt, A & I, laborer, Monterrey, NL.
    Tomás; 23, Pvt, A, herdsman, d Feb 10, 1864 (Santa Rosa).
    Toribio; 23, Pvt, C & L, laborer.
    Vicente; 23, Pvt, E, laborer, b Reynosa, Tamps, d May 20, 1864 (Brownsville).
GASIO
    James; 20, Pvt, F, d April 30, 1864 (Brownsville).
GATTAN
    Daniel; Pvt, G, d June 8, 1863 (Annunciation Square, New Orleans).
GÓMEZ
    Ángel; 36, Sgt, C & L, laborer.
    Calistro; 36, QM Sgt, D & M, ranchero, b Matamoros, Tamps,
        d June 19, 1864 (Brownsville).
    Frank; 27, Pvt, G, farmer, b Vera Cruz, VC, GCM, found guilty
        of attempted murder and sentenced to two years at Fort Jefferson,
        Fla; died of chronic diarrhea at Fort Jefferson, Nov 7, 1865.
    Guillermo; 35, Pvt, E & H, herdsman, d April 8, 1864 (Brownsville),
        returned September 19, 1864; 1890 UVC, Hidalgo, Hidalgo Cty;
        applied for pension, February 28, 1895.
    Hermenegildo; 27, Pvt, E & H, laborer, b Tula, Tamps.
    Jesús; 36, Pvt, C & L, laborer, d Jan 26, 1864 (Brownsville).
    José María; 24, 1st Sgt, IPR, mason, b Matamoros, Tamps;
        1890 UVC, San Antonio, Bexar Cty.
    Luciano; 29, Cpl, C & L, laborer, b Bexar Cty, Tex.
    Mauricio; 32, Pvt, A & I.
    Perfecto; 20, Pvt, G, farmer, b Bustamante, NL;
        disability discharge, June 24, 1864 (Baton Rouge).
    Tomás; 21, Pvt, A, laborer; died of pneumonia, April 10, 1864
        (Post Hospital, Brownsville).
GONZALEZ (Gonzales)
    Abraham; 24, Pvt, E & H, d Dec 1864 (Morganza, La).
    Alemán Antonio; 30, Cpl (cook), C & L, laborer.
    Anastacio; 37, Pvt, B & K, b Mier, Tamps, d June 17, 1865;
        dishonorably discharged.
    Andrés; 28, Sgt, D & M, vaquero, d May 19, 1864 (Edinburg).
    Andrew; 26, Pvt, E & G, ranchero, b Morelos, Mex.
    Antonio; 30, Pvt, C & L, herdsman, b Nueces Cty, Tex.
    Benancio; 21, Pvt, IPR, farmer, d July 28, 1864
        (march from Brownsville to Brazos Santiago).
    Cenobio; 23, Pvt, A & I, laborer, b Mier, Tamps, d Aug 14, 1865 (Houston).
    Concepción; 29, Pvt, IPR, teamster.
    Cosmé; 23, Pvt, A & I, laborer, b Agualeguas, NL, d Aug 14, 1865 (Houston).

GONZALEZ (Gonzales) *[continued]*
    Cypriano; 30, Pvt, C, laborer; GCM, May 13, 1865, sentenced to one year's hard labor at Fort Jefferson, Fla; released Nov 4, 1865.
    Félix; Pvt, H, d. March 28, 1864 (Brownsville).
    Fermín; 25, Pvt, G, farmer, b Linares, NL.
    Francisco; 36, Sgt, C & L, laborer.
    Gregorio; 23, Pvt, E & H, laborer; 1890 UVC, Brownsville, Cameron Cty.
    Jesús; 28, Pvt, B, stockraiser; 1890 UVC, San Antonio, Bexar Cty.
    Jesús; 23, Pvt, G, farmer, b Zacatecas, Zac.
    José María; 31, Pvt, C & L, d March 31, 1864 (Brownsville).
    José María; 25, Pvt, IPR, farmer, d May 28, 1864 (Edinburg).
    Juán; 25, Pvt, IPR, carpenter, d Feb 10, 1864.
    Juan; 26, Pvt, IPR, farmer; 1890 UVC, San Diego, Duval Cty.
    Luis; 23, Sgt, D & M, herdsman, b Mier, Tamps.
    Luis; 45, QM Sgt, D, ranchero.
    Nieves; 22, Sgt, C & L, herdsman; disability discharge, Dec 12, 1864, inguinal hernia (New Orleans).
    Onofre; 23, Pvt, A & I.
    Pablo; 26, Pvt, B & K, laborer, d May 21, 1864 (Santa Rosa).
    Pedro; 25, Pvt, B & K, herdsman, b Higuera, NL.
    Pedro; 25, Pvt, D & M, d July 25, 1864 (Morganza, La).
    Perfecto; 33, Pvt, G, farmer, b Linares, NL.
    Ramón; 25, Pvt, C & L. laborer.
    Reducindo; 25, Corp, C & L, herdsman, d Feb 3, 1864 (Brownsville).
    Refugio; 21, Pvt, C,L. laborer.
    Sacramento; 19, Pvt, B & K, herdsman, b San Antonio, Tex.
    Timoteo; 26, Pvt, A & I, laborer, b Linares, NL; GCM, June 17, 1865; dishonorably discharged (Shreveport).
    Tomás; 22, bugler, E & H, b Zacatecas, Zac; 1890 UVC, San Diego, Duval Cty.
    Venancio; Pvt, IRP, d [date unknown].
    Ventura; 25, Pvt, B & K, herdsman, b Ramos, Coah.
    Vicente; 24, Pvt, A & I, laborer.
    Ynocencio; 36, Sgt, B & K, herdsman; MIA, March 16, 1864 (Santa Rosa).

GRANADO
    S; Natchez, Miss, Hospital, June 1865.

GUAJARDO
    Anicleto; 36, Pvt, E & H, b Monclova, Coah.
    Juan; 31, Pvt, B & K, laborer, d May 21, 1864 (Santa Rosa).

GUERRA
    Cecilio; 38, Pvt, C & L, laborer, d March 31, 1864 (Brownsville).
    Eduardo; 22, Pvt, D, herdsman, b Linares, NL, d May 19, 1864 (Brownsville).
    Francisco; 30, Pvt, D & M, vaquero, d June 21, 1864 (Brownsville).

GUERRERO
    Melchor; 25, Pvt, IPR, carpenter, d Feb 6, 1864 (Brownsville).
    Miguel; 22, Pvt, F.
    Rosalio; 27, Pvt (cook), G, farmer, b Goliad Cty, Tex.
    Ventura; 22, Pvt, D & M, laborer, d Jan 30, 1864 (Brownsville); returned May 14, 1864.

GUERTO
: Tefrón; 26, Pvt, A & I, laborer, b Guerrero, Tamps.
GUEVARA
: Antonio; 22, Pvt, E & H, b. China, Tamps, d Dec 29, 1864 (Morganza, La).
: Antonio; 36, Pvt, D & M, herdsman, b Bexar Cty, Tex.
: Refugio; 30, Pvt, G, tailor, b Rio Verde, SLP.
GUTIÉRREZ
: Agapito; 50, Pvt, C, laborer; died July 10, 1864 from an internal injury after being thrown to the ground by a companion (Post Hospital, Brownsville).
: José María; 24, Sgt, E, b Guerrero, Tamps, d May 14, 1864 (Brownsville).
: Manuel; 18, Pvt, G, farmer, b Cerralvo, NL.
: Rafael; 21, Sgt, B & K, herdsman.
GUZMÁN
: Eugenio; 37, 2d Lt, D, I & M.
: Eugenio; 32, Pvt, B & K, laborer, d Feb 7, 1864 (Santa Rosa).
: Félix; 29, Pvt, A & I, laborer, b Sabinas, NL.
: Santiago; 33, Pvt, B & K, laborer, d Dec 25, 1864 (Morganza, La).

H

HERNÁNDEZ
: Alejo; 32, Pvt, D & H, stonemason, b San Antonio, Tex, d Oct 23, 1864 (Brazos Santiago).
: Andrés; 25, Pvt, D, G & H, teamster, b Lampazos, NL.
: Antonio; 22, Pvt, M, carpenter, b Saltillo, Coah.
: Antonio; 38, Pvt, IPR, farmer.
: Antonio; 23, Pvt, IPR, farmer, d May 26, 1864 (Edinburg).
: Antonio; 22, Corp, D, herdsman, b Linares, NL.
: Basilio; 22, Pvt, A,I, laborer, b Ciudad Victoria, Tamps, died Sept 30, 1864 of disease (Reg Hospital, Morganza, La).
: Benito; 33, Pvt, B, herdsman, b Sabinas, NL; died of disease.
: Benito; 33, Pvt, K, herdsman, died of disease, Oct 21, 1864 (Reg Hospital, Morganza, La).
: Dolores; 28, Pvt, D & M, laborer, b Palmillas, Tamps.
: Felipe; 28, Sgt, C & L, laborer.
: Fermín; 24, 1st Sgt, E & H, herdsman.
: Francisco; 20, Pvt, C & L.
: J; Pvt, G, d Feb 5, 1864 (Brownsville).
: Jesús; 26, Pvt, A & I, laborer, b Guerrero, Tamps, d [date unknown].
: Juan; 26, Pvt, A & I, laborer, b Monterrey, NL.
: Marjil; 33, Pvt, B, laborer; died of accidental gunshot, July 16, 1864 (New Orleans), buried in Monument Cemetery.
: Miguel; 42, Pvt (cook), C & K, died of disease, July 16, 1864 (New Orleans).
: Narciso; 22, Pvt, A, laborer.
: Nicolás; 28, Pvt, IPR, farmer.
: Paulino; 26, Pvt, G.
: Pedro; 25, Pvt, D & L, vaquero, d April 14, 1864 (Brownsville).
: Ramón; 23, Pvt, D & M.
: Santiago; 44, Pvt, D & H, d Oct 24, 1864 (Brazos Santiago).

HERNÁNDEZ [continued]
    Santos; 21, Pvt, D, G & H, teamster, b Laredo, Tex.
    Sicario; Pvt, G, d Feb 7, 1864 (Brownsville).
    Simón; 41, Pvt, B, herdsman.
    Sóstenes; 22, Pvt, A & I, laborer, b Mier, Tamps, d Aug 14, 1865 (Houston).
HERRERA
    Crecento; 25, Cpl, A & I, herdsman; died June 20, 1864 while on leave (Camargo, Tamps).
    Macario; 24, Pvt, E & H, laborer, b Chapa de Mota, Mex.
HIPÓLITO
    León; Pvt, D, d Dec 28, 1863 (Brownsville).
HINOJOSA
    Antonio; Pvt, B & K, herdsman, d May 21, 1864 (Santa Rosa).
    Damasio; 32, Cpl, D & N, laborer, d May 13, 1864 (Brownsville).
    José; 32, Pvt, B & K, laborer.
    Julio; 27, Cpl, A & I, herdsman, d June 16, 1864 (Brownsville).
    Leandro; 19, Pvt, A & I, herdsman.
    Lino; 27, QM Sgt, A & I, herdsman.
    Martín; 28, 2d Lt.
    Urbano; 25, Pvt, D & H, wagoner, b San Antonio, Tex; died Jan 2, 1865 of chronic dysentery (Brazos Santiago).
    Victor; 25, Pvt, D & M, laborer, d April 14, 1864 (Brownsville).
HOLGUÍN
    Antonio; Pvt, D & H, d Oct 23, 1864 (Brazos Santiago).
    Pedro; Pvt, G.
HUERTA
    Trifón; 26, Pvt, laborer.

I

IBARRA
    Julio; 25, Pvt, A, laborer, b Cadereyta, NL.
    Refugio; 30, Pvt, G.
    Santos; 36, Sgt, A & I.
    Silverio; 24, Cpl, E & H, ranchero.
    Valeriano; 21, Pvt, C & L, d [date unknown].

J

JACKSON
    James; Pvt, A, laborer, b Camargo, Tamps.
JIMÉNEZ
    Francisco Zuñiga; 22, Cpl, C & L, laborer, b Bexar Cty, Tex.
    Jesús; 20, bugler, C & L.
    Juan; 30, Cpl, B & K, laborer, d May 21, 1864 (Santa Rosa).
    Perfecto; 25, Pvt, A & I.
JOSSIA
    John; Pvt, IPR, d Feb 1, 1864 (Brownsville).
JUÁREZ
    Ascencio; 30, Pvt, B & K,, laborer, d April 24, 1864 (Santa Rosa).
    Cosmé; 22, Pvt, A & I, herdsman, d June 16, 1864 (Brownsville).
    Cenobio; 21, Pvt, D & M, herdsman, b Santa Ana, Tamps.

JUÁREZ [continued]
 George; 18, Pvt, D & M, workman, b Monterrey, NL.
 Juan; 28, Pvt, B & K, laborer.
 Rafael; 21, Pvt, B, laborer.

L

LARA
 Juan; 38, Pvt, F, d Jan 19, 1864 (Brownsville).
 Sylvestre; 37, Cpl, B & K, laborer, d April 24, 1864 (Santa Rosa).
LEACADIO
 James; 25, Pvt, I, d Jan 13, 1864 (Brownsville).
LEAL
 Fernando; 22, Cpl, IPR, teamster, b Mexico City, Mex,
  d July 26, 1864 (Brownsville).
 Gabino; 26, Pvt, IPR, stockraiser, d May 26, 1864.
 Pedro; 24, QM Sgt, IPR, carpenter, d July 28, 1864 (march from
  Brownsville to Brazos Santiago).
LEOS
 Sanatana; 25, Pvt, D,M, vaquero.
LONGORIA
 Lorenzo; 23, Pvt, C & L, d May 31, 1864 (Brownsville).
 Victoriano; 39, Pvt, B & K, laborer, b Cerralvo, NL.
LÓPEZ
 Abraham; 22, Pvt, E & H, b Guerrero, Tamps.
 Augustín; 26, Pvt, C & L.
 Benigno; 23, Cpl, E & H, farmer, b Saltillo, Coah, d 10 Feb 1864;
  rejoined Sept 16, 1865.
 Benito; 28, Pvt, IPR, carpenter, d Feb 10, 1864.
 Caspio; 25, Cpl, E, ranchero, d May 20, 1864 (Brownsville).
 Corpio; 23, Pvt, A, laborer, d May 24, 1864 (Edinburg).
 Isidro; 35, Pvt, H, d Feb 6, 1864 (Brownsville).
 John; Pvt, G, d April 4, 1864 (Santa Rosa).
 Mariano; Pvt, G, d April 4, 1864 (Santa Rosa).
 Matías; 32, Pvt, C, herdsman.
 Seferino; 32, 1st Sgt, A, herdsman, d June 16, 1864 (Brownsville).
 Tomás; 23, Pvt, C & L, laborer.
LOSSIAN
 LP; Pvt, IPR, d Feb 8, 1864 (Brownsville).
LOYA
 José María; 33, IPR, farmer, d July 28, 1864 (march from
  Brownsville to Brazos Santiago).
LOZA
 Asencio; 23, Sgt, IPR, farmer.
LOZANO
 Juan de Diós; 36, Pvt, B, herdsman.
 Manuel; 21, Pvt, E, laborer, d March 28, 1864 (Brownsville).
 Vidal; Pvt, B & K.
LUGANO
 Juan; 30, Pvt, K.

LUNA
- Ciriaco; 36, Pvt, B & K, laborer.
- Francisco; 29, Pvt, B & K, laborer, b Mier, Tamps.
- Tomás de; 25, Pvt, C & L, herdsman.

M

McDONALD
- Miguel; 21, QM Sgt, C, blacksmith, died from effects of accidental gunshot, Feb 4, 1864 (Brownsville).

MACÍAS
- Pablo; 30, Pvt, B, laborer.

MALDONADO
- José; Pvt, H.
- Juan; 26, Cpl, E & K, laborer, b Monterrey, NL.
- Reyes; 25, Pvt, C, D, H & L, teamster, b San Nicolás de Hidalgo, NL.

MANCHO
- Cristóbal; 40, Pvt, D & M, laborer, b Monterrey, NL.

MANCILLAS
- Salomón; 25, Pvt, IPR, farmer.
- Francisco; 22, Pvt, D & L, laborer, d March 31, 1864 (Ringgold Barracks).
- Ignacio; 25, Pvt, E, herdsman, d May 12, 1864 (Brownsville).
- Pablo; 30, Pvt, B & K.

MATÍAS
- Salomón; Pvt, IPR.

MARCOS
- F; Pvt, F.

MARÍN
- Isador; 34, Pvt, A.

MARMIDES
- Patricio; 25, Pvt, IPR, farmer; 1890 UVC, Corpus Christi, Nueces Cty.

MARROQUÍN
- Feliciano; 34, Pvt, A & I, d Feb 18, 1864 (Brownsville).

MARTÍNEZ
- Alejandro; 35, Pvt (nurse), M.
- Anastacio; 25, Pvt, IPR, farmer, d July 15, 1864.
- Antonio; 26, Pvt, H, farmer.
- Augustín; 44, Sgt, B & K, laborer.
- Benito; 19, Pvt, F, wounded June 18, 1864.
- Cornelio; 32, Pvt, A & I, laborer, b Agualeguas, NL, disability discharge Dec 4, 1864 (Greenville, La).
- Crecencio; 21, Pvt, E, stockraiser, d Feb 20, 1864 (Brownsville).
- Enno; 37, Pvt, IPR, farmer, d July 15, 1864.
- Faustino; 47, Pvt, B, laborer, d May 29, 1864 (Brownsville).
- Faustino; 22, Pvt, K, butcher, b Bexar Cty, Tex, d Oct 28, 1864 (Morganza, La).
- Feliciano; 21, Pvt, D & M, cartman, b Chipinque, NL [?].
- Francisco; 24, Pvt, A & I, b San Luis Potosí, d [date unknown].
- Francisco; 30, Comm Sgt, IPR, farmer, d July 28, 1864 (march from Brownsville to Brazos Santiago); later filed for removal of desertion charge, request denied.

MARTÍNEZ [continued]
    Francisco; 22, Pvt, D & M, herdsman, b Bexar Cty, Tex,
        d 28 Oct 1864 (Morganza).
    George; 21, Pvt, C & L, laborer, d May 29, 1864 (Edinburg).
    Jesse; 37, Cpl, E & F, carpenter, b San Antonio, Tex.
    José; 37, Cpl, E & F.
    José Alejandro; 35, Pvt, D, vaquero.
    José María; 36, Capt, E, mustered out by special order, July 14, 1864.
    Juan; 25, Pvt, D & M, herdsman, b Camargo, Tamps.
    Lázaro; 25, Pvt, IPR, farmer, d Feb 15, 1864 (Brownsville).
    Lorenzo; 28, Pvt, IPR, farmer, d July 28, 1864
        (Brownsville to Brazos Santiago).
    Manuel; 30, Pvt, C & L, herdsman, b Matehuala, SLP.
    Macario; 22, Sgt, A, laborer, b Brownsville, Tex.
    Pedro; 23, Pvt, E & L, d May 30, 1864 (Brownsville).
    Pedro; 25, Pvt, C, laborer.
    Pilar; 27, Cpl, IPR, farmer, d May 26, 1864 (Edinburg).
    Quereno; 23, Pvt, IPR, farmer.
    Rafael; 21, Pvt, B & K, farmer, b Río Blanco, NL.
    Severtino; 25, Pvt, G, farmer, b Piedras Negras, Coah; GCM, July 17, 1865.
    Ventura; 22, Pvt, IPR, farmer, d July 28, 1864 (march from
        Brownsville to Brazos Santiago).
MEDELES
    Alfonso; 30, Pvt, B & K, herdsman.
MEDINA
    Brigido; 22, Pvt, D & M, d Jan 17, 1864 (Brownsville).
MELLARDO
    Teodoro; 18, Cpl, D, herdsman, b Irimson [?], Guadalajara, Jal.
MENDIOLA
    José María; 20, Pvt, D & M, soldier, b Matamoros, Tamps,
        d Feb 18, 1864 (Brownsville).
MÉNDEZ
    Antonio; 28, Pvt, IPR, farmer, d March 8, 1864 (Brownsville).
    Domingo; 20, Pvt, G, teamster, b San Antonio, Tex.
MENDOZA
    Albino; 30, Pvt, E, laborer.
    Antonio; 26, Pvt, H, d December 29, 1864 (Morganza, La).
    Manuel; 50, Pvt, F.
    Michael; Pvt, G, d Jan 12, 1864 (Brownsville).
    Teodoro; 25, Pvt, D, substitute.
MERITO
    Francisco; 21, Pvt, H, d March 14, 1864 (Brownsville).
MIRELES
    Jesús; 22, Cpl, D & M, laborer, b Linares, NL.
MOLINA
    Calistano; 35, Cpl, IPR, farmer, d July 28, 1864 (March from
        Brownsville to Brazos Santiago).
    Doroteo; 28, Pvt, D & M, laborer, b Palmillas, Tamps.
    Jacobo; 22, Pvt, B & K, laborer, d April 24, 1864 (Santa Rosa).
    Juan; 24, Cpl, B, laborer, d May 30, 1864 (Brownsville).

MOLINA [continued]
    Matilde; 22, Pvt, A & I, laborer, b Agualeguas, NL,
        d Aug 14, 1865 (Houston).
MONTALVO
    Benancio; 21, Pvt, E & H.
    Facundo; 33, Pvt, C & L.
    José; 36, Pvt, E & H, laborer.
    Rafael; 25, bugler, A & I, laborer; 1890 UVC, Hidalgo, Hidalgo, Cty.
MONTES
    Francisco; 21, Cpl, A & I.
MONTOSA
    Antonio; 26, Pvt, E, laborer.
MONTOYA
    Anastacio; 23, Cpl, C & L, laborer, b Bexar Cty, Tex.
MORALES
    Cipriano; 21, Pvt, B & K, herdsman, d May 17, 1864 (Brownsville).
    Jesús; 32, Pvt, B & K, laborer, b Camargo, Tamps; died of disease
        (ptosis pulmonalis) Sedgwick Gen Hospital, Greenville La).
    Juan; 29, Cpl, B & K, herdsman.
MORENO
    Benigno; 23, Pvt, D & M, laborer, b Pesqueria Chico, NL.
    José; 45, Pvt, IPR, farmer, d May 28, 1864 (Edinburg).
    Ysidro; 23, Pvt, C & L, laborer, d Feb 15, 1864 (Brownsville).
MORÍN
    Juan; 26, Pvt, E, laborer, b Matamoros, Tamps,
        d March 29, 1864 (Brownsville).
MOYA
    Blas; 21, bugler, D, G & H, stockraiser, b San Antonio, Tex.
    Mogonio; 23, Pvt, B & K, laborer, d Feb 7, 1864 (Santa Rosa).
MUÑOZ
    Antonio; 23, Pvt, H, miner, b Viesca, Coah, June 8, 1864 (Brownsville).
    Juan Nepomuceno; 45, Pvt, B & K, herdsman.
MÚSQUEZ
    Camilo; 21, Pvt, D & M, herdsman, b Laredo, Tex, d 1864 (Brownsville).

N

NAVARRO
    Ignacio; 21, Pvt, D & M, laborer.
    Juan; 21, Cpl, B, laborer, d March 6, 1864 (Santa Rosa).
NIETO
    Andrés; 41, Pvt, IPR, tailor, b Bexar Cty, Tex.
NUÑEZ
    Francisco; 22, Pvt, C & L, herdsman.
    Santiago; 38, QM Sgt, E & H, herdsman, b Matamoros, Tamps.

O

OLIVARES
    Catarino; 35, Cpl, IPR, farmer; duplicate discharge furnished
        by War Department in 1888.
    Juan Antonio; Pvt, E & H.

OLIVARES [continued]
    Marcelino; 21, Pvt, IPR, farmer, b Mexico City, Mex,
        d July 28, 1864 (march from Brownsville to Brazos Santiago).
    Mario; 21, Pvt, E, laborer, b Morelos, Coah.
OLIVO
    Vicente; 29, Pvt, IPR, farmer, d June 14, 1864.
OROZCO
    Darío; 30, Pvt, G, farmer, b Guadalajara, Jal.
    Santiago; 25, Cpl, D & M, laborer, b Mier, Tamps.
ORTEGA
    Juan; 22, Pvt, E, b San Antonio Reynosa, Tamps,
        d Dec 24, 1864 (Morganza, La).
ORTIZ
    Abrám; 24, Cpl, D & M.
    Pedro; 25, Pvt, D, ranchero.
OSUNA
    Juan Manuel; 21, Pvt, C & L, laborer, d March 15, 1864 (Brownsville).
    Pascual; 21, Pvt, C & L, laborer, d March 21, 1864 (Ringgold Barracks).
OTELO
    Moncivais; 23, Pvt, B & K.
OTERO
    Ángel; 20, bugler, D & M, ranchero.

P

PAIS
    Valentine; 21, Pvt, B & K, herdsman, b Matamoros, Tamps,
        d Jan 20, 1864 (Brownsville).
PALACIO
    Encarnación; 23, Pvt, IPR, farmer.
    Leandro; 20, Comm Sgt, C & L, herdsman, b Mier, Tamps.
PANTHONA [?]
    Jesus; Pvt, IPR, d Jan 24, 1864 (Brownsville).
PARRAS
    Lución; Pvt, G, d Feb 5, 1864 (Port Isabel).
    Manuel; Pvt, B, substitute.
PARROLA
    Esteván; 44, Pvt, H, d [date unknown].
PATIÑO
    Leandro; 23, QM Sgt, B & K, laborer.
PAZ
    Andrés; 23, Pvt, C & L, laborer, d Jan 7, 1864 (Brownsville).
PEÑA
    Facundo; 23, Pvt, C & L, laborer, d March 15, 1864.
    Francisco; 40, Pvt (baker), A & L.
    Gregorio; 29, Pvt, A & I.
    Ignacio; Cpl, M, confined at Houston awaiting trial, Aug 30, 1865.
    Juan; 25, Pvt, E & H, ranchero.
    Luis; 25, Sgt, IPR, tailor, d July 15, 1864.
    Miguel; 25, Pvt (co tailor), E & H, tailor, b Cadereyta, NL;
        died of disease, April 28, 1865 (Baton Rouge).

PEÑA [continued]
    Ramón; 22, Pvt, H, d June 8, 1864 (Brownsville).
    Ygnacio; 35, Pvt, D, laborer.
PÉREZ
    Amalio; 35, Pvt, B & K, laborer.
    Blas; 27, Pvt, C & L, d Jan 20, 1864 (Brownsville).
    Cicel; 19, Pvt, G.
    Felipe; 23, Pvt, E & H, laborer.
    Jesús; 21, Cpl, E & H.
    John; 42, Pvt, G & H.
    José Ángel; 31, Pvt, C & L, laborer, d Jan 7. 1864 (Brownsville).
    Julio; 42, Pvt, D, G & H, farmer, b Goliad, Tex.
    Natividad; 27, Pvt, D & M, herdsman, b Santa Rosa, Tex.
    Patricio; 32, 1st Sgt, A & I, herdsman, b Rancherías, Tamps.
    Pedro; 21, Pvt, E, farmer, d Feb 8, 1864 (Brownsville).
    Severiano; 35, Pvt, IPR, carpenter, d May 26, 1864 (Edinburg).
    Tiburcio; 30, Pvt, A & I, laborer, d May 24, 1864 (Edinburg).
PIÑA
    José María; 40, Pvt, B & K, laborer.
PINEDA
    Clemente; 40, Pvt, B & K.
PORRAS
    Juan; 23, Comm Sgt, D & M, painter, b Bexar Cty, Tex.
PORTUGAL
    Manuel; unassigned recruit, d May 17, 1864 (Brownsville); 1860
        Cameron Cty Census; age 21, baker, b Tex.
PRESAS
    Tranquilino; 32, Pvt, B & K, laborer, d Feb 7. 1864 (Santa Rosa).
PRONTRO [?]
    Santiago; 23, Pvt, E, laborer, b Mante, Tamps, Mex,
        d March 7, 1864 (Brownsville).
PUEBLA
    Guillermo; 28, Sgt, D & M, ranchero.

Q

QUESADA
    Julián; 21, Pvt, D & M, laborer.
QUINTANILLA
    Filomeno; 24, Pvt, D & M, laborer.
QUIROGA
    Pablo; 32, Pvt, C & L, laborer; disability discharge,
        Dec 12, 1864 (Marine Gen Hospital, New Orleans).

R

RABAJOSA
    Fernando; Pvt, A & I, d [date unknown].
RAMÍREZ
    Andrés; 26, Pvt, A & I, laborer, d 8 Aug 1865 (Beaumont).
    Antonio; 33, Pvt, IPR, tailor, d April 13, 1864 (Brownsville).

RAMÍREZ [continued]
　Benito; Pvt, G, farmer, b San Antonio, Tex; disability discharge,
　　August 8, 1864, for reason of accidental wound (Brownsville).
　Feliciano; 23, Pvt, D & M, herdsman, b Corpus Christi, Tex.
　Guillermo; 27, Sgt, E, b Camargo, Tamps, d May 18, 1864 (Brownsville).
　Julián; 18, Pvt, A & I, laborer, b Alaquines, SLP.
　Lucio; 30, Pvt, IPR, farmer, d June 1, 1864 (Edinburg).
　Martín; 26, Cpl, A & I, herdsman, d May 20, 1864 (Edinburg).
　Tereso; 26, Pvt, A & I, laborer, b Alaquines, SLP;
　　d Sept 29, 1864 (Salado Creek near San Antonio, Tex).
　Sóstenes; 31, Pvt, A, herdsman.
RAMÓN
　Antonio; 37, Pvt, IPR, farmer.
　José; 25, Cpl, A & I, laborer, d June 16, 1864.
RAMOS
　Basilio; 33, Cpl, D & M, laborer, d June 6, 1865 (Natchez, Miss),
　　returned June 22, 1865.
　Calixto; 19, Pvt, D & M, herdsman, b Morelos, NL.
　Juan; 27, Pvt, D & M, laborer.
　Manuel; 26, Pvt, B & K, d May 29, 1864 (Brownsville).
　Pedro; 37, Pvt, B & K, laborer, b Alaquines, SLP.
　Santiago; 26, Cpl, B & K, laborer, d [date unknown].
　Telano; 29, Comm Sgt, B & K, laborer; left in Brownsville
　　Hospital upon evacuation, Sept 1, 1864.
REGALADO
　Esteban; 32, Cpl, E & H, laborer.
　Trinidad F; 36, Pvt, A, herdsman, d Feb 10, 1864 (Santa Rosa).
RENDÓN
　Doroteo; 27, Cpl, IPR, farmer, d July 15, 1864.
　Rosalio; 23, Pvt, IPR, laborer, d Jan 30, 1864, (Brownsville).
　Teófilo; 31, bugler, IPR, blacksmith, d July 28, 1864 (march
　　from Brownsville to Brazos Santiago).
RESÉNDEZ
　Juan Antonio; 37, Sgt, A & I, laborer.
　Severo; 20, Pvt, IPR, farmer, d May 26, 1864 (Edinburg).
REYES
　Camilo; 20, Pvt, D & M, laborer, b Camargo, Tamps.
　Catarino; 20, Cpl, K, soapmaker, b Monterrey, NL; disability
　　discharge, July 25, 1865 (Sedgwick Gen Hospital, Greenville,
　　La), for reason of accidental gunshot of right hand.
　Cristóbal; 21, Pvt, H, d June 6. 1864 (Brownsville Post Hospital).
　Maldonado; 25, Pvt, D.
REYNA
　Pedro; 49, Pvt, IPR, K, herdsman, b Sabinas, NL.
　Pedro; 25, Pvt, IPR, farmer, d April 17, 1864 (Brownsville).
　Ramón; 23, Pvt, A,I, herdsman, d Aug 8, 1865 (Beaumont).
REYNAS
　Antonio; Pvt, G, d Jan 15, 1864 (Brownsville).
RINCÓN
　Arcadio; 31, Sgt, IPR, farmer, d [date unknown].

RÍOS
- Bernardo; 32, Pvt, IPR, farmer, d July 15, 1864.
- Juan; 29, Cpl, IPR, farmer, b Mexico City, Mex.
- Manuel; 25, Pvt, IPR, farmer.
- Víctor; 26, Cpl, C & L, laborer.

RIVAS
- Merced; 22, pvt, A & I, laborer, d Aug 14, 1865 (Houston); captured Aug 14, 1865 (Victoria).
- Nabor; 32, Pvt, E & H, herdsman.

RIVERA
- Francisco; 33, Pvt, B & K, herdsman, d Jan 30, 1864 (Brownsville); captured Feb 1, 1864 (Brownsville); GCM, June 17, 1865 dishonorably discharged.

ROBLES
- Agapito; 28, Pvt (co clerk), D & M, herdsman, b Louisiana.
- Juan; 35, Pvt, D & M, b Puebla, Pue.

ROCHA
- Gavino; 25, Pvt, D, laborer, b Camargo, Tamps.

RODRÍGUEZ
- Alejandro; 24, Cpl, D & M, laborer, b Agualeguas, NL.
- Anastacio; 30, Pvt, G, laborer, b Realito Alamo, Tamps.
- Antonio; 26, Cpl, B & K, laborer.
- Carlos; unassigned recruit, d May 17, 1864.
- Casimiro; 34, Pvt, B & K, d May 28, 1864 (Santa Rosa).
- Clemente; 31, Pvt, IPR, d July 28, 1864 (march from Brownsville to Brazos Santiago).
- Damacio; 21, Pvt, B & K, d Feb 7, 1864 (Santa Rosa).
- Francisco Torres; 22, Pvt, D & M, laborer; killed while involved in marauding at Houston, Aug 23, 1865.
- Francisco; 42, Cpl, D & M, ranchero, d 21 June 1864 (Brownsville).
- Gregorio; 49, Pvt, C & L., laborer.
- Ildefonso; 27, Pvt, D & M.
- Jesús; 27, Pvt, IPR, farmer, d July 28, 1864 (march from Brownsville to Brazos Santiago); application for removal of desertion charges and applied for pension July 20, 1895, both denied.
- Jesús; 40, Pvt, B & K.
- José; 19, Pvt, A & I, laborer, b Albuquerque, SLP.
- José María; 25, Pvt, C & L, herdsman.
- José María; 32, Pvt, C & L, laborer.
- José María; 30, Cpl, A & I, laborer, d Aug 14, 1865 (Houston).
- Juan; 24, Pvt, B & K.
- Juan; 26, Pvt (cook), E & H, b Laredo, Tex.
- Marcelo; 24, Pvt, D, farmer, b Jalapa, Vera Cruz.
- Marcelo; 24, Pvt (co tailor), IPR, M.
- Martín; 40, Pvt, A & I, laborer.
- Nasirat; 30, Pvt, F.
- Pedro; 24, Pvt, D & M, laborer, b Guerrero, Tamps; disability discharge, June 24, 1865 (Baton Rouge).
- Rafael; 27, Sgt, IPR, drover, d July 15, 1864.
- Ramón; 27, Pvt, A & I, laborer, d May 9, 1864 (Brownsville).

RODRÍGUEZ [continued]
    Ramón; 22, bugler, D & M, laborer, b Monterrey, NL; disability discharge, June 24, 1865 (Baton Rouge); wounded in the chest at Clinton, La, May 6, 1865.
    Sabas; 30, Pvt, IPR, farmer.
    Santa Ana; 26, Sgt (co sadder), D & M, laborer, b Mier, Tamps.
    Santiago; 17, Pvt, E & H, d Dec 29, 1864 (Morganza, La).
    Trinidad; 23, Pvt, IPR, farmer; confined in brig at Tortugas, Fla, March-May 1864.

ROMAIN
    Joseph; Corp, G.
    Nicholás; Pvt (regimental orderly), G.
    Vicente; 17, Pvt, G, b San Antonio, Tex; wounded by accident and died of congestive chills, May 24, 1864 (Brownsville).

ROSA
    Dionisio; 30, Pvt, B & K, laborer.
    Juan de la; 25, Cpl, B, laborer, d June 21, 1864.

ROSAS
    José; 36, Pvt, B & K, laborer, d June 9, 1864 (Brownsville).

ROSTERO
    Santiago; Pvt, E.

RUBALCABA
    Francisco; 40, Pvt, C & L, laborer.

RUIZ
    Adriano; 30, Pvt, B & K.
    Alcario; 26, Pvt, D & M, laborer, b Candela, Coah, d Dec 25, 1864 (Morganza, La).
    Felipe; 18, Pvt, A & I, laborer, San Buenaventura, Chi.
    Florencio; 32, Sgt, D & M, laborer, b Matamoros, Tamps; 1890 UVC, Lagarto, Live Oak Cty.
    Leandro; 22, 1st Sgt Maj, C, L & M, staff, laborer.
    Santos; 25, Pvt, B & K, laborer.

S

SAIS
    Antonio; 22, Cpl, C & L, laborer.
    Félix; 27, Pvt, B & K, laborer.
    Pedro; 27, 1st Sgt, A & I, herdsman.
    Porfirio; 25, Cpl, D & M, laborer, d. 1 Feb 1864 (Brownsville).

SALAS
    Encarnación; 30, Pvt, B & K, herdsman, b Guerrero, Tamps, d March 11, 1864 (Brownsville).

SALAZAR
    Crecencio; 30, Pvt, C & G, herdsman, d Feb 4, 1864 (Brownsville).
    Dolores; 23, Pvt (teamster in ambulance corps), G, shoemaker, b Sabinas, NL.
    Francisco; 40, Pvt, C & L, laborer.
    Gabriel; Pvt, C.
    Gregorio; 18, Pvt, IPR, farmer, killed December 8, 1863.

SALAZAR [continued]
  Isabel; 24, Pvt, D, G & H, wagoneer, b Goliad, Tex; disability discharge, June 26, 1865 (New Orleans), accidentally wounded in the arm.
  Matías; 25, Pvt, D, G & H, laborer, b Goliad, Tex.
  Peter; 21, Pvt, D, b Goliad, Tex.
SALDÍVAR
  Rafael; 25, Cpl, D & M, vaquero.
SALINAS
  Alejandro; 25, Pvt (cook), A & I, herdsman.
  Celestino; 22, Pvt (cook), B & K, herdsman, b Ramos, NL.
  Eugenio; 23, Pvt, A & I, laborer, d June 16, 1864.
  José María; 23, Pvt, D & M, laborer, b Monterrey, NL.
  Matías; 23, Pvt, E & H, b Ramos, NL.
  Melitón; 26, Pvt, E & H, laborer, b Cerralvo, NL; disability discharge, Dec 12, 1864 (New Orleans) from inguinal hernia.
  Rafael; 30, Pvt, E & H, laborer.
SÁNCHEZ
  Ángel; 28, Pvt, IPR, farmer, d Feb 2, 1864 (Brownsville).
  Antonio; 21, Pvt, farmer; died of disease, Jan 20, 1864.
  Fernando; 28, Pvt, D & M, b San Antonio Reynosa, Tamps.
  Francisco; 35, Pvt, A, drover, b Monterrey, NL.
  Francisco; 30, Pvt, B & K, laborer.
  Jesús; 35, Pvt, D & M, herdsman, b Saltillo, Coah,
      d July 1, 1864 (Reg Hospital, Morganza, La).
  José; 25, Pvt, E, b Chihuahua, substitute.
  Pilar; 25, B & K, laborer, d Feb 7, 1864 (Santa Rosa).
SANDOVAL
  Benigno; 29, Cpl (cook), B & K, herdsman.
  Francisco; 25, Pvt, C & L, herdsman, b Monterrey, NL,
      d Feb 3, 1864 (Brownsville).
SANTOS
  Abraham de los; 24, Sgt, E & H, farmer, b Ramireño, Tex,
      d Aug 1, 1864 (Brownsville Post Hospital).
  Francisco de los; 43, Pvt, B & K, herdsman.
  Gabriel de los; 22, Pvt, A & I, laborer, d April 1, 1864 (Brownsville).
  Luciano de los; 22, Pvt, C & L, herdsman.
  Rafael; 19, Pvt, B & K, herdsman, b Candela, Coah.
SAROLA
  Esteban; Pvt, H, d July 8, 1864 (Brownsville Post Hospital).
SAUCEDO
  Alvino; 25, Pvt, H, farmer, b La Vaca, Mex; disability discharge, Feb 8, 1865 (New Orleans).
  Joseph; 30, Pvt, G, farmer, b Labarrillo, NL.
SAYAS
  Sixto; 30, Sgt, C & M, ranchero, b Matamoros, Tamps, d June 2, 1864 (Brownsville).
SEGURO
  Tiburcio; Pvt, G & D, June 19, 1864 (Brownsville).
SICÓN
  Pedro; Pvt, G, died July 12, 1865 (Baton Rouge) of chronic diarrhea.

SIERRA
    Damasio; 26, Pvt, C & M.
    Pololio; 21, Pvt, D, herdsman, b San Antonio, Tex.
SIFUENTES
    Felipe; Pvt, A.
    Macedonio; 21, Pvt, B & K, herdsman, b San Fernando, Tamps,
        d May 12, 1864 (Brownsville).
SILVA
    Martín; 19, Pvt, A & I, herdsman, b Matamoros, Tamps.
SOLÍS
    Julián; 27, Pvt, A & I, laborer, b Agualeguas, NL.
    Sixto; 26, Pvt, A & I, d Feb 18, 1864 (Santa Rosa).
    Tomás; 23, Pvt, A & I, laborer, d February 7, 1864 (Santa Rosa).
SOSA
    Francisco; 22, Cpl, D & M, ranchero, d Dec 28, 1863 (Brownsville).
    Martín; 27, Pvt, D & M, laborer, b Camargo, Tamps.
    Santiago; 22, Bugler, C & L, laborer, b Bexar Cty, Tex.
SOTO
    Hilario; 22, Pvt (cook), E & H, herdsman.
    Lino; 24, bugler, IPR, farmer, d March 13, 1864 (Brownsville).
SUÁREZ
    Evaristo; 24, Pvt, E & H, laborer.

T

TAMEZ
    Ángel; bugler, E & H, laborer, b Vallecillo, NL.
    Leandro; 30, Pvt, A, laborer, d January 13, 1864 (Brownsville).
    Pedro; 25, Pvt, IPR, farmer, d February 18. 1864.
TAPIA
    John; Pvt, G, d. Feb 12, 1864 (Brownsville).
THOMAS
    Pedro; Sgt, IPR, d Feb 2, 1864 (Brownsville).
TORRES
    Bernardo; 27, Pvt, IPR, farmer, d Feb 16, 1864 (Brownsville).
    Cosmé; 33, Pvt, D & M, herdsman, b Goliad Cty, Tex.
    Francisco; 34, Pvt, IPR, farmer, d July 28, 1864 (march from
        Brownsville to Brazos Santiago).
    Juan; 29, Pvt, B & K, herdsman, d May 28, 1865 (Baton Rouge).
    Natividad; 22, Pvt, laborer, b Guayamco, Gto, d May 21, 1864 (Brownsville).
    Solustriano; 26, Pvt, C, laborer.
TREVIÑO
    Alvino; 26, Pvt, C & L, herdsman.
    Antonio; 21, Pvt, D, G & H, stockraiser, b San Antonio, Tex.
    Cayetano; 43, Pvt, B & K, herdsman, b Mier, Tamps.
    Feliciano; 24, Pvt, A & I.
    Fermeno; 20, Pvt, E, shoemaker; disability discharge December 9,
        1864 (New Orleans Gen Hospital), inguinal hernia.
    Florencio; 23, Pvt, carpenter, b Matamoros, Tamps.
    Francisco; 23, Pvt, E, farmer, b Monterrey, NL.
    George; 45, Capt, A & I.

TREVIÑO [continued]
    Gregorio; 22, Pvt, D & H.
    Juan; 40, Pvt, D & M, laborer, Sabinas, NL.
    Leocadio; 25, Cpl, A & I, laborer.
    Loreto; 31, Pvt, IPR, farmer, d July 17, 1864.
    Mariano; 21, Pvt, A, herdsman, d Feb 18, 1864 (Santa Rosa).
    Rafael; 20, Pvt, A & I, laborer, b Cadereyta, NL; disability discharge, June 24, 1865 (Post Hospital, Baton Rouge).
    Simón; 21, Pvt, E, laborer, b San Antonio Reynosa, Tamps, d May 12, 1864 (Brownsville).
TRINIDAD
    Sogan; Pvt, G; taken as a deserter from the Mexican Army, March 18, 1864.

U

URBANO
    Josué; Pvt, H.
UTIRAS
    Chatarino; 22, Pvt, H, d June 8, 1864 (Brownsville).
    José; 21, Pvt, H, d June 8, 1864 (Brownsville).

V

VALDASO
    L; Pvt, IPR, d March 2, 1864.
VALDÉS
    Adenógines; 30, Pvt, C & L, herdsman, d July 15, 1864 (Brownsville Hospital).
VALDEZ
    Ángel; 27, Comm Sgt, D & M, b Havana, Cuba, d May 2, 1865 (Baton Rouge).
    Febarcio; 30, Pvt, IPR, farmer, d Feb 1, 1864.
    Juan; 23, Comm Sgt, D & M, ranchero.
    Pedro; Pvt, L,H.
VALVERDE
    Fernando; 25, Pvt, D, G & H, stockraiser, b Goliad, Tex.
VARGAS
    Andrés; 33, Pvt, IPR, farmer, d July 28, 1864 (march from Brownsville to Brazos Santiago).
    Nemincio; 29, Pvt, A & I, laborer, d May 23, 1864 (Edinburg).
VÁSQUEZ
    Juan; 22, Pvt, A & I, laborer, b Monterrey, NL, d June 12, 1864 (Brownsville).
    Lamilo; 21, Pvt, D.
    Severiano; 22, Pvt, C & L, laborer, d July 15, 1864 (Brownsville).
VELA
    Albino; 26, Sgt, E & H, ranchero.
    Cecilio; 44, 1st Lt, A & I, dishonorable discharge, May 20, 1864 by Special Order 261 for desertion.
    Francisco; 26, Pvt, A & I, laborer, b Reynosa, Tamps, d Aug 14, 1865 (Houston); captured and confined at Victoria, Aug 17, 1865.
    Hypólito; 40, Sgt, B & K, herdsman, d April 24, 1865 (Brownsville).

VELA [continued]
    Juan; 30, Pvt, A & I, herdsman, d April 24, 1865 (Brownsville).
    Santos; 50, Cpl, A & I, herdsman.
    Teodoro; 35, Pvt, A & I, herdsman.
VELÁSQUEZ
    Macedonio; 33, Cpl, A & I, herdsman.
VESSAY
    Florencio; 25, Pvt, IPR, farmer.
VIDAL
    Adrián J; 23, Capt, IPR, pilot, b Monterrey, NL, d June 19, 1864 (Brownsville); honorable discharge, June 9, 1864; dishonorable discharge, August 5, 1864; accused of being a spy for Cortina and executed at Camargo by the French Imperialists on June 14, 1865; interred at Matamoros remains later moved to Brownsville Cemetery.
    Albino; Pvt, A.
VIDALES
    Francisco; 33, Pvt, IPR, teamster, d July 17, 1864.
VILLAFRANCO
    Domingo; 21, Pvt, B & K, herdsman; died Jan 20, 1864 of smallpox (Brownsville).
VILLANUEVA
    Francisco; 20, Pvt, C & L, laborer, d Jan 20, 1864 (Brownsville).
    Francisco; 33, Pvt, IPR, C & L, teamster, d July 17, 1864.
    John; Pvt, G.
VILLARREAL
    Agapito; 30, Cpl, B & K.
    Amado; 26, Pvt, B & K, laborer.
    Antonio; Pvt, G, d Feb 12, 1864 (Brownsville).
    Concepción; 23, Pvt, A & I, laborer, b Camargo, Tamps.
    Desiderio; 26, Pvt, D, saddler, d March 9, 1864 (Brownsville).
    Esteban; 46, Pvt, B, farmer, b Roma, Tex.
    Francisco; 24, Sgt, B & K, laborer, d May 9, 1864 (Brownsville).
    Gavino; 22, Pvt, D & M, herdsman, d March 9, 1864 (Brownsville).
    Ignacio; 23, Pvt, B, herdsman.
    Juan; 26, Sgt, D & G, farmer, b Los Adobes, NL.
    Juan; 24, Pvt, D & M, d [date unknown].
    Leonardo; 40, Pvt, F.
    Manuel; 47, Pvt, B, d [date unknown].
    Manuel; 21, Pvt, H, d [date unknown].
    Mauricio; 29, Pvt, E & H.
    Ricardo; 35, Pvt, B & K, died of disease [date unknown].
    Timoteo; 28, Pvt, A & I, d [date unknown].
    Tomás; 22, Pvt, B & K.
    Tomás; 24, Cpl, D & M.
    William; 25, Pvt, E, peddler, b Monclova, Coah.
    Ygnacio; 23, Pvt, K.
VILLEGAS
    Apolino; 29, Pvt, B & K.
    Silverio; 36, Pvt, D & M, laborer.

Y

YAÑEZ
John; Pvt, D.
YBARRA
Julio; Pvt.
Pablo; 23, Pvt, IPR, farmer, d April 14, 1864 (Brownsville).
YNFANTE
Santiago; 42, Pvt, D & M.
YZAZAGA
Francisco; 25, Pvt, E, sailor, substitute for John D. Crawford.

Z

ZACARÍAS
Simón; Pvt (cook), IPR.
ZAMORA
Ignacio; 26, Sgt, E & H.
Juan; 18, Pvt, C & M, laborer, b Padilla, Tamps; died Nov 28, 1865 (Galveston Post Hospital) of chronic diarrhea.
Luciano; 40, Pvt, C & L.
Timoteo; 21, Pvt, B & K, laborer, b Reynosa, Tamps.
ZAPATA
Clemente; 50, Capt, B & K.
Rafael; 48, Pvt, B & K.
ZARAGOZA
Francisco; Pvt, E, substitute.
ZARATE
Guadalupe; 28, Pvt, G, killed, April 4, 1865 by unknown person (Baton Rouge).
Vicente; 25, Sgt (cook), H.
ZAVALA
Francisco; 26, Pvt, C, b Tex; disability discharge, May 24, 1865 (Baton Rouge).
ZEPEDA
J; d December 14, 1864.
ZUÑIGA
Nasario; 25, 1st Sgt, D & L.

Footnotes

1. *Corpus Christi Ranchero*, December 8, 1860.
2. *Ibid.*
3. *Ibid.*, December 22, 1860.
4. *Ibid.*
5. *Ibid.*, January 12, 1861.
6. Ernest William Winkler (ed.), *Journal of the Secession Convention of Texas, 1861* (Austin, 1912). Marcus J. Wright, *Texas in the War, 1861-1865*, ed. Harold B. Simpson (Hillsboro, 1965), 175-182.
7. *Ibid.* Two Mexican Texans, Basilio Benavides from Laredo and Jose Antonio Navarro from San Antonio, were members of the state legislature at the time of secession. J. M. Rodriguez, *Rodriguez Memois of Early Texas* (San Antonio, 1913), 21.
8. Bette Gay Hunter Ash, "Mexican Texans in the Civil War," M. S. Thesis, East Texas State University, Commerce, Texas, 1972, 23.
9. W. J. Hughes, *Rebellious Ranger, Rip Ford and the Old Southwest* (Norman, 1964), 187-197. John Salmon Ford, *Rip Ford's Texas*, ed. Stephen B. Oates (Austin, 1963), 324-329.
10. Santos Benavides to Edward Clark, April 22, 1861, Papers of Governor Edward Clark, Texas State Archives, Austin, Texas. Hereafter referred to as Clark Papers.
11. *Corpus Christi Ranchero*, November 17, 1860
12. Sketches of Santos Benavides may be found in: John Henry Brown, *Indian Wars and Pioneers of Texas* (Austin, 1891-1892), 613-614. L. E. Daniell, *Types of Successful Men of Texas* (Austin, 1890), 324-330. *A Legislative manual for the State of Texas* (Austin, 1883), 267. *Record of Southwest Texas* (Chicago, 1894, 477-478. *The Mexican Texans* (San Antonio: The University of Texas Institute of Texan Cultures, 1971), 23.
13. Ford, *Rip Ford's Texas*, 323.
14. Lyman L. Woodman, *Cortina, Rogue of the Rio Grande* (San Antonio, 1950), 70. Charles W. Goldfinch, *Juan N. Cortina, 1824-1892: A re-appraisal* (Chicago, 1949) 52. Wayne Moquin (ed.), *A Documentary History of the Mexican Americans* (New York, 1971), 272. Ford, *Rip Ford's Texas*.

15. Henry Redmond to John S. Ford, April 12, 1861, Clark Papers.
16. *Ibid.*
17. Mat Nolan to John S. Ford, April 16, 1861, John S. Ford Papers, Museum of the Daughters of the Confederacy, Austin, Texas. Hereafter referred to as Ford Papers.
18. *Ibid. Corpus Christi Ranchero*, April 27, 1861.
19. John S. Ford to Edward Clark, April 21, 1861, Clark Papers.
20. John S. Ford to Edward Clark, May 8, 1861, Clark Papers. Also, Ford to Clark, May 12, 1861.
21. Santos Benavides to J. S. Ford, May 14, 1861, Broadside file, Texas State Archives. Hereafter referred to as Broadside file.
22. Ysidro Vela to John S. Ford, May 14, 1861, Broadside file.
23. Noah Cox to John S. Ford, May 7, 1861, Clark Papers. *Corpus Christi Ranchero*, May 18, 1861.
24. H. Clay Davis to Mat Nolan, May 5, 1861, Ford Papers.
25. Henry Redmond to John S. Ford, May 14, 1861, Broadside file.
26. *Corpus Christi Ranchero*, May 18, 1861.
27. Ysidro Vela to Ford, May 14, 1861, Broadside file.
28. Santos Benavides to John S. Ford, May 14, 1861, Broadside file.
29. Henry Redmond to John S. Ford, May 23, 1861, Broadside file.
30. *Ibid.*
31. *Corpus Christi Ranchero*, June 8, 1861.
32. Henry Redmond to John S. Ford, May 23, 1861, Broadside file.
33. Santos Benavides to John S. Ford, May 23, 1861, Broadside file. Same letter, Ford Papers. Muster and Pay Rolls of Santos Benavides' Company of Texas State Troops, Muster Roll File, Texas State Archives.
34. *Ibid.*
35. John S. Ford, Orders No. 21, Broadside file.
36. John S. Ford to Santos Benavides, May 27, 1861, Ford Papers.
37. Daniell, L. E. *Types of Successful Men of Texas*, 327. Wallace E. Oakes to Clark, August 27, 1861, Clark Papers. Santos Benavides to Edward Clark, October 24, 1861, Clark Papers.
38. Harold B. Simpson, *Hood's Texas Brigade: Lee's Grenadier Guard* (Waco, 1970).
39. Muster Roll of Trevanion T. Teel's Light Company (No. 1166), Texas State Archives, Austin, Texas. All muster rolls in the Texas State Archives are filed by numbers. Hereafter all muster rolls in the T.S.A. will be cited by number only. See also, Martin H. Hall, *Sibley's New Mexico Campaign* (Austin, 1960), 307-329. Jerry Don Thompson, "Mexican Americans in the Civil War: The Battle of Valverde," *Texana* X (No. 1, 1972), pp. 1-19. From Dalton, Georgia, in March, 1864, Antonio Bustillos wrote a moving letter home to San Antonio: "My esteemed mother. With much pleasure I take my pen in hand to write you these lines since a good opportunity offers itself in that someone is going to Texas on leave, and I am certain that it will arrive in your hands. I have only to tell you that we are all fine, and I pray to God that you are enjoying the same. We are now camped outside our quarters and are waiting for the enemy to try to advance. We left Mobile, Alabama, as reinforcements, but having arrived at Montgomery, we were counterordered here again. The Yankees made a vague advance, and that was the motive for our return, but then when we returned we had a small battle with them, and we made them retreat. We took several prisoners and we killed several others and we only lost one in all our brigade. I must also tell you that I have enlisted for the duration of the war and not to expect me soon, only if I am fortunate to get a leave. Everyone assures me that this bloody war ought to end in this year at the latest, and I hope it turns out that way since I have a great desire

to see all of you, since it is now going on two years since I have been gone from my home. We expect to have an election for second lieutenant today or tomorrow, and we hope to get Eugenio Navarro elected to this position so notify Don Antonio Navarro or family that we will do all that is possible to see that he gets this distinction. I think that he will win because we have the majority of the company in his favor. He is thinking of going to see his uncle in Richmond, Virginia, and already has a leave. I don't have any more news to send you so I am ending this letter by sending my best expressions to my sisters and brothers and to all my relatives in general and to all my friends. I hope they remember me. And I remain your son who esteems you, loves you, and desires to see you." Antonio Bustillos to Petra Martines de Bustillos, March 1, 1864, Antonio Bustillos Papers, Daughters of the Republic of Texas Library, San Antonio, Texas.

40. M. R. No. 95, T.S.A. Also, "Compiled Service Records of Joseph M. Penaloza and Angel Navarro," in Complied Service Records of Confederate Soldiers who Served in Organizations From the State of Texas; War Department Collection of Confederate Records, Record Group 109; The National Archives, Washington, D.C. Hereafter all compiled military service records will be cited by the soldiers' name and the Record Group. A survey of all Spanish surnamed individuals who fought in the Confederate Army (or their next of kin) and later applied for pensions from the state of Texas reveals that Webb County had the largest number of applicants with 44, followed by Bexar County with 25; Wilson with 11; Dallas and Goliad with three; Potter, Travis, Victoria, Washington, and Matagorda with two; Gregg, Red River, Callahan, Leon, Limestone, Nacogdoches, Tom Green, Atascosa, Reedville, Starr, San Patricio, Trinity, Cherokee, and Harrison, all with one. This survey is not necessarily a true demographic reflection of the percentage or numbers of Mexican-Texans who served in the Confederate Army. This is due in part to the post Civil War migration of Mexican-Texans, the probably prejudice of some county officials toward Mexican-Texan applicants, as well as the number of eligible Tejanos who never applied for pensions for various other reasons. For example, no Spanish surnamed individual applied for a pension from Refugio County, whereas that county sent large numbers of Mexican-Texans into the war. This is also true although to a lesser degree, of Zapata, Cameron, Bee, Nueces, and Hidalgo Counties. John M. Kinney (comp.), *Index to Applications for Texas Confederate Pensions* (Austin: Archives Division Texas State Library, 1975).

41. *Corpus Christi Ranchero*, Extra, August 19, 1862. Report of Captain Jack Sands, August 27, 1862, *The War of the Rebellion: A Compilation of the Official Records of the Union and Confederate Armies* (Washington, 1889), Series I, Volume IX, 618. Hereafter referred to as *O.R.* H. P. Bee to C. M. Mason, August 21, 1862, *O.R.*, I, IX, 618-619. H. P. Bee to C. M. Mason, August 26, 1862, *O.R.*, I, IX, 619-620. A. M. Hobby to E. F. Gray, August 16, 1862, *O.R.*, I, IX, 621-623. A. M. Hobby to E. F. Gray, August 18, 1862, *O.R.*, I, IX, 623.

42. A. M. Hobby to E. F. Gray, May 5, 1863, *O.R.*, I, XV, 404. Benjamin F. Neal to A. M. Hobby, May 5, 1863, *O.R.*, I, XV, 405. E. E. Hobby to Benjamin F. Neal, May 4, 1863, *O.R.*, I, XV, 405.

43. M.R. 481, T.S.A.
44. M.R. 1547, T.S.A.
45. M.R. 649, T.S.A.
46. M.R. 1556, T.S.A.
47. *Corpus Christi Ranchero*, June 29, 1861.
48. M.R. 6, T.S.A.
49. M.R. 626, T.S.A.
50. M.R. 337, T.S.A.
51. M.R. 249, T.S.A.

52. M.R. 1486, T.S.A.
53. M.R. 259, T.S.A.
54. M.R. 967, 796, and 966, T.S.A.
55. M.R. 631, T.S.A.
56. M.R. 92, 93, 94, 311, 172, 539, and 1614, T.S.A.
57. M.R. 279, T.S.A.
58. M.R. 157, T.S.A.
59. John S. Ford to Edward Clark, June 23, 1861, Clark Papers.
60. John S. Ford to Santos Benavides, May 29, 1861, Ford Papers.
61. John S. Ford to Edward Clark, July 14, 1861, Clark Papers.
62. Ibid.
63. Santos Benavides to Edward Clark, October 24, 1861, Clark Papers.
64. Charles Lovenskiold to Francis Lubbock, November 6, 1861, Lubbock Papers.
65. Francis Richard Lubbock, *Six Decades in Texas or the Memoirs of Francis Richard Lubbock*, ed. C. W. Raines (Austin, 1900), 380.
66. Charles Lovenskiold to Francis Lubbock, November 6, 1861, Lubbock Papers.
67. Charles Callaghan to Charles Lovenskiold, November 6, 1861, Lubbock Papers.
68. Charles Lovenskiold to Francis Lubbock, December 5, 1861, Lubbock Papers.
69. Santos Benavides to Francis Lubbock, December 28, 1861, Lubbock Papers.
70. Charles Lovenskiold to Santos Benavides, January 25, 1862, Ford Papers.
71. *Ibid.*, The Laredo deserters were Francisco Flores, Nicolas Flores, Manuel Pruneda, and Nestor Filan.
72. *Ibid.*
73. Charles Lovenskiold to Francis Lubbock, January 19, 1862, Lubbock Papers.
74. *Ibid.*
75. *Ibid.*
76. *Ibid.*
77. Muster Roll of Refugio Benavides' Company, University of Texas Archives, Austin, Texas.
78. A. Buchel to Samuel Boyer Davis, December 5, 1861, *O.R.*, I, IV, 152.
79. *Ibid.*
80. Brownsville *Fort Brown Flag*, January 2, 1863.
81. *Ibid.*
82. Hamilton P. Bee to Albino Lopez, February 3, 1863, *O.R.*, I, XV, 967.
83. *Corpus Christi Ranchero*, January 23, 1863.
84. *Corpus Christi Ranchero*, January 23, 1863.
85. *Ibid.*
86. Hamilton P. Bee to A. G. Dickinson, February 25, 1863, *O.R.*, I, IV, 992.
87. Santos Benavides to E. J. Gray, March 13, 1863, Confederate Treasury Department Records, R.G. 365, N.A.
88. *Ibid.*
89. *Ibid.*
90. Albino Lopez to Hamilton P. Bee, March 15, 1863. *O.R.*, I, IV, 1129.
91. *Ibid.*
92. Albino Lopez to Hamilton P. Bee, March 17, 1863. *O.R.*, I, IV, 1131.
93. Hamilton P. Bee to Albino Lopez, March 16, 1863, *O.R.*, I, IV, 1129.
94. Hamilton P. Bee to Albino Lopez, March 18, 1863, *O.R.*, I, IV, 1132.
95. Hamilton P. Bee to Albino Lopez, March 22, 1863, *O.R.*, I, IV, 1135.

96. W. M. Walton, *Life and Adventures of Ben Thompson* (Austin, 1956), 37-45. J. B. Wilkinson, *Laredo and the Rio Grande Frontier* (Austin, 1975), 285. Miscellaneous Notes, Seb Wilcox Papers, St. Mary's University Library, San Antonio, Texas.
97. Santos Benavides to E. F. Gray, *O.R.*, I, IV, 1040.
98. *Ibid.*
99. *Ibid.*
100. *Ibid.*
101. Albino Lopez to Hamilton P. Bee, *O.R.*, I, IV, 1044.
102. *Ibid.*
103. Hamilton P. Bee to Albino Lopez,*O.R.*, I, IV, 1052.
104. *Ibid.*
105. Joint Resolution of the Texas Legislature, Quoted in General Order No. 56, March 30, 1863, *O.R.*, I, XV, 221.
106. *Corpus Christi Ranchero*, April 23, 1863.
107. *Ibid.*
108. *Ibid.*
109. *Ibid.*
110. *Corpus Christi Ranchero*, April 23, 1863.
111. Orders Issued by General J. B. Magruder, December 16, 1862, Lubbock Papers.
112. Hamilton P. Bee to Edmund P. Turner, April 27, 1863, *O.R.*, I, XV, 1056-1057.
113. *Ibid.*
114. *Corpus Christi Ranchero*, November 17, 1863.
115. *Ibid.*
116. *Ibid.*
117. *Corpus Christi Ranchero*, August 13, 1863.
118. *Ibid.*
119. Brownsville *Fort Brown Flag* quoted in *Corpus Christi Ranchero*, September 3, 1863.
120. *Ibid.*
121. Santos Benavides to William O. Yager, September 3, 1863, *O.R.*, I, XXVI, I, 285.
122. *Ibid.*
123. Hamilton P. Bee to Edmund P. Turner, September 11, 1863, *O.R.*, I, XXIV, I, 284.
124. *Ibid.*
125. "Compiled Service Record of Adrian J. Vidal," (Union), R.G. 94; N.A. Benjamin F. McIntyre, *Federals on the Frontier*, ed. Nannie M. Tilley (Austin, 1963), 325.
126. E. W. Williams, *With the Border Ruffians* (London, 1907), 290.
127. Adrian J. Vidal (Confederate), R.G. 109; N.A.
128. James Duff to E. R. Tarver, November 11, 1863, *O.R.*, I, XXVI, I, 439-443. Hamilton P. Bee to Edmund P. Turner, October 28, 1863, *O.R.*, I, XXVI, I, 448-449.
129. *Ibid.* Also, Williams, *With the Border Ruffians*, 201.
130. *Ibid.*
131. *Ibid.*
132. Hamilton P. Bee to Manuel Ruiz, October 28, 1863, *O.R.*, I, XXVI, I, 450.
133. James Duff to E. R. Tarver, November 11, 1863, *O.R.*, I, XXVI, I, 440.
134. Hamilton P. Bee to Manuel Ruiz, October 28, 1863,*O.R.*, I, XXVI, I, 450. Manuel Ruiz to Hamilton P. Bee, October 28, 1863, *O.R.*, I, XXVI, I, 450. Hamilton P. Bee to Manuel Ruiz, October 30, 1863, *O.R.*, I, XXVI, I, 451.
135. Hamilton P. Bee to Edmund P. Turner, October 31, 1863, *O.R.*, I, XXVI,

I, 451-452.

136. Nathaniel P. Banks to Abraham Lincoln, November 3, 1863, *O.R.*, I, XXVI, I, 396. Banks to H. W. Halleck, November 4, 1863, *O.R.*, I, XXVI, I, 397-398. Banks to Halleck, November 6, 1863, *O.R.*, I, XXVI, I, 399-400.

137. Hamilton P. Bee to Edmund P. Turner, November 5, 1863, *O.R.*, I, XXVI, I, 433. Richard Taylor to James Duff, November 3, 1863, *O.R.*, I, XXVI, I, 443-444. Henry T. Davis to George W. Caldwell, November 11, 1863, *O.R.*, I, XXVI, I, 444-445.

138. Hamilton P. Bee to Edmund P. Turner, November 8, 1863, *O.R.*, I, XXVI, I, 434-435.

139. Adrian J. Vidal (Union), R.G. 94. N.A. *Adjutant General's Report, 1873* (Austin: 1875), 111-112. Muster Roll of Vidal's Partisan Rangers, Adjutant General's Records; T.S.A.

140. N. J. T. Dana to Charles P. Stone, December 2, 1863, *O.R.*, I, XXVI, I, 840.

141. McIntyre, *Federals on the Frontier*, 325-332.

142. Adrian J. Vidal (Union), R.G. 94.

143. *Ibid.*

144. *Ibid.*

145. *Adjutant General's Report, 1873*, 111-112.

146. McIntyre, *Federals on the Frontier*, 349-350.

147. *Ibid.*, 359.

148. Tom Lea, *The King Ranch* (Boston, 1957), I, 447.

149. Muster Rolls of the First and Second Regiments of Texas Cavalry Volunteers and Adrian J. Vidal's Partisan Rangers, Adjutant General's Records; T.S.A. These muster rolls can also be found in the *Adjutant General's Report, 1873*, (Austin: Adjutant General's Office, 1875). Reference to these records will be by letter of the individual company. A number of those who served in the Union Army were, in reality, citizens of Mexico rather than Texas.

150. Leonard Pierce to W. H. Seward, April 8, 1862, Consular Dispatches, Matamoros, Mexico: Records of the U.S. Department of State, Record Group 59, National Archives.

151. Leonard Pierce to W. H. Seward, August 26, 1862, *Ibid.* John L. Waller, *Colossal Hamilton of Texas* (El Paso, 1968), 35.

152. Frank H. Smyrl, "Texans in the Union Army, 1861-1865," *Southwestern Historical Quarterly*, LXV (October, 1961), 235.

153. Leonard Price to W. H. Seward, September 21, 1862, Consular Dispatches, Matamoros, Mexico: R. G. 59, N.A.

154. Leonard Price to W. H. Seward, September 22, 1862, Consular Dispatches, Matamoros, Mexico: R. G. 59, N.A. R. H. Williams and John W. Sansom, *The Massacre on the Nueces River* (Grand Prairie), 35. Williams, *With the Border Ruffians*.

155. Horatio C. Hunt, "The 1st Texas Cavalry of U.S. Volunteers — Its History," Newspaper clippings in John L. Haynes Papers: University of Texas Archives, Austin, Texas. These papers will hereafter be referred to as Haynes Papers.

156. *Ibid.*

157. *Ibid.*

158. Recruiting Handbill signed by Antonio Abad Dias, December 7, 1863; Ford Papers.

159. "Minority Report to the Honorable M. K. Taylor, Speaker of the House of Representatives," Haynes Papers.

160. Austin *State Gazette*, January 14, 1860; *Galveston News*, February 23, 1860, both in Haynes Papers.

161. The Brownsville *American Flag*, March 17, 1860; Haynes Papers.
162. *Ibid.* February 9, 1860; Haynes Papers.
163. New Orleans *Picayune*, December, 1860; Haynes Papers.
164. *Southern Intelligencer*, no date; Haynes Papers.
165. *Paris Press*, no date; Brownsville *Rio Grande Sentinel*, February 27, 1861; *Indianola Courier*, no date; Haynes Papers.
166. Muster Rolls of Second Regiment of Texas Cavalry; Regimental Order Book; A.G.R.; T.S.A.
167. *Ibid.*
168. *Ibid.*
169. *Ibid.*
170. John L. Haynes to E. J. Davis, December 31, 1863, Regimental Papers of the Second Regiment of Texas Cavalry, R.G. 93; N.A.
171. Edmund J. Davis to E.O.C. Ord, February 10, 1864, *O.R.*, I, XXXIV, II, 288.
172. *Ibid.*
173. Court Martial Findings and Sentence in the Case of Pedro Garcia; Ford Papers.
174. McIntyre, *Federals on the Frontier*, 353-354.
175. *Ibid.*, 347.
176. John L. Haynes to F. J. Herron, May 2, 1864, Regimental Papers of the Second Regiment, R.G. 94, N.A.
177. *Ibid.*
178. *Ibid.*
179. Hunt, "History of the 1st Texas Cavalry," Haynes Papers.
180. *Ibid.*
181. George Trevino (Union), R.G. 94, N.A.
182. Muster Rolls of the First Regiment of Texas Cavalry; A.G.R., T.S.A.
183. John L. Haynes (Union), R.G. 94, N.A.
184. Units Comprising the Northern Division of Louisiana, March, 1865, *O.R.*, I, XLVIII, I, 1021.
185. Hunt, "History of the 1st Texas Cavalry," Haynes Papers.
186. Muster Roll of Company I, 1st Texas Cavalry (Union), T.S.A.
187. B. Wilson to John L. Haynes, October 2, 1864, *O.R.*, I, XLI, III, 552. Hunt, "History of the 1st Texas Cavalry," Haynes Papers.
188. Cesario Falcon, R.G. 94, N.A.
189. M. R. of Company L, 1st Texas Cavalry (Union), T.S.A.
190. John L. Haynes, R.G. 94, N.A.
191. M. R. of Company I, 1st Texas Cavalry (Union), T.S.A.
192. James Arthur Irby, "Line of the Rio Grande: War and Trade on the Confederate Frontier, 1861-1865," Ph.D. Dissertation, University of Georgia, Athens, Georgia, 1969, 210.
193. Farewell address of John L. Haynes; Haynes Papers.
194. N. J. T. Dana to L. Pierce, December 1, 1863, *O.R.*, I, XXVI, 830.
195. N. J. T. Dana to Charles P. Stone, December 2, 1863, *O.R.*, I, XXVI, 830-831.
196. J. C. McFerran to General in Chief, March 27, 1864, *O.R.*, I, XXXIV, 755-756. James H. Carleton to H. W. Halleck, March 20, 1864, *O.R.*, I, XXXIV, II, 671-672.
197. E. Kirby Smith to Santos Benavides, November 3, 1863; Ford Papers.
198. J. Bankhead Magruder to W. R. Boggs, January 6, 1864, *O.R.*, I, XXXIV, II, 830-836.
199. S. Hart to George Williamson, December 24, 1863, *O.R.*, I, LIII, 933-935. Patricio Milmo to C. C. Thayer, December 17, 1863, *O.R.*, I, LIII, 933. Patricio Milmo to S. Hart, December 11, 1863, *O.R.*, I, LIII, 936. E. Kirby Smith to Jef-

ferson Davis, January 20, 1864, *O.R.*, I, LIII, 930.

200. Register of Imports at the Port of Laredo, Confederate District of Brazos Santiago, January, 1864, R.G. 365, N.A.

201. Santos Benavides to John B. Magruder, April 4, 1864, R. G. 365, N.A. James Arthur Irby, "Line of the Rio Grande: War and Trade on the Confederate Frontier," Ph.D. dissertation, University of Georgia, Athens, Georgia, 1969, 131-132.

202. John S. Ford to Santos Benavides, December 27, 1863, Ford Papers.

203. Ford, *Rip Ford's Texas*, 357.

204. John S. Ford to Santos Benavides, February 7, 1864, Ford Papers.

205. John S. Ford to Santos Benavides, December 28, 1863, Ford Papers.

206. John S. Ford to E. P. Turner, February 7, 1863, *O.R.*, I, XXXIV, II, 948.

207. John S. Ford to Santos Benavides, February 4, 1864, Ford Papers.

208. Santos Benavides to John S. Ford, January 10, 1864, Ford Papers.

209. Santos Benavides to John S. Ford, February 7, 1864, *O.R.*, I, XXXIV, II, 949.

210. Santos Benavides to John S. Ford, February 13, 1864, Ford Papers.

211. F. J. Herron to Charles P. Stone, January 15, 1864, *O.R.*, I, XXXIV, II, 84-87.

212. T. P. McManus to N. J. T. Dana, February 13, 1864, *O.R.*, I, XXXIV, II, 316-320.

213. *Ibid.*

214. G. H. Giddings to John S. Ford, February 15, 1864, Ford Papers.

215. Thomas A. Dwyer to John S. Ford, March 21, 1864, Ford Papers.

216. George Pfeuffer to Santos Benavides, February 22, 1864, Ford Papers.

217. Santos Benavides to James E. Slaughter, March 14, 1864, *O.R.*, I, XXXIV, II, 1043.

218. J. B. Magruder to Juan N. Cortina, May 22, 1864, *O.R.*, I, LIII, 1002.

219. Ford, *Rip Ford's Texas*, p. 355. "John S. Ford Memoirs," University of Texas Archives, Austin, Texas, 1058.

220. Mat Nolan to John S. Ford, March 15, 1864, *O.R.*, I, XXXIV, I, 638-639.

221. *Ibid.*

222. Mat Nolan to John S. Ford, March 21, 1864, *O.R.*, I, XXXIV, I, 642-643.

223. Santos Benavides to John S. Ford, March 19, 1864, *O.R.*, I, XXXIV, I, 647. Santos Benavides to John S. Ford, March 21, 1864, *O.R.*, I, XXXIV, I, 648-649. Copies of these letters are also found in the Ford Papers.

224. Thomas A. Dwyer to John S. Ford, March 21, 1864, Ford Papers.

225. Ford, *Rip Ford's Texas*, 357.

226. Thomas A. Dwyer to John S. Ford, March 21, 1864, Ford Papers.

227. Santos Benavides to John S. Ford, March 21, 1864, *O.R.*, I, XXXIV, I, 648.

228. *Ibid.*

229. Thomas A. Dwyer to John S. Ford, March 21, 1864, Ford Papers.

230. *Ibid.*

231. W. W. Camp to John S. Ford, March 20, 1864, Ford Papers.

232. John S. Ford to Santos Benavides, March 31, 1864, Ford Papers.

233. J. E. Slaughter to Santos Benavides, March 24, 1864, *O.R.*, I, XXXIV, II, 1079.

234. Santos Benavides to James E. Slaughter, April 10, 1864, *O.R.*, I, LIII, 980-981.

235. Ford, *Rip Ford's Texas*, 360.

236. John S. Ford to E. P. Turner, April 17, 1864, *O.R.*, I, XXXIV, III, 776.

237. John S. Ford to E. P. Turner, May 5, 1863, *O.R.*, I, XXXIV, III, 807-808.

238. Special Order No. 60, May 8, 1864, *O.R.*, Ford Papers.

239. John S. Ford to E. P. Turner, May 5, 1864, *O.R.*, I, XXXIV, III, 808.

240. John S. Ford to J. E. Slaughter, July 2, 1864, *O.R.*, I, XXXIV, I, 1055.
241. *Ibid.*
242. *Ibid.*
243. *Ibid.*
244. F. J. Herron to William Dwight, July 2, 1864, *O.R.*, I, XXXIV, I, 1054.
245. J. B. Weyman to E. P. Turner, April 5, 1864, *O.R.*, I, XXXIV, III, 736.
246. James A. Ware to Bart J. DeWitt, June 20, 1864, *O.R.*, I, XXXIV, I, 1034.
247. *Ibid.*
248. Special Order No. 110, July 31, 1864, Ford Papers.
249. Santos Benavides to John S. Ford, July 18, 1864, Ford Papers.
250. Santos Benavides to John S. Ford, July 19, 1864, Ford Papers.
251. Ford, *Rip Ford's Texas*, 366.
252. John S. Ford to W. Kearny, August 16, 1864, *O.R.*, I, XLI, II, 1069.
253. Refugio Benavides to Felix Blucher, August 19, 1864, Ford Papers.
254. James H. Fry to Santos Benavides, August 27, 1864, Ford Papers.
255. James H. Fry to Santos Benavides, September 2, 1864, Ford Papers.
256. W. L. Newsom to W. Kearny, September 4, 1864, Ford Papers.
257. E. Kirby Smith to E. P. Turner, December 27, 1864, *O.R.*, I, XLI, IV, 1123-1124.
258. Ford, *Rip Ford's Texas*, 385.
259. *Ibid.*
260. Hughes, *Rebellious Ranger*, 232.
261. C.S.R. of John Z. Leyendecker, R.G. 109; N.A.
262. A. L. Cashell to George H. Giddings, September, 1864, Ford Papers.
263. G. H. Giddings to Ed Duggan, January 25, 1865, Ford Papers.
264. T. E. Cater to John S. Ford, February 1, 1865, Ford Papers.
265. Special Order No. 32, February 7, 1865, Ford Papers. Cristobal Benavides was in command of Company A; Refugio Benavides, Company B; J. M. Penaloza, Company C; G. A. Gibson, Company D; S. E. Navarro, Company E; H. A. Mitchell, Company F; A. C. Jones, Company G; H. C. Davis, Company H; Julian Garcia, Company I; and P. B. Watson, Company K.
266. Records of a Board of Inquiry, December 1, 1864, Ford Papers.
267. *Ibid.*
268. Letter to L. G. Aldrich, May 6, 1865, Ford Papers.
269. *Ibid.*
270. W. H. D. Carrington to John S. Ford, May 8, 1865, Ford Papers.
271. Santos Benavides to John Z. Leyendecker, May 16, 1865, Leyendecker Papers.

Bibliography

UNPUBLISHED MATERIAL

Ash, Bette Gay Hunter. "The Mexican-Texans in the Civil War," M.A. Thesis, East Texas State University, 1972.
Cowling, Annie. "The Confederate Cotton Trade With Mexico," M.A. Thesis, University of Texas, 1926.
Downs, Fane. "The History of Mexicans in Texas, 1820-1845," Ph.D. Dissertation, Texas Tech University, 1970.
Ford, John Salmon. "Memoirs of John Salmon Ford." Seven volumes. University of Texas Archives, Austin, Texas.
Graf, LeRoy P. "The Economic History of the Lower Rio Grande Valley, 1820-1875," Ph.D. Dissertation, Harvard University, 1942.
Hastings, Virginia M. "A History of Arizona During the Civil War, 1861-1865," M.A. Thesis, University of Arizona, 1943.
Kitchen, Carr P. "Mexican Depredations on the Lower Rio Grande Valley, 1835-1885," M.A. Thesis, Baylor University, 1933.
Riley, Mary C. "The History of the Development of the Port of Corpus Christi," M.A. Thesis, University of Texas, 1951.
Sutherland, Thomas S. "Historical Sketch of Webb County." St. Mary's University Library, San Antonio, Texas.

ARCHIVAL COLLECTIONS

Broadside File of Civil War Materials. Texas State Archives, Austin, Texas.
Bustillos, Antonio. Antonio Bustillos Papers. Daughters of the Republic of Texas Library, San Antonio, Texas.
Clark, Edward. Clark Papers. Texas State Archives, Austin, Texas.
Compiled Service Records. Benavides' Regiment. Records of the Confederate Department of War. Adjutant General's Office. Record Group 109. The National Archives, Washington, D.C.
Compiled Service Records of Confederate Generals and Staff Officers, and Non-regimental Enlisted Men. Records of the Confederate Department of War.

Adjutant General's Office. Record Group 109. The National Archives, Washington, D.C.

Compiled Service Records. Eighth Texas Infantry. Records of the Confederate Department of War. Adjutant General's Office. Record Group 109. The National Archives, Washington, D.C.

Compiled Service Records. Second Regiment of Texas Cavalry. Records of the United States Department of War. Adjutant General's Office. Record Group 94. The National Archives, Washington, D.C.

Compiled Service Records. Third Texas Infantry. Records of the Confederate Department of War. Adjutant General's Office. Record Group 109. The National Archives, Washington, D.C.

Compiled Service Records. Thirty-Third Texas Cavalry. Records of the Confederate Department of War. Adjutant General's Office. Record Group 109. The National Archives, Washington, D.C.

Confederate Pension Records. Texas State Archives, Austin, Texas.

Davis, Edmund J. Davis Papers. Texas State Archives, Austin, Texas.

Dispatches From the U.S. Consuls in Matamoros, Mexico. Records of the United States Department of State. Record Group 59. The National Archives, Washington, D.C.

Ford, John Salmon. Ford Papers. Museum of the United Daughters of the Confederacy, Austin, Texas.

Haynes, John L. Haynes Papers. University of Texas Archives, Austin, Texas.

Index to Compiled Service Records of Confederate Soldiers Who Served in Organizations From the State of Texas. Records of the Confederate Department of War. Adjutant General's Office. Record Group 109. The National Archives, Washington, D.C.

Index to Compiled Service Records of Volunteer Soldiers Who Served in Organizations From the State of Texas. Records of the United States Department of War. Adjutant General's Office. Record Group 94. The National Archives, Washington, D.C.

Laredo Archives. St. Mary's University Library, San Antonio, Texas.

Letters Received by the Confederate Adjutant and Inspector General and by the Confederate Quartermaster General. Records of the Confederate Department of War. Adjutant General's Office. Record Group 109. The National Archives, Washington, D.C.

Letters Received, 1861-1865. District of Texas, New Mexico and Arizona. Records of the Confederate Department of War. Record Group 109. The National Archives, Washington, D.C.

Letters Received by the Secretary of War. Records of the Confederate Department of War. Record Group 109. The National Archives, Washington, D.C.

Leyendecker, John Z. Leyendecker Papers. St. Mary's University Library, San Antonio, Texas.

Lubbock, Francis R. Lubbock Papers. Texas State Archives, Austin, Texas.

Muster Roll of Company Commanded by Cristobal Benavides. Texas State Archives, Austin, Texas.

Muster Rolls of the First and Second Texas Cavalry (Union). Texas State Archives, Austin, Texas.

Muster Rolls and Returns. Regimental Papers, Second Regiment of Texas Cavalry. Records of the United States Department of War. Adjutant General's Office. Record Group 94. The National Archives, Washington, D.C.

Order Book. Second Texas Cavalry (Union). Texas State Archives, Austin, Texas.

Pickett Papers. Manuscript Division, Library of Congress, Washington, D.C.

Register of Imports at the Port of Laredo. District of Brazos Santiago. Confederate

Treasury Department. Record Group 365. The National Archives, Washington, D.C.
Records of the Cotton Bureau. Confederate Treasury Department. Record Group 365. The National Archives, Washington, D.C.
San Roman, Jose. San Roman Papers. University of Texas Archives, Austin, Texas.
Various Confederate Muster Rolls. Texas State Archives, Austin, Texas.
Wilcox, Seb S. Wilcox Papers. St. Mary's University Library, San Antonio, Texas.

NEWSPAPERS

Austin *Southern Intelligencer.*
Austin *State Gazette.*
Austin *Tri-Weekly State Gazette.*
Brownsville *American Flag.*
Brownsville *La Bandera.*
Brownsville *Rio Grande Sentinel.*
Cincinnati Daily Commercial.
Corpus Christi *Ranchero.*
Daily Austin Republican.
Galveston News.
Houston *Daily Telegraph.*
Indianola Courier.
Laredo Times.
New Orleans *Picayune.*
New York *Evening Post.*
New York Herald.
New York Times.
Paris Press.
San Antonio News.

BOOKS

Acuna, Rodolfo. *Occupied America, the Chicano's Struggle Toward Liberation.* San Francisco, 1972.
Adjutant General's Office. *Adjutant General's Report, 1873.* Texas State Archives, Austin, Texas.
Ashford, Gerald. *Spanish Texas, Yesterday and Today.* Austin, 1971.
Bancroft, Hubert H. *History of the North Mexican States and Texas.* San Francisco, 1886-1889.
Bartlett, John R. *Personal Narrative of Explorations and Incidents in Texas, New Mexico, California, Sonora, and Chihuahua.* Two volumes. New York, 1854.
Beers, Henry Putney. *Guide to the Archives of the Government of the Confederate States of America.* Washington, 1968.
Boatner, Mack M. *The Civil War Dictionary.* New York, 1969.
Bradley, Haldeen. *Mexico and the Old Southwest.* Port Washington, New York, 1971.
Brown, John Henry. *Indian Wars and Pioneers of Texas.* Austin, 1891-1892.
Callahan, James M. *American Foreign Policy in Mexican Relations.* New York, 1932.
_____. *The Diplomatic History of the Southern Confederation.* Baltimore, 1901.

Castaneda, Carlos E. *Our Catholic Heritage in Texas, 1519-1936.* Seven volumes. Austin, 1936.
Chatfield, W.H. *The Twin Cities on the Border.* New Orleans, 1893.
Clendenen, Clarence C. *Blood on the Border, the United States Army and the Mexican Irregulars.* London, 1969.
Dabbs, Jack Autrey. *The French Army in Mexico, 1861-1867: A Study in Military Government,* The Hague, 1963.
DaCamara, Kathleen. *Laredo on the Rio Grande.* San Antonio, 1949.
Daniell, L.E. *Successful Men of Texas.* Austin, 1890.
Davis, Burke. *The Incredible Civil War.* New York, 1960.
Dobie, J. Frank. *The Mustangs.* Boston, 1952.
_____. *A Vaquero of the Brush Country.* Boston, 1957.
Durham, George. *Taming the Nueces Strip.* Austin, 1962.
Evans, Clement A. *Confederate Military History.* Twelve volumes. Atlanta, 1899.
Flint, Henry M. *Mexico Under Maximilian.* Philadelphia, 1867.
Ford, John Salmon. *Rip Ford's Texas.* Edited by Stephen B. Oates. Austin, 1963.
Frayer, Robert. *Forts of the West.* Norman, 1972.
Fremantle, Arthur James Lyon. *The Fremantle Diary: Being the Journal of Lieutenant-Colonel James Arthur Lyon Fremantle, Coldstream Guards, on his Three Months in the Southern States.* Edited by Walter Lord. Boston, 1954.
Fugate, Francis. *The Spanish Heritage of the Southwest.* El Paso, 1952.
Galarza, Ernesto, Herman Gallegos, and Julian Samora. *Mexican-Americans in the Southwest.* Santa Barbara, 1969.
Gallaway, B.P., ed. *The Dark Corner of the Confederacy.* Dubuque, Iowa, 1972.
Garcia, Rogelia O. *Dolores, Revilla, and Laredo.* Laredo: 1970.
_____. *The Bells of St. Augustine.* Laredo: 1963.
_____. *Song of La Grande Agua.* Laredo: 1973.
Goff, Richard D. *Confederate Supply.* Durham, 1969.
Goldfinch, Charles W. *Juan N. Cortina, 1824-1892: A Re-appraisal.* Chicago, 1951.
Grebler, Leo, John W. Moore and Ralph C. Guzman. *The Mexican-American People, The Nation's Second Largest Minority.* New York, 1970.
Grimm, Agnes C. *Llanos Mestenos, Mustang Plains.* Waco, 1968.
Hall, Martin Hardwick. *Sibley's New Mexico Campaign.* Austin, 1960.
Heitman, Francis B. *Historical Register and Dictionary of the United States Army.* Two volumes. Urbana, Illinois, 1955.
Henderson, Harry McCorry. *Texas in the Confederacy.* San Antonio, 1955.
Horgan, Paul. *Great River: The Rio Grande in North American History.* Two volumes. New York, 1954.
Hughes, W.J. *Rebellious Ranger: Rip Ford and the Old Southwest.* Norman, 1964.
Hunt, Aurora. *Major General James Henry Carleton, 1814-1873, Western Frontier Dragoon.* Glendale, California, 1958.
Johnson, Francis W. *A History of Texas and Texans.* Edited by Eugene C. Barker. Five volumes. New York, 1914.
Kielman, Chester V. Ed. *The University of Texas Archives.* Austin, 1967.
Lamb, Ruth S. *Mexican-Americans: Sons of the Southwest.* Claremont, 1970.
Lea, Tom. *The King Ranch.* Two volumes. Boston, 1957.
Lonn, Ella. *Desertion During the Civil War.* Gloucester, Mass., 1966.
_____. *Foreigners in the Confederacy.* Gloucester, Mass., 1965.
_____. *Foreigners in the Union Army and Navy.* Baton Rouge, 1952.
Lowrie, Samuel H. *Culture Conflict in Texas, 1821-1935.* New York, 1967.
Lubbock, Francis Richard. *Six Decades in Texas or Memoirs of Francis Richard Lubbock.* Edited by C.W. Raines. Austin, 1900.
Madsen, William. *The Mexican-Americans of South Texas.* New York, 1964.

Matthussen, Peter. *Sal Si Puedes*. New York, 1968.
McCampbell, Coleman. *Saga of a Frontier Seaport*. Dallas, 1934.
McWilliams, Carey. *al Norte de Mexico: El Conflicto Entre Anglos e Hispanos*. Mexico, D.F., 1968.
_____. *North from Mexico: The Spanish-Speaking People of the United States*. New York, 1968.
McIntyre, Benjamin F. *Federals on the Frontier: the Diary of Benjamin F. McIntyre*. Edited by Nannie M. Tilley. Austin, 1963.
Monaghan, Jay. *Civil War on the Western Border, 1854-1865*. New York, 1960.
Moquin, Wayne, Ed. *A Documentary History of the Mexican-Americans*. New York, 1972.
Morfi, Juan A. *History of Texas, 1673-1779*. Albuquerque, 1935.
Morin, Raul. *Among the Valiant. Mexican-Americans in World War II and Korea*. Los Angeles, 1963.
Morrow, William W. *Spanish and Mexican Private Land Grants*. San Francisco, 1923.
Munden, Kenneth W. and Beers, Henry Putney. *Guide to Federal Archives Relating to the Civil War*. Washington, 1962.
Nance, Joseph Milton. *After San Jacinto: the Texas-Mexican Frontier, 1836-1841*. Austin, 1963.
_____. *Attack and Counterattack: the Texas-Mexican Frontier, 1842*. Austin, 1964.
Nava, Julian. *Mexican-Americans: A Brief Look at Their History*. New York, 1969.
Nichols, James L. *The Confederate Quartermaster in the Trans-Mississippi*. Austin, 1964.
Oates, Stephen B. *Confederate Cavalry West of the River*. Austin, 1961.
Olmsted, Frederick Law. *A Journey Through Texas*. New York, 1857.
Owsley, Frank Lawrence. *King Cotton Diplomacy: Foreign Relations of the Confederate States of America*. Chicago, 1959.
Paredes, Americo. *With His Pistol in His Hand*. Austin, 1966.
Perrigo, Lynn I. *The American Southwest*. New York, 1971.
_____. *Our Spanish Southwest*. Dallas, 1960.
Pierce, Frank F. *A Brief History of the Lower Rio Grande Valley*. Menasha, Wisconsin, 1917.
Rayburn, Virginia Kemp and John C. Eds. *Century of Conflict*. Waco, 1966.
Record of Southwest Texas. Chicago, 1894.
Report of the Committee who Visited Washington on the Affairs of Western Texas. New York: n.p., 1862.
Rippy, J. Fred. *The United States and Mexico*. New York, 1926.
Rivera, Feliciano and Meier, Matt S. *A Bibliography for Chicano History*. San Francisco, 1972.
_____. *The Chicanos: A History of Mexican-Americans*. New York, 1972.
Rodriguez, J.M. *Rodriguez Memoirs of Early Texas*. San Antonio, 1961.
Ruiz, Ramon E. and Tebbell, J. *South by Southwest: The Mexican-American and His Heritage*. Garden City, New York, 1969.
Samora, Julian. *La Raza: the Forgotten Americans*. South Bend, Indiana, 1966.
Santleben, August A. *A Texas Pioneer: Early Staging and Overland Freighting Days on the Frontier of Texas and Mexico*. Edited by I.D. Affleck. New York, 1910.
Schmitt, Karl M. *Mexico and the United States, 1821-1973*. New York, 1974.
Scholes, Walter V. *Mexican Politics During the Juarez Regime, 1855-1872*. Columbia, 1957.
Scott, Florence J. *Historical Heritage of the Lower Rio Grande*. Waco, 1966.

Seguin, John N. *Personal Memoirs, 1834-1842.* San Antonio, 1858.
Servin, Manuel P. *The Mexican-Americans: An Awakening Minority.* New York, 1970.
Simpson, Harold B. *Hood's Texas Brigade: Lee's Grenadier Guard.* Waco, 1970.
Stambaugh, J. Lee and Stambaugh, Lillian J. *The Lower Rio Grande Valley of Texas.* San Antonio, 1954.
Steiner, Stan. *La Raza.* New York, 1970.
Sumpter, Jesse. *Paso del Aguila: A Chronicle of Frontier Days on the Texas Border.* Edited by Ben E. Pingenot. Austin, 1969.
The Texas Album of the Eighth Legislature. Austin, 1860.
Thompson, Jerry. *Colonel John Robert Baylor: Texas Indian Fighter and Confederate Soldier.* Hillsboro, Texas, 1971.
_____. *Sabers on the Rio Grande.* Austin, 1974.
Thompson, Samuel Bernard. *Confederate Purchasing Operations Abroad.* Chapel Hill, 1935.
Tyler, Ronnie C. *Santiago Vidaurri and the Southern Confederacy.* Austin, 1973.
University of Texas Institute of Texan Cultures. *Mexican-Texans.* San Antonio, 1971.
Waller, John L. *Colossal Hamilton of Texas.* El Paso, 1968.
War of the Rebellion: A Compilation of the Official Records of the Union and Confederate Armies. 128 volumes. Washington, 1880-1901.
Warner, Ezra J. *Generals in Gray.* Baton Rouge, 1959.
Webb, Walter P. *The Texas Rangers.* Austin, 1965.
_____ and Carroll, H. Bailey, Eds. *Handbook of Texas.* Two volumes. Austin, 1952.
Weber, David J., Ed. *Foreigners in Their Native Land.* Albuquerque, 1973.
Weigley, Russell F. *History of the United States Army.* London, 1967.
Wilcox, J.B. *Laredo and the Rio Grande Frontier.* Austin, 1975.
Williams, R.H. *With the Border Ruffians: Memories of the Far West, 1852-1868.* Edited by E.W. Williams. London, 1908.
_____ and Sansom, John W. *The Massacre on the Nueces River.* Grand Prairie, n.d.
Winkler, E.W., Ed. *Journal of the Secession Convention of Texas.* Austin, 1912.
Woodman, Lyman L. *Cortina, Rogue of the Rio Grande.* San Antonio, 1950.
Wright, Kathleen. *The Other Americans.* Greenwich, Conn., 1971.
Wright, Marcus Joseph. *Texas in the War, 1861-1865.* Edited by Harold B. Simpson. Hillsboro, Texas, 1965.

ARTICLES

Almaraz, Felix D. "Historical Origin of the Mexican in Texas: An Interpretation." Austin: Office of Bilingual and International Education, Texas Education Agency, 1968.
Blumenthal, Henry. "Confederate Diplomacy: Popular Notions and International Realities." *Journal of Southern History,* XXXII (May, 1966), 151-171.
Broussard, Ray F. "Vidaurri, Juarez and Comonfort's Return from Exile," *Hispanic American Historical Review,* XLIX (May, 1969), 268-280.
Clendenen, Clarence C. "Mexican Unionists: A Forgotten Incident of the War Between the States," *New Mexico Historical Review,* XXXIX (1964), 32-39.
Cohen, Barry M. "The Texas-Mexico Border, 1858-1867," *Texana,* VI (Summer, 1968), 153-165.
Davenport, Herbert. "General Jose Maria Jesus Carbajal," *Southwestern Historical Quarterly,* LV (April, 1952), 475-483.

_____. "Notes on Early Steamboating on the Rio Grande," *Southwestern Historical Quarterly*, XLIX (October, 1945), 286-289.
Delaney, Robert W. "Matamoros, Port for Texas During the Civil War," *Southwestern Historical Quarterly*, LVIII (April, 1955), 473-487.
Diamond, William. "Imports of the Confederate Government from Europe and Mexico," *Journal of Southern History*, VI (November, 1940), 470-503.
Elliott, Claude. "Union Sentiment in Texas, 1861-1865," *Southwestern Historical Quarterly*, (April, 1947), 449-477.
Ellis, L. Tuffly. "Maritime Commerce on the Far Western Gulf, 1861-1865," *Southwestern Historical Quarterly*, LXXVII (October, 1973), 167-226.
Hall, Martin Hardwick. "Colonel James Reily's Diplomatic Missions to Chihuahua and Sonora," *New Mexico Historical Review*, XXXI (July, 1956), 232-242.
Hanna, Kathryn Abbey. "The Roles of the South in the French Intervention in Mexico," *Journal of Southern History*, XX (February, 1954), 3-21.
Harby, Lee C. "Mexican-Texas Types and Contrasts," *Harpers Magazine*, (July 1890), 229-246.
Kenny, W.R. "Mexican-American Conflict on the Mining Frontier, 1848-1852." *Journal of the West*. (October, 1967), 582-592.
Larios, Avila. "Brownsville-Matamoros: Confederate Lifeline," *Mid-America*, XL (April, 1958), 67-89.
Moseley, Edward H. "Indians From the Eastern United States and the Defense of Northeastern Mexico: 1855-1864," *Southwestern Social Science Quarterly*, LXVI (December, 1965), 273-280.
Oates, Stephen B. "Los Diablos Tejanos!" *American West*, (Summer, 1965), 41-50.
Porter, Kenneth W. "The Seminole in Mexico, 1850-1861," *Hispanic American Historical Review*, XXXI (February, 1951), 1-36.
Ramsdell, Charles W. "The Texas State Military Board, 1862-1865," *Southwestern Historical Quarterly*, XXVII (April, 1924), 253-275.
Rippy, J. Fred. "Border Troubles Along the Rio Grande, 1848-1860," *Southwestern Historical Quarterly*, XXIII (October, 1919).
Shearer, Ernest C. "The Callahan Expedition, 1855," *Southwestern Historical Quarterly*, LIV (April, 1951), 430-451.
_____. "The Carvajal Disturbances," *Southwestern Historical Quarterly*, LV (October, 1951), 201-230.
Sibley, Marilyn McAdams. "Charles Stillman: A Case Study of Enterpreneurship on the Rio Grande, 1861-1865," *Southwestern Historical Quarterly*, LXXVII (October, 1973), 225-240.
Smith, Mitchell. "The 'Neutral' Matamoros Trade, 1861-1865," *Southwest Review*, XXXVII (Autumn, 1952), 319-324.
Smyrl, Frank H. "Texans in the Union Army, 1861-1865," *Southwestern Historical Quarterly*, LXV (1961), 234-250.
_____. "Unionism in Texas, 1856-1861," *Southwestern Historical Quarterly*, LIV (April, 1951), 430-451.
Thompson, Jerry D. "Mexican-Americans in the Civil War: The Battle of Valverde," *Texana*, X (1972), 1-19.
Tyler, Ronnie C. "Cotton on the Border, 1861-1865," *Southwestern Historical Quarterly*, LXXIII (April, 1970), 456-477.
_____. "Santiago Vidaurri and the Confederacy," *The Americas*, XXVI (July, 1969), 66-76.
_____. "The Callahan Expedition of 1855: Indians or Negroes?" *Southwestern Historical Quarterly*, LXX (April, 1967), 574-585.
Weinert, Richard P. "Confederate Border Troubles with Mexico," *Civil War Times Illustrated*, III (October, 1964), 36-43.
Windham, William T. "The Problem of Supply in the Trans-Mississippi Confederacy," *Journal of Southern History*, XXII (May, 1961), 149-168.

Index

A

Alameda, Doretea: 100
Alderete, Acencio: 30
Alderete, Rafael: 29
Arellano, Cristobal: 28
Aresola, Dario: 22
Austin, Texas: 104

B

Banks, Nathaniel P.: 84, 92
Baton Rouge, Louisiana: 92
Bee, Hamilton P.: 48-49, 54, 55, 72 75, 76, 120
Benavides, Basilio: 12, 21, 22
Benavides, Cristobal: 8, 59, 60, 111, 114, 117-122
Benavides, Jose: 8, 12
Benavides, Refugio: 8, 21, 23, 46-55, 59, 107, 109-117, 117-120
Benavides, Santos: 8, 11, 12, 16, 17-23, 32 (port.), 42, 43-48, 50-54, 85, 97-99, 101-106, 106-110, 110-112, 116, 118-120, 122-124
Bexar, County of: 10, 16, 30
Boca del Rio: 85
Brashear City, Louisiana: 85
Brazos Santiago: 78, 84, 85, 92, 93
Brownsville, Texas: 42, 47, 58, 59, (photo 68, 69), 72, 75-79, 98, 100, 103, 104, 105, 116, 117, 119, 123
Byrd, William: 28
Bustillo, Antonio: 20, 26
Bustillo, Clemente: 22, 28

C

Callaghan, Charles: 44
Camargo, Mexico: 17, 18, 27, 50, 103
Cameron, County of: 10, 11, 86, 90
Cantu, Flavio: 94
Carleton, James H.: 98, 104
Carrizo (Zapata): 10, 15-23, 85, 101, 107
Carrollton, Louisiana: 84
Cavazos, Juan: 100
Cave, E. W.: 117
Chattanooga, Battle of: 26
Chickamauga, Battle of: 26
Chihuahua, Mexico: 27
Ciudad Victoria, Mexico: 27
Corpus Christi, Texas: 82, 89, 105, 106
Clareno Ranch: 16, 41
Clark, Edward: 11, 23, 28, 43
Cortina, Juan Nepomuceno: 12, 13, 17-23, 43, 74, 86, 105
Cox, Noah: 18
Cuellar, Antonio: 28
Cuellar, John: 88, 96
Cuellar, Matias: 30

D

Dana, N. J. T.: 77, 97
Davis, Clay H.: 18
Davis, Edmund: 61, 83, 85, 87, 89, 90, 91, 93, 96, 97, 102, 120
Davis, Henry T.: 76
Davis, Jefferson: 87
Dias, Antonio Abad: 85

Dias, Pablo: 10, 83
De la Zada, Nuncio: 30
Duff, James: 59, 71, 73
Dunn, James: 114
Durand, Joseph A.: 30
Dwyer, Thomas: 107, 110

E

Eagle Pass: 26, 52, 100, 104, 105, 107, 115, 120
Escandon, Jose de: 8

F

Falcon, Cesario: 94
Falcon, Ramon: 30
Farias, Leonard: 29
Fisk, Jim: 108
Flores, Anselmo: 20
Flores, Pedro: 28
Ford, John: 12, 17-23, 42-43, 101-125
Fort Brown: 42, 76, 77, 82
Fort Duncan: 104, 116
Fort McIntosh: 110
Franklin, Louisiana: 84

G

Gamboa, Antonio: 100
Gamboa, Ramon: 47
Galvan, Jeremiah: 100
Garcia, Guadalupe: 42, 43
Garcia, Eugenio: 117
Garcia, Hipolito: 100
Garcia, Ildefonso: 47
Garcia, Pedro: 90, 91
Garza, Jesus: 28
Garza, Serapio: 29
Gettysburg, Battle of: 26
Glaneke, Adolphus: 29
Gonzalez, Yldefonzo: 100
Grant, Ulysses S.: 96, 123
Gray, E. N.: 28
Gray, James W.: 30
Guanajuato, Mexico: 27
Guerrero, Mexico: 17, 18, 27
Gutierrez, Jesus: 100
Guzman, Eugenio: 96

H

Hamilton, Andrew J.: 82, 87, 96
Halleck, Henry Wager: 87
Haynes, John L.: 77, 85-93, 96, 98, 104, 105
Hynes, John: 30
Herrera, Natividad: 60
Herrera, Manuel: 30
Hermann, Theodore: 29
Hidalgo, County of: 10, 11, 86
Houston, Texas: 95, 110, 119
Houston, Sam: 87
Herron, F. J.: 78, 91, 115

I

Ibarra, Juan: 108

J

Jimenez, Angel: 21, 22
Juarez, Benito: 110

K

Kenedy, Mifflin: 71, 100
King, Richard: 71, 100

L

Laredo, Texas: 10, 58, 64, 82, 100, 103, 105, 107, 110, 111, 117-119
Linares, Mexico: 27
Lincoln, Abraham: 75, 87
Lopez, Albino: 33, 34
Lochte, Henry: 88
Los Angeles, California: 6
Louisiana Pointe Coupee Artillery: 6
Lovenskiold, Charles Grimus Thorkelin de: 43-47
Lubbock, Francis R.: 44, 45
Luckett, Philip Nolan: 10, 48

M

Magruder, John B.: 105
Magruder, George A., Jr.: 73
Marmion, James R.: 48
Martin, Raymond: 100
Martinez, Fermin: 28

Marysville, California: 6
Matamoros, Mexico: 27, 50, 82, 87, 117
McIntyre, Benjamin: 78, 90
McManus, T. P.: 104
Mier, Mexico: 27, 71, 88
Milmo, Patricio: 99
Montemorelos, Mexico: 88
Monterrey, Mexico: 88, 110, 111
Moreno, Bartolo: 47
Morganza, Louisiana: 92, 93
Mussett, Fenis: 10, 19, 20

N

Navarro, Angel: 26
New Mexico Militia: 7
Ninety-Fourth Illinois Volunteers: 76, 85
New Orleans: 83, 84, 98
New Iberia, Louisiana: 84

O

Oakes, Wallace E.: 23
Ochoa, Antonio: 15-17, 41, 42
Ogden's Louisiana Cavalry: 6
Ortiz, Juan: 43

P

Palacios, A. M.: 10
Parker, F. J.: 55
Pedernales Cavalry: 31
Penaloza, Joseph M.: 26, 48
Piedras Negras, Mexico: 98, 103, 104, 115
Pierce, Garner: 46, 47
Pierce, Leonard: 82, 83
Port Isabel, Texas: 76
Puebla, Mexico: 27
Pyron, Charles: 26

Q

Quintero, Jose Agustin: 99, 110

R

Radetzki, Gustavo H.: 93

Ramon, Martin: 47
Redmond, Henry: 15-20
Refugio, County of: 5
Reyna, Pedro: 20
Reynosa, Mexico: 17, 27, 88, 93, 97
Ringgold Barracks: 47, 97, 112, 113, 115, 116, 122
Rio Grande City, Texas: 20, 29, 58, 77, 85, 86, 91, 97, 98, 100, 101, 112, 115, 118, 120, 122, 123
Rodriguez, Jesus: 28
Rodriguez, Papinesino: 31
Rodriguez, T. A.: 117
Roma, Texas: 85, 88, 98, 100
Ruiz, Manuel: 75
Russell, Charles: 45, 99

S

Sada, David: 100
Salinas, Jacob: 47
Salinas, Jose Maria: 54
Salmas, Monico: 60
Sanchez, Tomas: 12
Sandoval, Ignacio: 28
San Antonio, Texas: 11, 28, 48, 82, 96, 98, 103, 105, 115
San Luis Potosi, Mexico: 27
San Francisco, California: 6
San Patricio, County of: 5, 31
San Roman, Jose: 100
San Ygnacio, Texas: 21
Santa Anna, Antonio Lopez de: 8
Second Texas Cavalry (Union): 58, 81, 85
Seward, William H.: 82
Sibley, Henry H.: 26
Skidmore, Sam C.: 31
Slaughter, James: 73, 110, 120, 123
Smith, Kirby: 99, 100, 119
Stanfields, Silas S.: 29
Starck, Fred E.: 77
Starr, County of: 9, 10, 11, 18, 86, 88
Stillman, Charles: 71, 100

T

Tamaulipas, Mexico: 49, 53, 105
Tampico, Mexico: 27
Taylor, Richard: 72, 74, 75
Temple, Philip G.: 114
Thirteenth Maine Volunteers: 76
Thompson, Ben: 52, 53

Thompson, C. W.: 101
Trevino, Augustin: 100
Trevino, Jorge: 29, 88, 92
Trevino, Tomas: 119
Tubac, Arizona: 6
Tucson, Arizona: 6
Twiggs, David E.: 11

U

Upton, Edward P.: 29

V

Valerio, Cecilio: 106, 108
Vidal, Adrian J.: 7, 71, 75, 76-79, 81, 88, 90
Vidaurri, Santiago: 99, 100, 110
Villarreal, Juan: 17, 18
Vela, Cecilio: 88
Vela, Domingo: 10
Vela, Ysidro: 10, 15-20, 49
Vera Cruz, Mexico: 27

W

Wells, Angelica: 86
Webb, County of: 10, 11, 48
Weisenger, M.: 118, 119
Weyman, J. B.: 115

Y

Yturri, Manuel II: 26
Yturria, Francisco: 100

Z

Zacatecas, Mexico: 27
Zacate Creek: 108
Zapata, Clemente: 28, 88
Zapata, County of: 10, 11, 15-23, 41, 88, 96

www.ingramcontent.com/pod-product-compliance
Lightning Source LLC
Chambersburg PA
CBHW021057080526
44587CB00010B/279